Cooking Light®

Light and Easy
Cookbook

Oxmoor
House®

Cooking Light® Light and Easy Cookbook from the
  Today's Gourmet series
© 1997 by Oxmoor House, Inc.
Book Division of Southern Progress Corporation
P.O. Box 2463, Birmingham, Alabama 35201

Library of Congress Catalog Card Number: 97-68914
ISBN: 0-8487-1597-7

Manufactured in the United States of America
First Printing 1997

Be sure to check with your health-care provider before
making any changes in your diet.

Editor-in-Chief: Nancy Fitzpatrick Wyatt
Senior Foods Editor: Katherine M. Eakin
Senior Editor, Editorial Services: Olivia Kindig Wells
Art Director: James Boone

Light and Easy Cookbook

Editor: Kathryn M. Wheeler, R.D.
Copy Editor: Donna Baldone
Editorial Assistants: Julie A. Cole, Catherine S. Ritter
Associate Art Director: Cynthia R. Cooper
Senior Designer: Larry Hunter
Director, Test Kitchens: Kathleen Royal Phillips
Assistant Director, Test Kitchens: Gayle Hays Sadler
Test Kitchens Staff: Molly Baldwin,
  Susan Hall Bellows, Julie Christopher,
  Natalie E. King, Elizabeth Tyler Luckett,
  Jan Jacks Moon, Iris Crawley O'Brien,
  Jan A. Smith
Photographer: Brit Huckabay
Photo Stylist: Virginia R. Cravens
Publishing Systems Administrator: Rick Tucker
Production Director: Phillip Lee
Associate Production Manager: Theresa L. Beste
Production Assistant: Faye Porter Bonner

Cover: Chunky Chicken and Mushroom Soup (page 152)
Page 1: Cuban Black Beans (page 107)
Page 2: Roasted Peppers and Feta Pizza (page 112)
Page 5: Orange-Coconut Angel Food Cake (page 58)

We're Here For You!

We at Oxmoor House are dedicated
to serving you with reliable information that expands your imagination
and enriches your life. We welcome
your comments and suggestions.
Please write to us at:

Oxmoor House, Inc.
Editor, *Light and Easy Cookbook*
2100 Lakeshore Drive
Birmingham, AL 35209

To order additional publications, call
1-205-877-6560.

Contents

About This Book

This compilation of the best of the *Light and Easy Cooking Collection* plus over 100 new recipes brings you creative combinations of ordinary food. Now you'll have an enthusiastic answer to the question "What's for dinner?" And you can be confident that every recipe uses healthy, easy-to-find, basic ingredients for great-tasting food in record time. On these pages, you'll find:

SuperQuick **recipes**—as in 25 minutes or less from pantry to table. Need an appetizer *now?* Pull a few ingredients off your shelf and try *Quick Chicken Quesadillas* (page 17) or any one of the other 103 superquick recipes throughout the book.

Preparation and cooking times listed with every recipe. You can be assured that *Greek Salad* (page 125) will get you out of the kitchen in a record 15 minutes.

Nutrient Analyses and Diabetic Exchanges provided with every recipe. *Orange-Coconut Angel Food Cake* (page 58) and *Frosted Peppermint Brownies* (page 65) are just two of the showstopper desserts that will satisfy your sweet tooth and save your waistline. So you can indulge without the guilt.

Meal plans included with all 14 menus. If planning healthy meals is more challenging than actually preparing the recipes, then Quick Menus such as *Grill Out Tonight* (page 208) were created just for you.

Orange-Coconut Angel Food Cake (page 58)

Blushing Champagne Punch (page 23)

Hot Artichoke and Parmesan Spread (page 11)

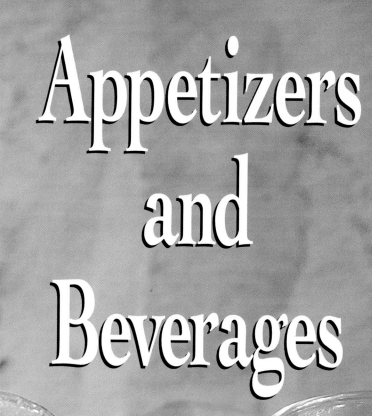

Appetizers and Beverages

Lemon Velvet (page 24)

Sweet-and-Sour Shrimp (page 18)

Marinated Mushrooms

Prep time: 8 minutes   Cook time: 20 minutes
Chill time: 8 hours

1½ pounds medium-size fresh mushrooms
    Vegetable cooking spray
2   tablespoons minced garlic
½   cup water
⅓   cup red wine vinegar
1½ tablespoons coriander seeds
¾   teaspoon dried thyme
¾   teaspoon dried oregano
½   teaspoon salt
½   teaspoon pepper

Clean mushrooms with damp paper towels; trim ends from stems. Set mushrooms aside.

Coat a large nonstick skillet with cooking spray; place over medium heat until hot. Add garlic; sauté 2 minutes. Add water and remaining 6 ingredients; bring to a boil. Add mushrooms. Cover, reduce heat to low, and cook 20 minutes or until mushrooms are tender, stirring occasionally.

Transfer mushroom mixture to a bowl; let cool. Cover and chill at least 8 hours. Drain mushroom mixture, discarding marinade.
Yield: 3 cups or 12 (¼-cup) appetizer servings.

Per Serving:

Calories 20	Carbohydrate 3.9g	Fiber 1.0g
Fat 0.4g	Cholesterol 0mg	Calcium 14mg
Protein 1.4g	Sodium 101mg	Iron 1.0mg

Exchange: Free

Appetizer Anyone?

Red wine vinegar and herbs infuse bold flavor into this easy mushroom recipe. It's the perfect complement to any appetizer tray.

Garbanzo Guacamole

SuperQuick
Prep time: 12 minutes

1   (15-ounce) can garbanzo beans, rinsed and drained
1   tablespoon lemon juice
1   large clove garlic, halved
¾   cup chopped onion
¾   cup peeled, cubed avocado (about 1 small)
1   (4.5-ounce) can chopped green chiles, drained
¼   teaspoon salt
¼   teaspoon pepper
1   cup seeded, chopped tomato
½   cup chopped green onions

Position knife blade in food processor bowl; add beans, lemon juice, and garlic. Process 20 seconds, stopping once to scrape down sides. Add onion and next 4 ingredients; pulse 10 times or until mixture is chunky.

Transfer mixture to a medium bowl; stir in tomato and green onions. Serve with no-oil baked tortilla chips. Yield: 3 cups.

Per Tablespoon:

Calories 14	Carbohydrate 2.3g	Fiber 0.6g
Fat 0.4g	Cholesterol 0mg	Calcium 4mg
Protein 0.5g	Sodium 39mg	Iron 0.2mg

Exchange: Free

Garbanzo Guacamole

Creamy Crab Dip

SuperQuick

Prep time: 12 minutes

½ cup plain low-fat yogurt
⅓ cup reduced-fat mayonnaise
1 tablespoon grated onion
1 tablespoon minced fresh parsley
2 teaspoons lemon juice
1 teaspoon Dijon mustard
¼ teaspoon dried dillweed
6 ounces fresh lump crabmeat, drained

Combine first 7 ingredients in a small bowl; stir well. Stir in crabmeat. Transfer mixture to a serving bowl. Serve with Melba rounds or fresh raw vegetables. Yield: 1½ cups.

Per Tablespoon:

Calories 19	Carbohydrate 0.7g	Fiber 0.0g
Fat 1.0g	Cholesterol 5mg	Calcium 14mg
Protein 1.7g	Sodium 110mg	Iron 0.1mg

Exchange: Free

Ham and Cheese Ball

Prep time: 15 minutes   Chill time: 1 hour

1 (8-ounce) package Neufchâtel cheese, softened
¼ cup plain low-fat yogurt
1 cup (4 ounces) reduced-fat sharp Cheddar cheese
¾ cup finely chopped lean cooked ham
2 tablespoons finely chopped green onions
2 teaspoons prepared horseradish
1 teaspoon country-style Dijon mustard
¼ cup chopped fresh parsley

Combine Neufchâtel cheese and yogurt in a large mixing bowl; beat at medium speed of an electric mixer until smooth. Add Cheddar cheese and next 4 ingredients; stir well. Cover and chill at least 1 hour.

Shape cheese mixture into a ball, and sprinkle with parsley. Press parsley gently into cheese ball. Wrap cheese ball in heavy-duty plastic wrap, and chill. Serve with fat-free crackers. Yield: 2 cups.

Per Tablespoon:

Calories 35	Carbohydrate 0.6g	Fiber 0.0g
Fat 2.5g	Cholesterol 10mg	Calcium 41mg
Protein 2.5g	Sodium 104mg	Iron 0.1mg

Exchange: ½ Fat

Crispy Dippers

Don't feel limited to crackers to accompany your healthy dips and spreads. When serving sweet dips, use banana slices, apple wedges, melon balls, and fat-free cookies. For savory dips, try carrot sticks, celery sticks, broccoli flowerets, and cherry tomatoes. Or for variety, use French bread, breadsticks, or tortilla, bagel, and pita chips. To make crispy chips, follow these easy instructions.

Bagel chips: Cut bagels in half; cut each half horizontally into thin slices. Place on a baking sheet; bake at 350° for 5 minutes.

Pita chips: Split pita rounds; cut each half into 8 wedges. Place on a baking sheet; bake at 400° for 5 minutes.

Tortilla chips: Cut each corn or flour tortilla into 8 wedges. Place on a baking sheet; bake at 350° for 10 minutes.

Hot Artichoke and Parmesan Spread

SuperQuick

Prep time: 5 minutes   Cook time: 20 minutes

1   cup 1% low-fat cottage cheese
½   cup grated Parmesan cheese
3   tablespoons nonfat mayonnaise
1   to 2 cloves garlic, minced
¼   teaspoon hot sauce
1   (14-ounce) can artichoke hearts, drained and finely chopped
    Vegetable cooking spray
48 whole wheat Melba rounds

Position knife blade in food processor bowl; add first 5 ingredients. Process until smooth, stopping once to scrape down sides. Transfer mixture to a bowl; stir in artichokes.

Spoon artichoke mixture into a 1-quart baking dish coated with cooking spray. Bake at 350° for 20 minutes or until thoroughly heated. Serve with Melba rounds. Yield: 16 appetizer servings.

Per Serving:

Calories 63	Carbohydrate 10.1g	Fiber 1.2g
Fat 0.9g	Cholesterol 3mg	Calcium 51mg
Protein 4.5g	Sodium 210mg	Iron 0.3mg

Exchanges: ½ Starch, ½ Vegetable

Hot Spinach Dip

Prep time: 15 minutes   Cook time: 20 minutes

1   (10-ounce) package frozen chopped spinach, thawed
2   tablespoons margarine
1½   tablespoons all-purpose flour
1   tablespoon chopped onion
¼   cup evaporated skimmed milk
3   ounces light process cream cheese
¼   cup (1 ounce) shredded Monterey Jack cheese with jalapeño peppers
1   tablespoon low-sodium Worcestershire sauce
¼   teaspoon garlic powder
¼   teaspoon pepper
⅛   teaspoon dried crushed red pepper
1   (2-ounce) jar diced pimiento, drained

Cook spinach according to package directions, omitting salt and fat; drain well, reserving ¼ cup liquid. Set spinach and liquid aside.

Melt margarine in a medium saucepan over medium heat. Add flour and onion; cook, stirring constantly, 1 minute. Gradually add reserved spinach liquid and evaporated milk; cook until slightly thickened, stirring constantly. Add cream cheese and next 5 ingredients, stirring until cheese melts. Stir in reserved spinach and pimiento. Cook 1 minute or until thoroughly heated. Serve with toasted bread cubes or fresh vegetables. Yield: 2 cups.

Per Tablespoon:

Calories 21	Carbohydrate 1.2g	Fiber 0.3g
Fat 1.5g	Cholesterol 2mg	Calcium 26mg
Protein 1.0g	Sodium 39mg	Iron 0.2mg

Exchange: Free

Spicy Bean Dip

SuperQuick

Prep time: 5 minutes   Cook time: 17 minutes

1   (15-ounce) can black-eyed peas, drained
½   cup 1% low-fat cottage cheese
1   teaspoon chili powder
½   teaspoon garlic powder
¼   to ½ teaspoon ground red pepper
    Vegetable cooking spray
½   cup (2 ounces) shredded reduced-fat sharp
    Cheddar cheese
1   tablespoon sliced green onions

Position knife blade in food processor bowl; add first 5 ingredients. Process 1 minute or until smooth, stopping once to scrape down sides.

Transfer bean mixture to a 1-quart baking dish coated with cooking spray. Bake at 400° for 15 to 20 minutes or until thoroughly heated. Sprinkle with cheese. Bake 2 additional minutes or until cheese melts.

Top with green onions. Serve with no-oil baked tortilla chips. Yield: 1½ cups.

Per Tablespoon:

Calories 21	Carbohydrate 1.9g	Fiber 0.2g
Fat 0.6g	Cholesterol 2mg	Calcium 27mg
Protein 2.0g	Sodium 75mg	Iron 0.2mg

Exchange: Free

Layered Southwestern Dip

Prep time: 12 minutes   Cook time: 20 minutes

2   cups (8 ounces) shredded part-skim
    mozzarella cheese
⅓   cup 1% low-fat cottage cheese
1   (4½-ounce) can chopped green chiles,
    drained
2   tablespoons reduced-fat mayonnaise
¼   teaspoon garlic powder
½   cup canned red kidney beans, drained
1   cup shredded lettuce
1   cup chopped tomato
1½ tablespoons sliced green onions
8   ripe olives, sliced

Combine first 5 ingredients in a medium bowl; stir well. Spread cheese mixture in a 9-inch baking dish. Bake at 350° for 20 minutes or until bubbly. Let cool about 3 minutes.

Layer beans, lettuce, and tomato on cheese mixture. Sprinkle evenly with green onions and olives. Serve warm with no-oil baked tortilla chips. Yield: 2 cups.

Per Tablespoon:

Calories 30	Carbohydrate 1.7g	Fiber 0.3g
Fat 1.5g	Cholesterol 5mg	Calcium 50mg
Protein 2.4g	Sodium 78mg	Iron 0.2mg

Exchange: Free

Tomato-Basil Bruschetta

SuperQuick

Prep time: 9 minutes   Cook time: 3 minutes

1   cup diced plum tomato
2   tablespoons finely chopped purple onion
1   tablespoon slivered fresh basil
1   clove garlic, minced
1   tablespoon balsamic vinegar
2   teaspoons olive oil
⅛   teaspoon freshly ground pepper
1   large clove garlic, halved
12   (½-inch) slices French baguette
     Olive oil-flavored vegetable cooking spray

Combine first 7 ingredients in a small bowl; set aside.

Rub garlic halves on both sides of bread slices. Coat each side of bread slices with cooking spray. Coat grill rack with cooking spray, and place on grill over medium-hot coals (350° to 400°). Place bread slices on rack; grill, uncovered, 1 to 2 minutes on each side or until toasted.

To serve, spoon 2 teaspoons tomato mixture onto each bread slice. Yield: 6 appetizer servings.

Per Serving:

Calories 106	Carbohydrate 17.8g	Fiber 1.1g
Fat 2.3g	Cholesterol 1mg	Calcium 16mg
Protein 3.0g	Sodium 168mg	Iron 0.8mg

Exchanges: 1 Starch, ½ Fat

Viva Italian!

Bruschetta comes from the Italian word *brus-care*, which means to roast over coals. The original version of bruschetta is a thick slice of country bread grilled over coals, then rubbed with a cut clove of garlic and drizzled with olive oil. We enhanced the flavor of the grilled bread by adding tomato, onion and basil for a delectable treat.

Baked Cheese with Tomato Chutney

Prep time: 15 minutes   Cook time: 25 minutes
Stand time: 5 minutes

1   (8-ounce) can no-salt-added whole
      tomatoes, undrained and chopped
¼   cup water
2   tablespoons red wine vinegar
2   tablespoons sugar
¼   teaspoon ground ginger
¼   teaspoon ground cloves
⅛   teaspoon ground cinnamon
2   cloves garlic, minced
1   tablespoon currants
1   egg, lightly beaten
½   teaspoon ground red pepper
1   (8-ounce) round farmer cheese
¼   cup toasted wheat germ
      Vegetable cooking spray
12 (½-inch) slices French baguette, toasted

Combine first 8 ingredients in a saucepan.
Bring to a boil over medium heat. Reduce heat,
and cook, uncovered, 15 minutes or until thickened, stirring occasionally. Remove from heat, and
stir in currants. Set aside, and keep warm.

Combine egg and red pepper in a medium
bowl; dip cheese round in egg mixture, and dredge
in wheat germ, coating well. Place cheese on a baking sheet coated with cooking spray.

Cut a piece of aluminum foil long enough to
fit around cheese, allowing a 1-inch overlap; fold
foil lengthwise into thirds. Lightly coat one side of
foil with cooking spray; wrap foil around outside of
cheese, coated side in, allowing foil to extend ¼
inch above cheese. Secure foil with string. Bake at
375° for 10 minutes or just until cheese melts. Let
stand 5 minutes. Transfer cheese to a serving plate;
remove foil. Serve with warm Tomato Chutney and
toasted bread slices. Yield: 12 appetizer servings.

Per Serving:

Calories 132	Carbohydrate 13.6g	Fiber 0.7g
Fat 5.7g	Cholesterol 20mg	Calcium 18mg
Protein 6.6g	Sodium 230mg	Iron 0.7mg

Exchanges: 1 Medium-Fat Meat, ½ Starch, ½ Vegetable

Tortellini with Spicy Tomato-Basil Sauce

SuperQuick
Prep time: 5 minutes   Cook time: 10 minutes

2   (9-ounce) packages fresh cheese-filled
      tortellini, uncooked
1   (26-ounce) jar fat-free spaghetti sauce
2   cloves garlic, crushed
¼   teaspoon dried crushed red pepper
¼   teaspoon pepper
¼   cup chopped fresh basil
¼   cup freshly grated Parmesan cheese

Cook tortellini according to package directions, omitting salt and fat. Drain and keep warm.

Combine spaghetti sauce and next 4 ingredients in a medium saucepan. Bring mixture to a
boil; reduce heat, and simmer, uncovered, 5 minutes. To serve, transfer basil sauce to a serving
bowl. Sprinkle with cheese. Serve tortellini with
warm sauce. Yield: 30 appetizer servings.

Per Serving:

Calories 40	Carbohydrate 6.0g	Fiber 0.4g
Fat 0.9g	Cholesterol 5mg	Calcium 12mg
Protein 2.1g	Sodium 124mg	Iron 0.0mg

Exchange: ½ Starch

Crunchy Snack Mix

Prep time: 8 minutes   Cook time: 30 minutes

- 2 cups corn-and-rice cereal
- 2 cups crispy wheat cereal squares
- 1½ cups fat-free bite-size pretzels
- ½ cup reduced-fat honey roasted peanuts
- 2 tablespoons reduced-calorie margarine, melted
- 2 teaspoons low-sodium Worcestershire sauce
- ½ teaspoon salt-free spicy pepper blend
- 1 cup raisins

Combine first 4 ingredients in a roasting pan. Combine margarine and Worcestershire sauce; pour over cereal mixture, tossing gently. Sprinkle with pepper blend.

Bake at 250° for 30 minutes, stirring every 10 minutes. Remove pan from oven; stir in raisins. Cool completely in pan on a wire rack, stirring occasionally. Store in an airtight container. Yield: 14 (½-cup) servings.

Per Serving:

Calories 115	Carbohydrate 23.4g	Fiber 1.7g
Fat 2.1g	Cholesterol 0mg	Calcium 9mg
Protein 2.6g	Sodium 190mg	Iron 1.8mg

Exchanges: 1 Starch, ½ Fat

Spicy Meatballs

Prep time: 18 minutes   Cook time: 14 minutes

- 1 pound ground chuck
- ½ cup soft breadcrumbs
- 2 tablespoons chopped green pepper
- 2 tablespoons skim milk
- 1 teaspoon low-sodium Worcestershire sauce
- 2 egg whites, lightly beaten
  Vegetable cooking spray
- 1 tablespoon plus 1 teaspoon cornstarch
- ¼ cup water
- ¼ cup firmly packed brown sugar
- ¼ cup red wine vinegar
- ¼ cup low-sodium soy sauce
- 1 teaspoon peeled, minced gingerroot
- ⅛ teaspoon garlic powder

Combine first 6 ingredients in a large bowl; stir well. Shape mixture into 42 (1-inch) meatballs. Arrange meatballs on rack of a broiler pan coated with cooking spray. Broil 5½ inches from heat (with electric oven door partially opened) 10 minutes or until browned, turning often.

Combine cornstarch and water in a large saucepan; stir well. Add brown sugar and remaining 4 ingredients; stir well. Place over medium heat; bring to a boil, stirring constantly. Reduce heat, and simmer 3 to 5 minutes, stirring constantly, until thickened. Add meatballs, stirring gently to coat. Transfer to a chafing dish, and serve warm. Yield: 3½ dozen.

Per Appetizer:

Calories 31	Carbohydrate 2.0g	Fiber 0.0g
Fat 1.4g	Cholesterol 7mg	Calcium 3mg
Protein 2.3g	Sodium 50mg	Iron 0.2mg

Exchange: Free

Freeze, if You Please

If you want to make this recipe in advance, or serve a few at a time, freeze the meatballs uncooked. When ready to eat, broil the frozen meatballs 5½ inches from heat (with electric oven door partially opened) 15 minutes. Proceed with recipe as directed.

Chicken Wontons

Chicken Wontons

Prep time: 22 minutes   Cook time: 16 minutes

 1 clove garlic
 2 (4-ounce) skinned, boned chicken breast
    halves, cut into small pieces
    Butter-flavored vegetable cooking spray
½ cup shredded carrot
¼ cup finely chopped celery
 1 tablespoon low-sodium soy sauce
 1 tablespoon dry sherry
 1 tablespoon fresh lime juice
 1 teaspoon ground ginger
 2 teaspoons cornstarch
40 wonton wrappers
    Green onion strips (optional)

Position knife blade in food processor bowl. Drop garlic through food chute with processor running; process until garlic is minced. Add chicken; process until chicken is ground.

Coat a large nonstick skillet with cooking spray. Place over medium-high heat until hot. Add chicken mixture; cook, stirring constantly, until chicken is done; drain. Combine chicken, carrot, and next 6 ingredients in a bowl, stirring well.

Spoon 1 rounded teaspoon chicken mixture into center of each wonton wrapper; moisten edges with water. Carefully bring 2 opposite points of wrapper to center over filling; pinch points together. Bring 2 remaining opposite points to center, and pinch together.

Place filled wontons on a baking sheet coated with cooking spray. Lightly coat each wonton with cooking spray. Bake at 375° for 8 to 10 minutes or until lightly browned. Garnish with green onion strips, if desired. Yield: 40 appetizers.

Per Appetizer:

Calories 32	Carbohydrate 5.0g	Fiber 0.0g
Fat 0.2g	Cholesterol 4mg	Calcium 5mg
Protein 2.1g	Sodium 60mg	Iron 0.3mg

Exchange: 1 Vegetable

Dip in Flavor

Low-fat condiments such as Chinese mustard, soy sauce, and sweet-and-sour sauce give an extra flavor kick. Find wonton wrappers in the produce section of your supermarket, or substitute egg roll wrappers, and cut them into quarters.

Quick Chicken Quesadillas

SuperQuick

Prep time: 10 minutes   Cook time: 8 minutes

 8 (8-inch) fat-free flour tortillas
 2 (5-ounce) cans chunk chicken in water,
    drained and flaked
1½ cups nonfat cottage cheese
 2 tablespoons chopped jalapeño pepper
¾ cup (3 ounces) shredded reduced-fat
    Monterey Jack cheese
⅔ cup sliced green onions
 1 cup chunky salsa
    Fresh cilantro sprigs (optional)

Place 4 tortillas on an ungreased baking sheet. Combine chicken, cottage cheese and jalapeño pepper; spoon mixture evenly over tortillas. Top each tortilla evenly with cheese, and green onions; top with remaining 4 tortillas.

Bake at 350° for 8 to 10 minutes or until cheese softens. Cut each tortilla into 6 wedges. Spoon salsa evenly over each wedge, and garnish with cilantro sprigs, if desired. Serve immediately. Yield: 24 appetizers.

Per Appetizer:

Calories 73	Carbohydrate 9.3g	Fiber 0.3g
Fat 1.1g	Cholesterol 3mg	Calcium 45mg
Protein 6.6g	Sodium 268mg	Iron 0.3mg

Exchanges: 1 Very Lean Meat, ½ Starch

Hot and Spicy Oysters

SuperQuick
Prep time: 5 minutes   Cook time: 2 minutes

12 oysters on the half shell
    Vegetable cooking spray
⅓   cup chopped green onions
½   cup soft breadcrumbs
3   tablespoons grated Parmesan cheese
½   teaspoon black pepper
¼   teaspoon ground red pepper

Place oysters on a baking sheet; set aside.
Coat a small nonstick skillet with cooking spray; place over medium-high heat until hot. Add green onions; sauté until tender. Add breadcrumbs, Parmesan cheese, black pepper, and red pepper, stirring well. Spoon breadcrumb mixture evenly over oysters. Broil 5½ inches from heat (with electric oven door partially opened) 2 minutes or until golden. Serve immediately. Yield: 12 appetizers.

Per Appetizer:

Calories 25	Carbohydrate 2.0g	Fiber 0.1g
Fat 1.0g	Cholesterol 7mg	Calcium 40mg
Protein 1.9g	Sodium 69mg	Iron 0.8mg

Exchange: Free

Ah, Shucks!

To shuck or open an oyster, hold the oyster, flat side up, firmly against a cutting board. Insert an oyster knife tip between the shells near the hinge. Twist the blade, and push it into the opening, prying the oyster open. Move the blade along the inside of the upper shell to free the muscle. Remove and discard the top shell of the oyster and any bits of shell. Enjoy!

Sweet-and-Sour Shrimp

Prep time: 17 minutes   Cook time: 10 minutes

1½ teaspoons ground coriander
1½ teaspoons chili powder
1   teaspoon curry powder
½   teaspoon ground cinnamon
¼   teaspoon sugar
¼   teaspoon salt
¼   teaspoon grated lemon rind
1½ pounds unpeeled large fresh shrimp
6   cups water
    Vegetable cooking spray
½   cup unsweetened pineapple juice
1   tablespoon plus 2 teaspoons cornstarch
⅓   cup cider vinegar
¼   cup reduced-calorie ketchup
2   tablespoons sugar
2   tablespoons low-sodium soy sauce
2   tablespoons dry sherry
⅓   cup thinly sliced green onions

Combine first 7 ingredients in a small bowl; stir well, and set aside.
Peel shrimp, and devein, if desired, leaving tails intact. Bring water to a boil; add shrimp, and cook 3 to 5 minutes or until shrimp turn pink. Drain; spray shrimp with vegetable cooking spray, and sprinkle with spice mixture.
Combine pineapple juice and cornstarch in a small bowl, stirring until smooth. Combine vinegar, and next 4 ingredients in a small saucepan. Stir in cornstarch mixture. Cook over medium heat, stirring constantly, until mixture is thickened and bubbly. Sprinkle with green onions, and serve with shrimp. Serve warm. Yield: 35 appetizers.

Per Appetizer:

Calories 26	Carbohydrate 2.2g	Fiber 0.1g
Fat 0.3g	Cholesterol 24mg	Calcium 11mg
Protein 3.2g	Sodium 64mg	Iron 0.5mg

Exchange: ½ Very Lean Meat

Rosemary Lemonade

Prep time: 8 minutes   Cook time: 10 minutes
Stand time: 10 minutes

9   **cups water**
3   **cups fresh lemon juice (about 12 large**
      lemons)
1½ **cups sugar**
1½ **teaspoons minced fresh rosemary**
      Fresh rosemary sprigs (optional)

Combine first 3 ingredients in a nonaluminum Dutch oven. Bring mixture to a boil, stirring occasionally. Remove from heat. Add 1½ teaspoons rosemary, and let stand 10 minutes. Strain mixture, discarding rosemary. Cover and chill. Serve over ice. Garnish with a rosemary sprig, if desired. Yield: 12 (1-cup) servings.

Per Serving:

Calories 112	Carbohydrate 30.3g	Fiber 0.0g
Fat 0.0g	Cholesterol 0mg	Calcium 5mg
Protein 0.2g	Sodium 1mg	Iron 0.0mg

Exchanges: ½ Starch, 1 Fruit

Spiced Iced Tea

Prep time: 3 minutes   Cook time: 10 minutes
Stand time: 20 minutes

2   cups brewed tea
1½   cups unsweetened orange juice
¾   cup unsweetened pineapple juice
5   whole cloves
1   (3-inch) stick cinnamon
¼   teaspoon whole allspice

Combine all ingredients in a medium saucepan. Bring to a boil. Remove from heat; cover and let stand 20 minutes. Strain mixture, discarding spices. Cover and chill. Serve over ice.
Yield: 4 (1-cup) servings.

Per Serving:

Calories 69	Carbohydrate 16.9g	Fiber 0.2g
Fat 0.1g	Cholesterol 0mg	Calcium 16mg
Protein 0.8g	Sodium 5mg	Iron 0.2mg

Exchange: 1 Fruit

Gingered Watermelon Spritzer

Prep time: 20 minutes

3   tablespoons peeled, grated gingerroot
2   cups seeded, cubed watermelon
3   tablespoons frozen orange juice concentrate, thawed and undiluted
1   tablespoon lemon juice
1¾   cups lemon-lime-flavored sparkling mineral water, chilled

Place gingerroot on an 8-inch square of cheesecloth. Bring edges together at top and hold securely. Squeeze cheesecloth over a small bowl, reserving 2 teaspoons juice; discard gingerroot.
Combine ginger juice, watermelon, orange juice concentrate, and lemon juice in container of an electric blender; cover and process until smooth, stopping once to scrape down sides. Pour into a pitcher. Stir in mineral water. Serve over ice.
Yield: 4 (1-cup) servings.

Per Serving:

Calories 29	Carbohydrate 6.7g	Fiber 0.3g
Fat 0.2g	Cholesterol 0mg	Calcium 7mg
Protein 0.5g	Sodium 13mg	Iron 0.1mg

Exchange: ½ Fruit

Bellini Cooler

SuperQuick
Prep time: 8 minutes

1½ cups frozen sliced peaches, thawed
1 cup apricot nectar
1 cup champagne, chilled
½ cup club soda, chilled

Combine peaches and apricot nectar in container of an electric blender; cover and process until smooth, stopping once to scrape down sides. Pour into a large pitcher. Gently stir in champagne and club soda just before serving.
Yield: 4 (1-cup) servings.

Variation:

Strawberry-Orange Cooler: Substitute 2 cups fresh or frozen strawberries for the peaches and 1 cup unsweetened orange juice for the apricot nectar. Proceed with recipe as directed.
Yield: 4 (1-cup) servings.

Per Serving:

Calories 102	Carbohydrate 14.4g	Fiber 2.7g
Fat 0.4g	Cholesterol 0mg	Calcium 23mg
Protein 1.2g	Sodium 10mg	Iron 0.7mg

Exchanges: ½ Starch, 1 Fruit

Per Serving:

Calories 111	Carbohydrate 17.8g	Fiber 1.5g
Fat 0.1g	Cholesterol 0mg	Calcium 11mg
Protein 0.9g	Sodium 10mg	Iron 0.6mg

Exchanges: ½ Starch, 1 Fruit

Blushing Champagne Punch

Blushing Champagne Punch

SuperQuick
Prep time: 5 minutes

1 (32-ounce) bottle cranberry juice cocktail, chilled
1 (32-ounce) bottle unsweetened apple juice, chilled
1 (750-milliliter) bottle champagne, chilled

Combine cranberry juice cocktail and apple juice in a large punch bowl; stir well. Add champagne just before serving. Yield: 23 (½-cup) servings.

Per Serving:

Calories 66	Carbohydrate 10.9g	Fiber 0.1g
Fat 0.1g	Cholesterol 0mg	Calcium 5mg
Protein 0.1g	Sodium 4mg	Iron 0.4mg

Exchange: ½ Fruit

Creamy Banana-Strawberry Sipper

SuperQuick
Prep time: 8 minutes

2 large frozen bananas
1 (6-ounce) can frozen apple juice concentrate, undiluted
1 (8-ounce) carton strawberry low-fat yogurt
⅓ cup instant nonfat dry milk powder
¼ cup water
⅛ teaspoon vanilla extract
   Ice cubes
   Fresh whole strawberries (optional)

Combine first 6 ingredients in container of an electric blender; cover and process until smooth, stopping once to scrape down sides. Gradually add enough ice to bring mixture to a 4-cup level; cover and process until smooth. Pour mixture into glasses. Garnish each serving with a fresh strawberry, if desired. Yield: 8 (½-cup) servings.

Per Serving:

Calories 115	Carbohydrate 25.0g	Fiber 1.1g
Fat 0.6g	Cholesterol 2mg	Calcium 109mg
Protein 3.4g	Sodium 47mg	Iron 0.3mg

Exchanges: 1 Fruit, ½ Skim Milk

Going Bananas!

Get a jump-start by freezing the bananas ahead. Cut bananas into ½-inch slices, and toss with 2 teaspoons lemon juice to keep them from darkening. Place banana slices on a baking sheet; cover and freeze at least 30 minutes.

Chocolate-Peppermint Shake

SuperQuick

Prep time: 8 minutes

2 cups 1% low-fat chocolate milk
2 cups vanilla nonfat frozen yogurt
½ cup peeled, sliced banana (about 1 small)
¼ teaspoon peppermint extract
1¼ cups crushed ice

Combine all ingredients in container of an electric blender; cover and process until smooth, stopping once to scrape down sides of blender. Serve immediately. Yield: 5 (1-cup) servings.

Per Serving:

Calories 150	Carbohydrate 30.0g	Fiber 0.5g
Fat 1.1g	Cholesterol 3mg	Calcium 231mg
Protein 6.5g	Sodium 115mg	Iron 0.3mg

Exchanges: 1½ Starch, ½ Skim Milk

Variation:

Piña Colada Shake: Substitute 2 cups skim milk for chocolate milk, and ½ cup canned crushed pineapple in juice, drained, for banana. Substitute ⅛ teaspoon rum extract and ⅛ teaspoon coconut extract for peppermint extract. Proceed with recipe as directed. Yield: 5 (1-cup) servings.

Per Serving:

Calories 118	Carbohydrate 23.5g	Fiber 0.1g
Fat 0.2g	Cholesterol 2mg	Calcium 238mg
Protein 6.5g	Sodium 105mg	Iron 0.1mg

Exchanges: 1 Starch, ½ Skim Milk

Lemon Velvet

SuperQuick

Prep time: 8 minutes

2½ cups skim milk
1 tablespoon sugar
1 teaspoon vanilla extract
1 (8-ounce) carton lemon low-fat yogurt
1 (6-ounce) can frozen orange juice concentrate, undiluted
Ice cubes

Combine half each of first 5 ingredients in container of an electric blender; cover and process until smooth, stopping once to scrape down sides. Gradually add enough ice to bring mixture to a 3½-cup level; cover and process until smooth, stopping once to scrape down sides. Pour mixture into glasses.

Repeat procedure with remaining half of ingredients. Serve beverage immediately. Yield: 7 (1-cup) servings.

Per Serving:

Calories 110	Carbohydrate 21.4g	Fiber 0.2g
Fat 0.6g	Cholesterol 3mg	Calcium 160mg
Protein 4.8g	Sodium 63mg	Iron 0.1mg

Exchanges: 1 Starch, ½ Skim Milk

Grand Marnier Cappuccino

Prep time: 8 minutes   Chill time: 30 minutes

¼ cup evaporated skimmed milk
½ teaspoon vanilla extract
3 cups strongly brewed hot coffee
2 tablespoons Grand Marnier or other
    orange-flavored liqueur
2 to 3 tablespoons sugar
    Grated semisweet chocolate (optional)

Place milk in a small narrow glass or stainless steel bowl; freeze 30 minutes or until a ⅛-inch-thick layer of ice forms on surface.

Add vanilla to partially frozen milk; beat at high speed of an electric mixer 5 minutes or until stiff peaks form.

Combine coffee, Grand Marnier, and sugar, stirring until sugar dissolves. Divide coffee mixture among 4 cups. Top with whipped milk mixture.

Sprinkle with grated chocolate, if desired. Serve immediately. Yield: 4 (¾-cup) servings.

Per Serving:

Calories 66	Carbohydrate 11.1g	Fiber 0.0g
Fat 0.1g	Cholesterol 1mg	Calcium 50mg
Protein 1.4g	Sodium 22mg	Iron 0.8mg

Exchange: ½ Starch

Hot Mocha

Prep time: 20 minutes

2½	cups brewed hot coffee
¾	teaspoon ground cinnamon
¼	teaspoon ground nutmeg
¼	cup unsweetened cocoa
3	tablespoons sugar
¾	cup water
3	cups skim milk
¾	teaspoon vanilla extract

Combine first 3 ingredients, stirring well. Set coffee mixture aside, and keep warm.

Combine cocoa and sugar in a large saucepan; add water, and stir well. Bring mixture to a boil over medium heat. Reduce heat, and simmer 3 minutes, stirring constantly. Gradually stir in milk, and cook over medium heat until thoroughly heated. Remove from heat; stir in vanilla and reserved coffee mixture. Serve immediately.
Yield: 6 (1-cup) servings.

Per Serving:

Calories 88	Carbohydrate 14.7g	Fiber 0.1g
Fat 0.7g	Cholesterol 3mg	Calcium 162mg
Protein 5.3g	Sodium 67mg	Iron 1.2mg

Exchanges: ½ Starch, ½ Skim Milk

Mulled Cranberry Cider

SuperQuick
Prep time: 10 minutes   Cook time: 10 minutes

2¼	cups unsweetened apple juice
2	cups cranberry juice cocktail
2	tablespoons lemon juice
1	lemon, sliced
4	coriander seeds
2	whole cloves
1	(3-inch) stick cinnamon, broken in half

Combine first 3 ingredients in a medium non-aluminum saucepan.

Tie sliced lemon and remaining 3 ingredients in a piece of cheesecloth; add to juice mixture. Bring to a boil; reduce heat, and simmer, uncovered, 10 minutes. Remove and discard spice bag. Pour cider into glass mugs; serve warm.
Yield: 4 (1-cup) servings.

Per Serving:

Calories 142	Carbohydrate 36.2g	Fiber 0.3g
Fat 0.2g	Cholesterol 0mg	Calcium 14mg
Protein 0.1g	Sodium 9mg	Iron 0.7mg

Exchange: 2 Fruit

Coriander vs. Cilantro

Actually both the dried form, coriander seeds, and the fresh form, cilantro, are from the same plant in the parsley family. But don't try to interchange the two since their flavor and form are so different. The mildly fragrant, peppery-flavored seeds enhance pickled foods and mulled beverages. Fresh cilantro has a very pungent, distinct flavor and is used frequently in Asian, Caribbean, and Latin American dishes.

Breads

Cinnamon-Sugar Popovers (page 32)

Garlic Bread

Prep time: 5 minutes   Cook time: 20 minutes

½ (1-pound) loaf Italian bread
   Butter-flavored cooking spray
⅛ teaspoon garlic powder
2 tablespoons grated Parmesan cheese

Slice bread horizontally into 2 halves. Spray each half with cooking spray; sprinkle with garlic powder and Parmesan cheese. Wrap in aluminum foil, and bake at 350° for 20 minutes or until thoroughly heated. Serve immediately.
Yield: 8 (1-inch) slices.

Per Slice:

Calories 87	Carbohydrate 16.1g	Fiber 0.8g
Fat 0.8g	Cholesterol 1mg	Calcium 26mg
Protein 3.2g	Sodium 194mg	Iron 0.6mg

Exchange: 1 Starch

Southern Cornbread

Prep time: 8 minutes   Cook time: 20 minutes

1 cup all-purpose flour
¾ cup yellow cornmeal
2 teaspoons baking powder
¾ teaspoon salt
2 tablespoons sugar
1 cup skim milk
2 tablespoons vegetable oil
1 egg, lightly beaten
   Vegetable cooking spray

Combine first 5 ingredients in a bowl; make a well in center of mixture. Combine milk, oil, and egg; stir well. Add to dry ingredients, stirring just until moistened.

Spoon batter into an 8-inch square baking pan coated with cooking spray. Bake at 425° for 20 minutes or until done. Cool 5 minutes in pan on a wire rack. Yield: 9 servings.

Per Serving:

Calories 145	Carbohydrate 23.0g	Fiber 0.9g
Fat 4.0g	Cholesterol 24mg	Calcium 78mg
Protein 3.9g	Sodium 217mg	Iron 1.2mg

Exchanges: 1½ Starch, ½ Fat

Ummm . . . Cornbread!

Ever wonder what makes cornbread irresistible? Maybe it's just the right combination of simple ingredients such as cornmeal, flour, eggs, oil, margarine, and sugar, which has created cornbread afficionados everywhere. Receive raves for your favorite cornbread recipe by remembering these baking basics.

• Cornmeal made from white or yellow corn can be used interchangeably in recipes, but yellow meal tends to make the cornbread slightly coarser.

• The proportion of cornmeal to flour in cornbreads determines the texture—more flour results in a softer, lighter texture.

• Eggs also add lightness and volume to cornbread.

• Fat such as oil or margarine added to cornmeal makes cornbread tender.

• Sugar is added to bring out the sweet nutlike flavor of cornmeal.

Jalapeño and Corn Cornbread

Prep time: 13 minutes   Cook time: 30 minutes

1   cup all-purpose flour
1   cup yellow cornmeal
2   tablespoons sugar
1   teaspoon baking soda
¾   teaspoon salt
1   cup nonfat buttermilk
2   tablespoons vegetable oil
2   egg whites, lightly beaten
1   egg, lightly beaten
1   cup frozen whole kernel corn
½   cup sliced green onions
3   tablespoons minced jalapeño pepper (about
      3 small peppers)
1   clove garlic, minced
      Vegetable cooking spray

Combine first 5 ingredients in a large bowl; make a well in center of mixture. Combine buttermilk and next 3 ingredients; stir in corn, green onions, jalapeño pepper, and garlic. Add to dry ingredients, stirring just until moistened.

Spoon batter into a 9-inch square pan coated with cooking spray. Bake at 375° for 30 to 35 minutes or until done. Cool 5 minutes in pan on a wire rack. Yield: 9 servings.

Per Serving:

Calories 182	Carbohydrate 30.5g	Fiber 1.8g
Fat 4.3g	Cholesterol 25mg	Calcium 44mg
Protein 5.8g	Sodium 337mg	Iron 1.5mg

Exchanges: 2 Starch, ½ Fat

Blueberry-Lemon Muffins

Prep time: 10 minutes   Cook time: 18 minutes

1¼ cups all-purpose flour
½ cup whole wheat flour
⅓ cup sugar
1 teaspoon baking powder
½ teaspoon baking soda
¼ teaspoon salt
½ teaspoon ground cardamom
½ cup unsweetened applesauce
⅓ cup nonfat buttermilk
1 egg, beaten
3 tablespoons margarine, melted
½ teaspoon grated lemon rind
½ teaspoon vanilla extract
1 cup frozen blueberries, thawed and drained
   Vegetable cooking spray
1 tablespoon sugar

Combine first 7 ingredients in a medium bowl; stir well. Combine applesauce, buttermilk, egg, margarine, lemon rind, and vanilla, stirring well. Add applesauce mixture to dry mixture, stirring just until dry ingredients are moistened. Gently fold in blueberries.

Spoon batter into muffin pans coated with cooking spray, filling two-thirds full. Sprinkle evenly with 1 tablespoon sugar. Bake at 375° for 18 to 20 minutes or until golden. Yield: 1 dozen.

Per Muffin:

Calories 138	Carbohydrate 23.5g	Fiber 1.6g
Fat 3.7g	Cholesterol 23.5mg	Calcium 40mg
Protein 2.9g	Sodium 149mg	Iron 1.0mg

Exchanges: 1 Starch, ½ Fruit, ½ Fat

Reheat It Right

For warm muffins in a jiffy, reheat one or two in a microwave at 50% power 10 seconds.

Orange Scones

Prep time: 12 minutes   Cook time: 16 minutes

2 cups all-purpose flour
2 teaspoons baking powder
½ teaspoon baking soda
¼ teaspoon salt
⅓ cup sugar
3 tablespoons chilled stick margarine, cut into small pieces
1 (8-ounce) carton lemon low-fat yogurt
2 teaspoons grated orange rind
¼ cup unsweetened orange juice
   Vegetable cooking spray
1 tablespoon sugar

Combine first 5 ingredients in a bowl; cut in margarine with a pastry blender until mixture resembles coarse meal. Combine yogurt, orange rind, and orange juice; add to dry ingredients, stirring just until dry ingredients are moistened. (Dough will be sticky.)

With floured hands, pat dough into a 9-inch circle on a baking sheet coated with cooking spray. Cut into 10 wedges, cutting to, but not through, bottom of dough. Sprinkle with 1 tablespoon sugar. Bake at 400° for 16 minutes or until golden. Yield: 10 scones.

Per Scone:

Calories 179	Carbohydrate 33.0g	Fiber 0.6g
Fat 3.9g	Cholesterol 0mg	Calcium 70mg
Protein 3.3g	Sodium 155mg	Iron 1.2mg

Exchanges: 2 Starch, ½ Fat

Cinnamon-Raisin Biscuits

Prep time: 12 minutes   Cook time: 14 minutes

2 **cups all-purpose flour**
1½ **tablespoons sugar**
2 **teaspoons baking powder**
¼ **teaspoon salt**
½ **teaspoon ground cinnamon**
¼ **cup chilled stick margarine, cut into small pieces**
½ **cup raisins**
¾ **cup 1% low-fat milk**
1 **tablespoon all-purpose flour**
   Vegetable cooking spray
½ **cup sifted powdered sugar**
1 **tablespoon 1% low-fat milk**

Combine first 5 ingredients in a bowl; cut in margarine with a pastry blender until mixture resembles coarse meal. Add raisins; toss well. Add ¾ cup milk, stirring just until dry ingredients are moistened.

Sprinkle 1 tablespoon flour evenly over work surface. Turn dough out onto floured surface; knead 4 or 5 times. Roll dough to ½-inch thickness; cut into rounds with a 2½-inch biscuit cutter. Place on a baking sheet coated with cooking spray, with sides slightly touching. Bake at 400° for 13 to 14 minutes or until golden.

Combine powdered sugar and 1 tablespoon milk; stir well. Drizzle over hot biscuits. Serve immediately. Yield: 1 dozen.

Per Biscuit:

Calories 157	Carbohydrate 27.4g	Fiber 0.9g
Fat 4.2g	Cholesterol 1mg	Calcium 58mg
Protein 2.8g	Sodium 103mg	Iron 1.1mg

Exchanges: 1 Starch, ½ Fruit, 1 Fat

Handle with Care

For fluffy biscuits, handle dough with a light touch. A good biscuit dough will be slightly sticky to the touch and should be kneaded gently just a few times.

Onion Pinwheels

Prep time: 20 minutes   Freeze time: 5 minutes
Cook time: 16 minutes

1¼ cups all-purpose flour
1   teaspoon baking powder
¼   teaspoon salt
3   tablespoons chilled margarine, cut into small pieces
3   tablespoons skim milk
1   egg, lightly beaten
     Vegetable cooking spray
¾   cup chopped green onions
¼   cup chopped fresh parsley
¼   teaspoon garlic powder
¼   teaspoon onion powder
⅛   teaspoon ground red pepper

Combine flour, baking powder, and salt in a bowl; cut in margarine with a pastry blender until mixture resembles coarse meal. Combine milk and egg; add to dry ingredients, stirring just until dry ingredients are moistened.

Turn dough out onto a lightly floured surface, and knead lightly 10 or 11 times. Shape dough into a ball; wrap in heavy-duty plastic wrap, and freeze 5 minutes to firm dough.

Coat a medium nonstick skillet with cooking spray; place over medium-high heat until hot. Add green onions and parsley; sauté 2 minutes. Stir in garlic powder and remaining ingredients. Set aside.

Roll dough into a 10- x 8-inch rectangle on a lightly floured surface. Spread dough evenly with onion mixture. Carefully roll up dough, jellyroll fashion, starting with long side. Pinch seam to seal.

Cut roll into 12 (1-inch) slices. Place, cut side down, in muffin cups coated with cooking spray. Bake at 400° for 16 minutes or until golden. Serve warm. Yield: 12 pinwheels.

Per Pinwheel:

Calories 85	Carbohydrate 10.8g	Fiber 0.5g
Fat 3.6g	Cholesterol 18mg	Calcium 38mg
Protein 2.2g	Sodium 91mg	Iron 0.9mg

Exchanges: ½ Starch, 1 Fat

Cinnamon-Sugar Popovers

Prep time: 8 minutes   Cook time: 25 minutes

1   cup bread flour
1   cup skim milk
1   egg
2   egg whites
2   teaspoons vegetable oil
2   teaspoons sugar
½   teaspoon ground cinnamon
¼   teaspoon salt
     Vegetable cooking spray

Combine first 8 ingredients in a medium bowl; beat at low speed of an electric mixer just until blended and smooth. Fill 6 (6-ounce) custard cups coated with cooking spray three-fourths full. Bake at 425° for 25 to 30 minutes or until crusty and dark brown. Serve popovers immediately. Yield: 6 popovers.

Per Popover:

Calories 123	Carbohydrate 17.6g	Fiber 0.0g
Fat 3.0g	Cholesterol 36mg	Calcium 60mg
Protein 5.9g	Sodium 148mg	Iron 1.1mg

Exchanges: 1 Starch, ½ Fat

Variation:

Parmesan Popovers: Substitute 1 teaspoon dried basil for the cinnamon; stir 2 tablespoons Parmesan cheese into batter just before filling custard cups. Proceed with recipe as directed. Yield: 6 popovers.

Per Popover:

Calories 127	Carbohydrate 16.3g	Fiber 0.0g
Fat 3.6g	Cholesterol 38mg	Calcium 90mg
Protein 6.8g	Sodium 186mg	Iron 1.1mg

Exchanges: ½ Medium-Fat Meat, 1 Starch

Puffy Popovers

Don't be intimidated by popovers; they're easy to mix and bake. Leavened by eggs and steam, the batter bakes and "pops over" the sides of the pan. Popovers can be baked in custard cups or popover pans. Popovers are satisfying plain or filled with creamed chicken or fruit salad.

Buttermilk Pancakes

SuperQuick
Prep time: 10 minutes   Cook time: 15 minutes

1½ cups all-purpose flour
2 tablespoons sugar
1 teaspoon baking powder
¼ teaspoon baking soda
⅛ teaspoon salt
1 cup nonfat buttermilk
1 teaspoon vegetable oil
1 egg, lightly beaten
Vegetable cooking spray

Combine first 5 ingredients in a medium bowl; stir well, and set aside. Combine buttermilk, oil, and egg in a small bowl; stir well. Add to flour mixture, stirring just until dry ingredients are moistened.

Coat a large nonstick skillet with cooking spray; place over medium-high heat until hot. For each pancake, pour ⅓ cup batter onto hot skillet. Cook pancakes 2 to 3 minutes or until tops are covered with bubbles and edges look cooked; turn pancakes, and cook other side.
Yield: 7 (4-inch) pancakes.

Per Pancake:

Calories 134	Carbohydrate 24.3g	Fiber 0.7g
Fat 1.8g	Cholesterol 32mg	Calcium 74mg
Protein 4.7g	Sodium 117mg	Iron 1.3mg

Exchange: 1½ Starch

Belgian Waffles

SuperQuick
Prep time: 8 minutes   Cook time: 9 minutes

2 cups all-purpose flour
1 tablespoon plus 1 teaspoon baking powder
½ teaspoon salt
1 tablespoon sugar
2 eggs, lightly beaten
1½ cups skim milk
¼ cup reduced-calorie margarine, melted
Vegetable cooking spray

Combine first 4 ingredients in a medium bowl. Combine eggs, milk, and margarine. Add to flour mixture; beat well at medium speed of an electric mixer.

Coat a Belgian waffle iron with cooking spray; allow waffle iron to preheat. For each waffle, spoon ¼ cup batter onto hot waffle iron, spreading batter to edges. Bake 4 to 5 minutes or until steaming stops. Repeat procedure with remaining batter. Yield: 12 (4-inch) waffles.

Per Waffle:

Calories 126	Carbohydrate 19.0g	Fiber 0.6g
Fat 3.8g	Cholesterol 37mg	Calcium 135mg
Protein 4.3g	Sodium 162mg	Iron 1.3mg

Exchanges: 1 Starch, 1 Fat

Smart Tip

Freeze leftover Belgian Waffles in a zip-top freezer bag. To serve, pop them in a toaster with wide slots or reheat them in a toaster oven at 350° for about 9 minutes.

Lemon Dutch Baby

Prep time: 12 minutes   Cook time: 20 minutes

3   egg whites
1   cup skim milk
1   cup all-purpose flour
2   teaspoons grated lemon rind
½   teaspoon poppy seeds
     Butter-flavored vegetable cooking spray
1   tablespoon reduced-calorie margarine
1   teaspoon powdered sugar
     Reduced-calorie maple syrup (optional)

Place egg whites in container of an electric blender. Cover and process 1 minute on high. With blender on high, gradually add milk in slow, steady stream through opening in cover. Gradually add flour, 1 heaping tablespoon at a time; process 30 additional seconds. Add lemon rind and poppy seeds; process 5 seconds.

Coat a 10-inch cast-iron skillet with cooking spray; add margarine to skillet. Place skillet in a 425° oven for 5 minutes or until margarine melts. Pour batter into hot skillet. Bake 20 minutes or until puffy and browned.

Transfer pancake to a serving platter; sift powdered sugar over pancake, and serve immediately. Serve with maple syrup, if desired.
Yield: 4 servings.

Per Serving:

Calories 159	Carbohydrate 26.0g	Fiber 0.8g
Fat 2.5g	Cholesterol 1mg	Calcium 88mg
Protein 7.7g	Sodium 101mg	Iron 1.4mg

Exchanges: 1½ Starch, ½ Fat

Dutch What?

Cooked in a cast-iron skillet, this puffed and crispy-edged pancake will deflate quickly after removing from the oven, so serve immediately. Its slightly sweet lemony flavor is enhanced by powdered sugar and maple syrup.

Amaretto French Toast

Prep time: 4 minutes   Stand time: 16 minutes
Cook time: 15 minutes

¾   cup skim milk
2   eggs
1   egg white
2   tablespoons brown sugar
2   tablespoons amaretto
¼   teaspoon ground cinnamon
¼   teaspoon salt
     Vegetable cooking spray
8   **(1-inch) slices French bread**
     Reduced-calorie maple syrup (optional)

Combine first 7 ingredients in a small bowl, stirring well. Pour mixture into a 13- x 9- x 2-inch baking dish coated with cooking spray. Arrange bread slices in the bottom of dish; let stand 10 minutes. Turn and let stand 6 additional minutes.

Bake at 425° for 10 minutes; turn bread slices, and bake 5 additional minutes or until golden. Serve with maple syrup, if desired. Yield: 8 slices.

Per Slice:

Calories 127	Carbohydrate 19.7g	Fiber 0.6g
Fat 1.9g	Cholesterol 54mg	Calcium 49mg
Protein 5.1g	Sodium 254mg	Iron 0.8mg

Exchange: 1½ Starch

Liquid Almond Flavor

If you don't have amaretto, an almond-flavored liqueur, deliver the same powerful flavor impact with almond extract. Use ¼ to ½ teaspoon of the extract instead of 2 tablespoons amaretto.

Banana Bread

Prep time: 15 minutes   Cook time: 55 minutes

2   cups all-purpose flour
1½ teaspoons baking powder
½   teaspoon baking soda
½   teaspoon salt
½   cup sugar
1   (8-ounce) carton plain nonfat yogurt
1   cup mashed ripe banana (about 1 large
     banana)
¼   cup margarine, melted
1   teaspoon vanilla extract
2   egg whites, lightly beaten
1   egg, lightly beaten
     Vegetable cooking spray
2   teaspoons all-purpose flour

Combine first 5 ingredients in a large bowl;
make a well in center of mixture. Combine yogurt
and next 5 ingredients; add to dry ingredients, stirring just until dry ingredients are moistened.

Coat a 9- x 5- x 3-inch loafpan with cooking
spray; sprinkle with 2 teaspoons flour. Spoon batter into prepared pan. Bake at 350° for 55 to 60
minutes or until a wooden pick inserted in center
comes out clean. Cool in pan 10 minutes; remove
from pan, and let cool on a wire rack.
Yield: 18 (½-inch) slices.

Per Slice:

Calories 117	Carbohydrate 19.5g	Fiber 0.7g
Fat 3.0g	Cholesterol 12mg	Calcium 45mg
Protein 2.9g	Sodium 137mg	Iron 0.7mg

Exchanges: 1 Starch, 1 Fat

Honey Bran Bread

Prep time: 8 minutes   Stand time: 5 minutes
Cook time: 45 minutes

¾   cup wheat bran flakes cereal
1½ cups nonfat buttermilk
¼   cup fat-free egg substitute
2   tablespoons vegetable oil
2   cups all-purpose flour
¼   cup honey-flavored wheat germ
1   teaspoon baking powder
1   teaspoon baking soda
1   teaspoon ground cinnamon
¼   teaspoon salt
3   tablespoons brown sugar
    Vegetable cooking spray

Combine cereal and buttermilk in a small bowl; let stand 5 minutes. Add egg substitute and oil; stir well.

Combine flour and next 6 ingredients in a large bowl, stirring well; make a well in center of mixture. Add cereal mixture to dry ingredients. Stir just until dry ingredients are moistened.

Spoon batter into an 8½- x 4½- x 3-inch loafpan coated with cooking spray. Bake at 350° for 45 minutes or until a wooden pick inserted in center comes out clean. Cool in pan 10 minutes; remove from pan, and let cool on a wire rack. Yield: 15 (½-inch) slices.

Per Slice:

Calories 103	Carbohydrate 17.5g	Fiber 0.9g
Fat 2.3g	Cholesterol 1mg	Calcium 49mg
Protein 3.6g	Sodium 145mg	Iron 1.5mg

Exchanges: 1 Starch, ½ Fat

Seeded Bagel Breadsticks

Prep time: 27 minutes   Stand time: 20 minutes
Cook time: 18 minutes

¾   teaspoon fennel seeds
¾   teaspoon caraway seeds
¾   teaspoon poppy seeds
¾   teaspoon sesame seeds
½   (32-ounce) package frozen bread dough,
     thawed (1 loaf)
    Vegetable cooking spray
3½ quarts water
1   tablespoon sugar

Combine first 4 ingredients in a small bowl; set aside.

Cut bread dough crosswise into 12 equal portions. Roll each portion into a 6-inch rope. Place ropes on a baking sheet coated with cooking spray. Cover and let rise in a warm place (85°), free from drafts, 20 minutes.

Broil ropes 5½ inches from heat (with electric oven door partially opened) 2 minutes on each side or until lightly browned using tongs to turn ropes.

Bring water and sugar to a boil in a large Dutch oven. Reduce heat to medium, and drop breadsticks, 4 at a time, into gently boiling water. Simmer, uncovered, 3 minutes on each side, turning over using tongs; drain breadsticks on paper towels.

Place breadsticks on baking sheet coated with cooking spray. Sprinkle with seed mixture; lightly press seeds into breadsticks. Bake at 375° for 18 to 20 minutes or until golden. Yield: 1 dozen.

Per Breadstick:

Calories 95	Carbohydrate 17.2g	Fiber 0.1g
Fat 1.5g	Cholesterol 0mg	Calcium 27mg
Protein 3.1g	Sodium 172mg	Iron 0.8mg

Exchange: 1 Starch

Bread Toppers

If you don't have all four types of seeds on hand that this recipe calls for, just use a total of 1 tablespoon of the seeds listed.

Seeded Bagel Breadsticks

Lemon-Glazed Cranberry Rolls

SuperQuick
Prep time: 10 minutes   Cook time: 15 minutes

- 1 (10-ounce) can refrigerated pizza crust dough
- ½ cup orange marmalade
- ⅔ cup dried cranberries
  Vegetable cooking spray
- ½ cup sifted powdered sugar
- 1½ teaspoons lemon juice
- 1 teaspoon hot water

Unroll pizza dough; pat into a 12- x 9-inch rectangle. Spread marmalade over dough, leaving a ½-inch border. Sprinkle cranberries over marmalade, pressing gently into dough.

Beginning with a long side, roll up dough, jellyroll fashion; pinch seam to seal (do not seal ends of roll). Cut roll into 12 (1-inch) slices.

Place slices, cut sides up, in muffin cups coated with cooking spray. Bake at 375° for 15 minutes or until golden. Remove rolls from pan, and place on a wire rack.

Combine powdered sugar, lemon juice, and hot water in a small bowl, stirring until smooth. Drizzle over warm rolls. Yield: 1 dozen.

Per Roll:

Calories 155	Carbohydrate 34.7g	Fiber 3.0g
Fat 1.0g	Cholesterol 0mg	Calcium 15mg
Protein 2.9g	Sodium 229mg	Iron 0.3mg

Exchanges: 1½ Starch, ½ Fruit

Dental Floss-Not Just for Teeth Anymore

Just when you thought dental floss was for teeth only, we've discovered a use for it in the kitchen. Try using clean floss as an easy tool to make even, clean-cut rounds from bread dough. Simply place a 10-inch piece of dental floss under the dough and cross the 2 strands over the top to cut a 1-inch slice. You'll be amazed at how easy it is to use, not to mention the cleanup.

Zesty Orange Bread

Prep time: 22 minutes   Stand time: 40 minutes
Cook time: 20 minutes

- 2 to 2½ cups bread flour, divided
- 1½ cups medium rye flour
- 1 package rapid-rise yeast
- 1 teaspoon salt
- 2 teaspoons orange rind
- 1½ cups warm unsweetened orange juice (120° to 130°)
- 1 teaspoon bread flour
  Vegetable cooking spray
- 1 tablespoon cornmeal

Combine 1 cup bread flour, rye flour, and next 3 ingredients in a large mixing bowl; stir well. Gradually add orange juice to flour mixture, beating well at low speed of an electric mixer. Beat 2 additional minutes at medium speed. Gradually stir in enough remaining 1½ cups bread flour to make a soft dough.

Sprinkle 1 teaspoon bread flour evenly over work surface. Turn dough out onto floured surface, and knead until smooth and elastic (about 8 minutes). Cover dough; let rest 10 minutes.

Coat baking sheet with cooking spray. Sprinkle with cornmeal. Divide dough in half. Shape each half into an oval loaf. Place loaves on prepared baking sheet. Cover and let rise in a warm place (85°), free from drafts, 30 minutes or until doubled in bulk. Using a sharp knife, make three (¼-inch-deep) slits across top of each loaf. Bake at 375° for 20 minutes or until loaves sound hollow when tapped.

Remove loaves from baking sheet immediately; cool on wire racks. Yield: 24 (½-inch) slices.

Per Slice:

Calories 74	Carbohydrate 15.6g	Fiber 1.3g
Fat 0.3g	Cholesterol 0mg	Calcium 5mg
Protein 2.2g	Sodium 98mg	Iron 0.7mg

Exchange: 1 Starch

Desserts

Raspberry-Peach Topping (page 43)

Spiced Fruit with Vanilla Yogurt

SuperQuick

Prep time: 15 minutes   Cook time: 5 minutes

2   cups sliced fresh plums (about ½ pound)
1½ cups peeled, sliced fresh peaches (about ½ pound)
2   teaspoons lemon juice
2   tablespoons sugar
⅛   teaspoon ground cinnamon
1   tablespoon margarine
½   cup vanilla low-fat yogurt

Place plums and peaches in a 1½-quart baking dish; add lemon juice, and sprinkle with sugar and cinnamon, tossing gently to coat. Dot with margarine. Cover with heavy-duty plastic wrap, and vent. Microwave at HIGH 5 to 6 minutes or until fruit is tender, stirring once.

To serve, spoon fruit into 6 individual dessert dishes; top with yogurt. Yield: 6 servings.

Per Serving:

Calories 109	Carbohydrate 21.1g	Fiber 1.7g
Fat 2.7g	Cholesterol 1mg	Calcium 40mg
Protein 1.8g	Sodium 36mg	Iron 0.1mg

Exchanges: 1 Fruit, ½ Fat

Creamy Fruit Ambrosia

Prep time: 15 minutes   Chill time: 30 minutes

4   cups cubed fresh pineapple
2   cups peeled, coarsely chopped fresh peaches
1   (8-ounce) carton vanilla low-fat yogurt
¼   cup no-sugar-added peach spread
2   tablespoons shredded unsweetened coconut, toasted
1   tablespoon finely chopped pecans, toasted

Combine pineapple and peaches in a large bowl; cover and chill.

Combine yogurt and peach spread in a small bowl; stir well.

Spoon fruit mixture evenly into 6 desserts dishes. Top with yogurt mixture; sprinkle with coconut and pecans. Yield: 6 servings.

Per Serving:

Calories 146	Carbohydrate 29.9g	Fiber 2.6g
Fat 2.9g	Cholesterol 2mg	Calcium 76mg
Protein 2.9g	Sodium 37mg	Iron 0.6mg

Exchanges: 2 Fruit, ½ Fat

Grilled Peaches with Raspberry Sauce

Prep time: 20 minutes   Cook time: 15 minutes

½ **(10-ounce) package frozen raspberries in light syrup, slightly thawed**
1½ **teaspoons lemon juice**
2 **medium peaches, peeled, halved, and pitted**
1½ **tablespoons brown sugar**
¼ **teaspoon ground cinnamon**
1½ **teaspoons rum extract**
2 **teaspoons margarine**
    Fresh mint sprigs (optional)

Combine raspberries and lemon juice in container of an electric blender or food processor; cover and process until smooth, stopping once to scrape down sides. Press berry mixture through a wire-mesh strainer, discarding seeds. Cover and chill.

Cut 1 (18- x 18-inch) sheet of heavy-duty aluminum foil. Place peach halves, cut side up, on foil.

Combine brown sugar and cinnamon; spoon evenly into center of each peach half.

Sprinkle peaches with rum extract, and dot with margarine. Fold foil over peaches, and loosely seal.

Place grill rack over medium coals (300° to 350°); place peach bundles on rack, and cook 15 minutes or until peaches are thoroughly heated.

To serve, spoon 2 tablespoons raspberry puree over each peach half. Garnish with fresh mint sprig, if desired. Yield: 4 servings.

Per Serving:		
Calories 93	Carbohydrate 17.7g	Fiber 3.2g
Fat 2.0g	Cholesterol 0mg	Calcium 13mg
Protein 0.6g	Sodium 24mg	Iron 0.4mg

Exchanges: 1 Fruit, ½ Fat

Spiced Apple Topping

SuperQuick

Prep time: 5 minutes   Cook time: 10 minutes

1¼ cups water
½ (12-ounce) can frozen unsweetened apple
     juice concentrate, thawed and undiluted
1½ cups peeled, chopped cooking apple (about 2
     large apples)
1 tablespoon dark brown sugar
½ teaspoon apple pie spice
2 tablespoons cornstarch
½ teaspoon vanilla extract

Combine water and juice concentrate.

Combine 1¾ cups juice mixture, chopped apple, brown sugar, and apple pie spice in a medium saucepan; bring to a boil. Reduce heat, and simmer 5 to 8 minutes or until apple is just tender.

Combine cornstarch and remaining ¼ cup juice mixture; add to apple mixture. Bring to a boil; cook, stirring constantly, until mixture is thickened and bubbly. Remove from heat; stir in vanilla. Serve warm or chilled over vanilla frozen yogurt or fat-free pound cake. Yield: 10 (¼-cup) servings.

Per Serving:

Calories 48	Carbohydrate 11.7g	Fiber 0.4g
Fat 0.1g	Cholesterol 0mg	Calcium 6mg
Protein 0.1g	Sodium 5mg	Iron 0.2mg

Exchange: ½ Fruit

Chunky Apple-Ginger Topping

Prep time: 15 minutes   Cook time: 12 minutes

¼ cup reduced-calorie margarine
2 medium Granny Smith apples, peeled,
     cored, and finely chopped
2 tablespoons finely chopped crystallized
     ginger
½ cup firmly packed brown sugar
2 tablespoons water
⅓ cup finely chopped walnuts, toasted

Melt margarine in a saucepan over medium heat; add apple and ginger. Cook, uncovered, 7 to 8 minutes or until apple is tender, stirring occasionally. Stir in brown sugar and water. Bring to a boil; reduce heat, and simmer 2 minutes or until sugar melts. Remove from heat, and stir in walnuts. Serve warm over fat-free pound cake or low-fat ice cream. Yield: 7 (¼-cup) servings.

Per Serving:

Calories 169	Carbohydrate 26.1g	Fiber 1.7g
Fat 7.7g	Cholesterol 0mg	Calcium 27mg
Protein 1.6g	Sodium 71mg	Iron 1.3mg

Exchanges: 1 Starch, ½ Fruit, 1 Fat

Don't Shop 'til You Drop

Don't wear yourself out looking for crystallized ginger; just look for it in the spice section of your supermarket. Crystallized ginger is fresh gingerroot that has been cooked in a sugar syrup and dipped in coarse or granulated sugar.

Blueberry Topping

Prep time: 5 minutes   Cook time: 7 minutes

2   cups fresh blueberries, divided
1½ cups unsweetened grape juice, divided
1   tablespoon frozen unsweetened orange juice concentrate, thawed and undiluted
⅛   teaspoon ground ginger
⅛   teaspoon ground cinnamon
1   tablespoon plus 2 teaspoons cornstarch

Combine 1 cup blueberries, 1 cup grape juice, orange juice concentrate, ginger, and cinnamon in a medium saucepan; bring to boil, stirring occasionally. Reduce heat, and simmer 3 minutes, stirring occasionally.

Combine cornstarch and remaining ½ cup grape juice; stir into blueberry mixture. Bring to a boil; cook, stirring constantly, 1 minute. Cool completely. Stir in remaining 1 cup blueberries before serving. Serve over vanilla or lemon frozen yogurt, pancakes, or waffles. Yield: 10 (¼-cup) servings.

Per Serving:

Calories 52	Carbohydrate 13.2g	Fiber 1.6g
Fat 0.1g	Cholesterol 0mg	Calcium 8mg
Protein 0.3g	Sodium 4mg	Iron 0.2mg

Exchange: 1 Fruit

Raspberry-Peach Topping

SuperQuick

Prep time: 5 minutes   Cook time: 7 minutes

2   cups chopped fresh peaches (about 2 large peaches)
1   cup water, divided
½   (12-ounce) can frozen unsweetened apple juice concentrate, thawed and undiluted
3   tablespoons cornstarch
¼   teaspoon almond extract
1   cup fresh raspberries

Combine chopped peaches, ⅔ cup water, and juice concentrate in a medium saucepan; cook over medium heat 5 minutes or until peaches are tender.

Combine cornstarch and remaining ⅓ cup water; stir into peach mixture. Bring to a boil; cook, stirring constantly, 1 minute or until mixture is thickened and bubbly. Remove from heat; stir in almond extract. Cool completely. Stir in raspberries before serving. Serve over vanilla frozen yogurt, angel food cake, or fat-free pound cake. Yield: 14 (¼-cup) servings.

Per Serving:

Calories 44	Carbohydrate 10.9g	Fiber 1.1g
Fat 0.1g	Cholesterol 0mg	Calcium 6mg
Protein 0.4g	Sodium 3mg	Iron 0.2mg

Exchange: ½ Fruit

Baked Apples with Cinnamon Ice Cream

Prep time: 20 minutes   Cook time: 10 minutes
Chill time: 2 hours

1½   cups low-fat vanilla ice cream, softened
½   teaspoon ground cinnamon
6   small Rome apples
¼   cup plus 2 tablespoons firmly packed brown
      sugar
¼   cup reduced-calorie margarine
2   tablespoons raisins
      Ground cinnamon (optional)

Combine softened ice cream and ½ teaspoon cinnamon; spoon mixture into a 9-inch square pan. Cover and freeze 2 hours or until firm.

Core apples, cutting to, but not through, the bottom of each apple. Spoon 1 tablespoon brown sugar, 2 teaspoons margarine, and 1 teaspoon raisins into center of each apple. Place apples in an 11- x 7- x 1½-inch baking dish; cover with heavy-duty plastic wrap. Microwave at HIGH 10 minutes or until apples are tender, giving dish a half-turn after 5 minutes.

Place apples in individual serving dishes; drizzle cooking liquid in baking dish evenly over apples. Top each apple with ¼ cup ice cream mixture. Sprinkle with cinnamon, if desired.
Yield: 6 servings.

Per Serving:

Calories 226	Carbohydrate 43.7g	Fiber 5.2g
Fat 6.8g	Cholesterol 5mg	Calcium 69mg
Protein 1.7g	Sodium 105mg	Iron 0.6mg

Exchanges: 1 Starch, 1½ Fruit, 1 Fat

A Baking Tip

If you don't have a microwave, bake the apples, uncovered, at 350° for 40 minutes.

Cherries Jubilee

SuperQuick
Prep time: 5 minutes   Cook time: 12 minutes

2   tablespoons sugar
1   tablespoon plus 1 teaspoon cornstarch
¼   cup unsweetened apple juice
¼   cup water
1   (16-ounce) package frozen unsweetened
      dark cherries, partially thawed
¼   cup brandy
3   cups vanilla nonfat ice cream

Combine sugar and cornstarch in a saucepan; stir well. Stir in apple juice and water; place over medium heat, and bring to a boil, stirring constantly. Add cherries; reduce heat, and simmer 10 minutes, stirring gently. Remove from heat.

Place brandy in a small long-handled saucepan, and heat just until warm (do not boil). Ignite brandy with a long match, and pour over cherry mixture. Stir gently until flame dies down. Scoop ½ cup ice cream into each individual dessert bowl. Spoon cherry mixture evenly over ice cream. Serve immediately. Yield: 6 servings.

Per Serving:

Calories 173	Carbohydrate 35.0g	Fiber 0.3g
Fat 3.2g	Cholesterol 9mg	Calcium 102mg
Protein 3.2g	Sodium 58mg	Iron 0.5mg

Exchanges: ½ Starch, 1 Fruit

Praline Bananas Foster

SuperQuick
Prep time: 15 minutes

¼ cup firmly packed dark brown sugar
1½ teaspoons cornstarch
½ cup evaporated skimmed milk
2 tablespoons chopped pecans, toasted
1 tablespoon praline liqueur or dark rum
2 teaspoons reduced-calorie margarine
1 teaspoon vanilla extract
2 medium-size firm ripe bananas
2 cups vanilla low-fat frozen yogurt

Combine brown sugar and cornstarch in a medium saucepan. Gradually stir in milk. Cook over medium heat, stirring constantly, until mixture comes to a boil and thickens slightly. Remove from heat. Add pecans, liqueur, margarine, and vanilla, stirring until margarine melts.

Cut each banana in half crosswise; cut each piece in half lengthwise. Spoon ½ cup frozen yogurt into each of 4 dessert dishes. Top each serving with 2 slices banana; spoon 3 tablespoons praline sauce over bananas. Yield: 4 servings.

Per Serving:

Calories 272	Carbohydrate 49.8g	Fiber 2.0g
Fat 6.0g	Cholesterol 11mg	Calcium 205mg
Protein 6.2g	Sodium 95mg	Iron 0.6mg

Exchanges: 1½ Starch, 1 Fat, ½ Skim Milk

Handy Substitution

Don't care for praline liqueur or don't have it on hand? You can still serve up this caramel delight by substituting ¼ teaspoon to ½ teaspoon rum extract for the liqueur.

Cranberry Ambrosia and Cream

Prep time: 10 minutes   Chill time: 2 hours

½ (12-ounce) package fresh cranberries
½ medium orange, seeded and quartered
1 cup fresh strawberries, quartered
⅓ cup sugar
1 small apple, diced
2½ cups vanilla nonfat ice cream

Position knife blade in food processor bowl; add cranberries and orange. Process until fruit is finely chopped. Transfer fruit mixture to a large bowl; stir in strawberries, sugar, and apple. Cover and chill at least 2 hours.

To serve, place ½ cup ice cream in each individual serving dish. Top each serving with ½ cup cranberry mixture. Yield: 5 servings.

Per Serving:

Calories 190	Carbohydrate 44.6g	Fiber 2.8g
Fat 0.3g	Cholesterol 0mg	Calcium 137mg
Protein 4.6g	Sodium 76mg	Iron 0.2mg

Exchanges: 1 Starch, 1 Fruit, ½ Skim Milk

The Bitter Truth

Do not peel the orange in this recipe. The rind adds a slightly bitter contrast to the sweet fruit.

Strawberries Romanoff

Prep time: 10 minutes   Chill time: 1 hour

3 cups fresh strawberries, hulled
2 tablespoons powdered sugar
1 tablespoon Cointreau or other
    orange-flavored liqueur
1 cup vanilla nonfat frozen yogurt, softened
¼ cup nonfat sour cream

Combine strawberries, powdered sugar, and Cointreau in a medium bowl, tossing gently. Cover and chill at least 1 hour.

Combine frozen yogurt and sour cream in a small bowl, stirring until smooth.

Spoon strawberries evenly into 4 individual serving dishes. Spoon yogurt mixture evenly over strawberries. Serve immediately.
Yield: 4 servings.

Per Serving:

Calories 116	Carbohydrate 23.7g	Fiber 2.9g
Fat 0.4g	Cholesterol 0mg	Calcium 87mg
Protein 3.6g	Sodium 45mg	Iron 0.4mg

Exchanges: 1 Starch, ½ Fruit

No Cointreau?

If you don't have Cointreau [KWAHN-troh], an orange-flavored liqueur, you can substitute equal amounts of frozen orange juice concentrate.

Strawberry Brûlée

Prep time: 5 minutes   Chill time: 30 minutes
Cook time: 12 minutes

⅓ cup sugar
2 tablespoons all-purpose flour
1 egg, lightly beaten
1½ cups 1% low-fat milk
1 teaspoon vanilla extract
1 cup sliced fresh strawberries
3 tablespoons brown sugar

Combine sugar, flour, and egg in a medium saucepan. Gradually stir in milk. Cook over medium heat, stirring constantly, until mixture thickens. Remove from heat; stir in vanilla. Cover and chill thoroughly.

Place strawberries evenly in 6 (¾-cup) oven-proof ramekins or custard cups.

Spoon custard mixture evenly over strawberries, and sprinkle evenly with brown sugar. Place ramekins on a baking sheet. Broil 5½ inches from heat (with electric oven door partially opened) 2 to 3 minutes or until sugar melts. Serve immediately. Yield: 6 servings.

Per Serving:

Calories 115	Carbohydrate 21.8g	Fiber 0.5g
Fat 1.6g	Cholesterol 39mg	Calcium 86mg
Protein 3.4g	Sodium 44mg	Iron 0.4mg

Exchanges: 1 Starch, ½ Fruit

Vanilla Custard

Prep time: 15 minutes   Chill time: 1 hour

2 cups skim milk
¼ cup sugar, divided
1 egg, beaten
1 tablespoon plus 1 teaspoon cornstarch
½ teaspoon vanilla extract

Combine milk and 3 tablespoons sugar in a 2-quart glass measure. Microwave, uncovered, at HIGH 5 to 6 minutes or just until mixture begins to boil, stirring every 3 minutes.

Combine egg and remaining 1 tablespoon sugar in a small bowl; stir well, using a wire whisk. Gradually add cornstarch, stirring constantly. Gradually stir one-fourth of hot milk mixture into egg mixture; add to remaining hot milk mixture, stirring constantly. Microwave at HIGH 2 to 3 minutes or until thickened, stirring every 30 seconds. Remove from microwave, and stir in vanilla.

Spoon mixture evenly into 5 dessert dishes; chill until set. Yield: 5 servings.

Per Serving:

Calories 98	Carbohydrate 16.9g	Fiber 0.0g
Fat 1.2g	Cholesterol 46mg	Calcium 126mg
Protein 4.6g	Sodium 64mg	Iron 0.2mg

Exchange: 1 Starch

Honey-Raisin Bread Pudding

Prep time: 7 minutes   Cook time: 33 minutes

2½ cups skim milk
6 (1-ounce) slices raisin bread, cubed
2 eggs, lightly beaten
2 tablespoons honey
1 teaspoon vanilla extract
¼ teaspoon salt
¼ teaspoon cinnamon
⅛ teaspoon nutmeg
   Vegetable cooking spray
¼ cup plus 2 tablespoons honey

Place milk in a large saucepan; cook over low heat until hot (do not boil). Remove from heat. Add bread and next 6 ingredients; stir well.

Spoon bread mixture into 6 (6-ounce) custard cups coated with cooking spray. Place custard cups in a 13- x 9- x 2-inch baking dish; add hot water to pan to depth of 1 inch. Bake at 350° for 20 minutes; shield with aluminum foil, and bake 10 additional minutes or until knife inserted in center comes out clean. Remove custard cups from water; transfer to a wire rack to cool. Top each serving with 1 tablespoon honey. Serve pudding warm or chilled. Yield: 6 servings.

Per Serving:

Calories 226	Carbohydrate 43.8g	Fiber 1.1g
Fat 2.8g	Cholesterol 74mg	Calcium 157mg
Protein 7.5g	Sodium 277mg	Iron 0.8mg

Exchange: 2½ Starch

Chocolate Pudding Cake

Prep time: 20 minutes   Cook time: 20 minutes

2 tablespoons margarine
½ cup sugar
⅛ teaspoon salt
1 egg
2 tablespoons all-purpose flour
⅓ cup unsweetened cocoa
¼ cup boiling water
1 teaspoon vanilla extract
4 egg whites
   Vegetable cooking spray
1½ cups vanilla nonfat ice cream

Beat margarine at medium speed of an electric mixer until creamy. Gradually add sugar and salt, beating well. Add egg; beat well. Add flour, beating until smooth.

Place cocoa in a small bowl; gradually add boiling water, stirring until smooth (mixture will be thick). Stir in vanilla. Gradually add cocoa mixture to margarine mixture, beating well.

Beat egg whites at high speed of an electric mixer until stiff peaks form. Fold beaten egg white into cocoa mixture. Pour batter into 6 (6-ounce) custard cups coated with cooking spray. Place cups in a 13- x 9- x 2-inch baking dish; add hot water to pan to depth of 1 inch. Bake at 325° for 20 minutes or until a wooden pick inserted in center comes out clean. Remove cups from water. Top each serving with ¼ cup ice cream. Serve immediately. Yield: 6 servings.

Per Serving:

Calories 201	Carbohydrate 30.9g	Fiber 0.1g
Fat 5.4g	Cholesterol 37mg	Calcium 75mg
Protein 7.0g	Sodium 177mg	Iron 1.1mg

Exchanges: 2 Starch, 1 Fat

Oohy, Gooey, Chocolatey

This dark chocolate cake has a creamy pudding-like fudgy layer on the bottom. Serve the cake warm right out of the custard cup, and let the ice cream melt over the chocolate.

Cappuccino Ice

Prep time: 10 minutes   Freeze time: 3 hours

3 cups brewed coffee
2 cups frozen reduced-calorie whipped topping, thawed
2 tablespoons sugar
2 tablespoons cocoa

Combine all ingredients in container of an electric blender; process until smooth. Pour mixture into an 8-inch square pan. Cover and freeze at least 3 hours or until mixture is almost frozen, stirring 2 or 3 times during freezing process. Scoop into individual dessert dishes; serve immediately. Yield: 6 servings.

Per Serving:

Calories 74	Carbohydrate 10.6g	Fiber 0.0g
Fat 3.1g	Cholesterol 0mg	Calcium 21mg
Protein 1.3g	Sodium 19mg	Iron 0.8mg

Exchanges: ½ Starch, ½ Fat

Mango-Pineapple Ice

Prep time: 10 minutes   Freeze time: 3 hours

2 ripe mangoes (about 2 pounds), peeled and coarsely chopped
1¾ cups unsweetened pineapple juice
3 tablespoons sugar
3 tablespoons lime juice

Place mango in container of an electric blender; cover and process until smooth, stopping once to scrape down sides. Add pineapple juice and remaining ingredients, and process until combined, stopping once to scrape down sides.

Pour mixture into an 8-inch square pan. Cover and freeze at least 3 hours or until mixture is almost frozen, stirring 2 or 3 times during freezing process. Scoop into individual dessert dishes; serve immediately. Yield: 8 servings.

Per Serving:

Calories 94	Carbohydrate 24.2g	Fiber 1.1g
Fat 0.2g	Cholesterol 0mg	Calcium 17mg
Protein 0.5g	Sodium 2mg	Iron 0.2mg

Exchanges: ½ Starch, ½ Fruit

Pineapple-Yogurt Pops

Prep time: 12 minutes   Freeze time: 8 hours

1 (20-ounce) can crushed pineapple in juice
1 (8-ounce) carton pineapple low-fat yogurt
1 (6-ounce) can unsweetened pineapple juice
1 teaspoon grated lemon rind
12 (3-ounce) paper cups
12 wooden craft sticks

Combine first 4 ingredients; spoon mixture evenly into paper cups. Cover with aluminum foil, and insert a wooden stick through foil into center of each cup. Freeze until firm.

To serve, remove foil; peel cup away from pop. Yield: 1 dozen.

Per Serving:

Calories 55	Carbohydrate 12.9g	Fiber 0.4g
Fat 0.3g	Cholesterol 1mg	Calcium 35mg
Protein 1.0g	Sodium 11mg	Iron 0.2mg

Exchange: 1 Fruit

Think There's No Substitute?

Pineapple low-fat yogurt works well in this recipe, but you can also substitute vanilla-flavored yogurt and still get the same great-tasting pineapple pops.

Citrus Shock

Prep time: 10 minutes   Freeze time: 8 hours

1 envelope unflavored gelatin
1½ cups cold water, divided
1 (16-ounce) carton vanilla low-fat yogurt
1 (6-ounce) can frozen lemonade concentrate, thawed and undiluted
⅓ cup sugar
1 tablespoon grated lemon rind
    Lemon slices (optional)
    Lemon rind strips (optional)

Sprinkle gelatin over ¼ cup cold water in a small saucepan; let stand 1 minute. Cook over low heat, stirring until gelatin dissolves, about 2 minutes. Combine gelatin mixture, remaining 1¼ cups water, yogurt, lemonade concentrate, sugar, and lemon rind in container of an electric blender or food processor; cover and process until smooth, stopping once to scrape down sides.

Pour mixture into freezer can of a 2-quart hand-turned or electric freezer. Freeze according to manufacturer's instructions. Remove mixture from freezer can; transfer to an airtight container, and freeze at least 8 hours. To serve, scoop mixture into individual dessert bowls, and serve immediately. Garnish with lemon slices and lemon rind strips, if desired. Yield: 10 servings.

Per Serving:

Calories 98	Carbohydrate 21.0g	Fiber 0.1g
Fat 0.6g	Cholesterol 2mg	Calcium 80mg
Protein 2.9g	Sodium 32mg	Iron 0.2mg

Exchange: 1 Starch

Variation:

Lime Shock: Substitute frozen limeade concentrate for lemonade concentrate and lime rind for lemon rind. Garnish with lime rind curls and lime rind strips, if desired. Yield: 10 servings.

Per Serving:

Calories 99	Carbohydrate 21.4g	Fiber 0.0g
Fat 0.6g	Cholesterol 2mg	Calcium 79mg
Protein 2.9g	Sodium 31mg	Iron 0.1mg

Exchange: 1 Starch

Lime Shock

Citrus Shock

Piña Colada Pie

Prep time: 15 minutes   Cook time: 10 minutes
Chill time: 1 hour, 30 minutes

¾   cup graham cracker crumbs
3   tablespoons reduced-calorie margarine,
      melted
1   tablespoon sugar
1   envelope unflavored gelatin
2   tablespoons cold water
¼   cup unsweetened pineapple juice
¾   cup part-skim ricotta cheese
¼   cup evaporated skimmed milk
1   tablespoon rum
1   teaspoon coconut extract
1   (20-ounce) can crushed pineapple in juice,
      undrained
⅓   cup shredded unsweetened coconut
2   tablespoons shredded unsweetened coconut,
      toasted

Combine graham cracker crumbs, margarine,
and sugar; press mixture in bottom and up sides of
a 9-inch pieplate. Bake at 350° for 8 to 10 minutes
or until lightly browned; let cool, and set aside.

Sprinkle gelatin over cold water in a saucepan;
let stand 1 minute. Add pineapple juice. Cook over
low heat, stirring until gelatin dissolves, about 2
minutes. Combine gelatin mixture, ricotta cheese,
and next 3 ingredients in container of an electric
blender or food processor; cover and process until
smooth, stopping once to scrape down sides.

Combine cheese mixture, pineapple, and ⅓
cup coconut in a medium bowl. Chill 30 to 40 minutes or until the consistency of unbeaten egg white,
stirring occasionally. Pour into crust. Cover; chill 1
hour or until set. Before serving, sprinkle toasted
coconut evenly over pie. Yield: 8 servings.

Per Serving:

Calories 192	Carbohydrate 24.0g	Fiber 0.8g
Fat 8.5g	Cholesterol 7mg	Calcium 102mg
Protein 5.2g	Sodium 142mg	Iron 0.9mg

Exchanges: 1½ Starch, 1 Fat

Toast in Flavor

To bring out the flavor of coconut, place
shredded coconut in a tray on a rack of a toaster
oven, and bake 3 minutes or until lightly browned,
stirring once.

Almond-Ginger Ice Cream Sandwiches

Prep time: 8 minutes   Freeze time: 3 hours

2   cups vanilla nonfat ice cream, softened
⅓   cup finely chopped almonds, toasted
⅛   teaspoon almond extract
16 (2-inch-round) thin gingersnaps

Combine first 3 ingredients in a bowl, stirring
well. Spread ¼ cup ice cream mixture onto each of
8 gingersnaps; top with remaining gingersnaps.
Place on a baking sheet, and freeze until firm.
Wrap sandwiches individually in plastic wrap, and
store in freezer. Yield: 8 servings.

Per Serving:

Calories 117	Carbohydrate 14.2g	Fiber 0.7g
Fat 6.1g	Cholesterol 5mg	Calcium 60mg
Protein 2.9g	Sodium 28mg	Iron 0.2mg

Exchanges: 1 Starch, 1 Fat

Caramel-Marshmallow Ice Box Pie

Prep time: 20 minutes   Freeze time: 3 hours

15   large marshmallows
¼   cup plus 2 tablespoons liquid fat-free
       hazelnut-flavored nondairy coffee
       creamer
4¾   ounces caramel candies (about 17 candies)
3   cups frozen reduced-calorie whipped
       topping, thawed and divided
1   (9-inch) reduced-fat graham cracker crust

Combine first 3 ingredients in top of a double boiler; bring water to a boil. Reduce heat to low; cook until marshmallows and caramels melt. Remove from heat; let cool.

Gently fold 2 cups whipped topping into caramel mixture. Spoon mixture into crust. Spread remaining whipped topping over caramel mixture. Freeze until firm. Yield: 8 servings.

Per Serving:

Calories 270	Carbohydrate 45.2g	Fiber 0.7g
Fat 8.1g	Cholesterol 2mg	Calcium 45mg
Protein 2.9g	Sodium 181mg	Iron 0.3mg

Exchanges: 2½ Starch, 1 Fat

Creamer Primer

Don't let the nondairy part fool you. Look for flavored creamers in the refrigerated dairy section of your supermarket.

Frozen Strawberry Margarita Squares

Prep time: 10 minutes   Freeze time: 8 hours

2   cups frozen unsweetened whole
       strawberries, halved
¼   cup lime juice
2   tablespoons tequila
2   tablespoons Triple Sec or other
       orange-flavored liqueur
6   cups vanilla nonfat ice cream, softened
       Vegetable cooking spray
20   unsalted pretzel sticks, crushed

Combine first 4 ingredients; fold into ice cream. Spread into an 8-inch square pan coated with cooking spray; sprinkle with pretzels. Cover and freeze until firm. Cut into squares. Yield: 9 servings.

Per Serving:

Calories 166	Carbohydrate 32.8g	Fiber 0.3g
Fat 0.1g	Cholesterol 0mg	Calcium 166mg
Protein 6.2g	Sodium 104mg	Iron 0.3mg

Exchanges: 1 Starch, ½ Fruit, ½ Skim Milk

Frozen Raspberry Brownie Dessert

Prep time: 5 minutes   Cook time: 20 minutes
Freeze time: 5 hours

1   (20.5-ounce) package light fudge brownie
     mix
     Vegetable cooking spray
4   cups raspberry low-fat frozen yogurt,
     softened
½   cup chocolate graham snacks crumbs (about
     44 cookies)
2   cups fresh raspberries

Prepare brownie mix according to package directions, using a 13-x 9-x 2-inch baking pan coated with cooking spray. Bake at 350° for 20 minutes. Remove from oven. Let cool in pan.

Spread softened yogurt evenly over cooled brownies in pan. Sprinkle crumbs over yogurt; cover and freeze 5 hours or until firm.

To serve, cut brownies into bars; top each with 2 tablespoons raspberries. Yield: 16 servings.

Per Serving:

Calories 221	Carbohydrate 42.7g	Fiber 4.4g
Fat 4.6g	Cholesterol 5mg	Calcium 51mg
Protein 4.1g	Sodium 162mg	Iron 0.1mg

Exchanges: 2 Starch, ½ Skim Milk

Double Chocolate Cupcakes

Prep time: 20 minutes   Cook time: 20 minutes

1   (18.25-ounce) package light 94% fat-free
     devil's food cake mix
1   cup water
3   eggs
     Vegetable cooking spray
¼   cup semisweet chocolate morsels
¼   cup skim milk
3   tablespoons unsweetened cocoa
2   cups sifted powdered sugar
2   teaspoons vanilla extract
2   tablespoons powdered sugar

Combine cake mix, water, and eggs in a bowl; beat at medium speed of an electric mixer 2 minutes. Divide batter among 24 muffin cups coated with cooking spray. Bake at 350° for 20 minutes or until a wooden pick inserted in center comes out clean. Cool in pans on wire racks 10 minutes; remove from pans, and let cool on wire racks.

Split each cupcake in half horizontally, using a serrated knife; set aside.

Combine chocolate morsels, milk, and cocoa in top of a double boiler; bring water to a boil. Reduce heat to low; cook until chocolate morsels melt, stirring occasionally. Remove from heat; stir in 2 cups powdered sugar and vanilla. Spread bottom half of each cupcake with 2 teaspoons chocolate mixture; place top half of cupcake on chocolate mixture. Sift 2 tablespoons powdered sugar over cupcakes. Yield: 2 dozen.

Per Cupcake:

Calories 115	Carbohydrate 20.2g	Fiber 0.0g
Fat 2.6g	Cholesterol 27mg	Calcium 28mg
Protein 2.7g	Sodium 217mg	Iron 0.7mg

Exchange: 1½ Starch

Apple-Cranberry Bake

Prep time: 15 minutes   Cook time: 25 minutes

3   cups chopped unpeeled Rome apple (about 4
    large apples)
2   cups fresh cranberries
    Vegetable cooking spray
½   cup sugar
⅓   cup all-purpose flour
¼   cup firmly packed brown sugar
3   tablespoons reduced-calorie margarine,
    softened
1   cup regular oats, uncooked
¼   cup chopped pecans
2   cups vanilla nonfat frozen yogurt

Layer apple and cranberries in an 8-inch square baking dish coated with cooking spray; sprinkle with sugar.

Combine flour and brown sugar; cut in margarine with pastry blender until mixture resembles coarse meal. Stir in oats and pecans. Sprinkle mixture over fruit.

Bake, uncovered, at 375° for 25 minutes or until bubbly and thoroughly heated. Let stand 5 minutes.

To serve, divide evenly among 8 individual dessert dishes; top each serving with ¼ cup frozen yogurt. Yield: 8 servings.

Per Serving:

Calories 255	Carbohydrate 48.4g	Fiber 3.0g
Fat 6.2g	Cholesterol 0mg	Calcium 78mg
Protein 4.2g	Sodium 73mg	Iron 1.0mg

Exchanges: 2 Starch, 1 Fruit, 1 Fat

Banana Cake

Prep time: 20 minutes   Cook time: 30 minutes

Vegetable cooking spray
2½ cups plus 1 tablespoon sifted cake flour, divided
1½ teaspoons baking powder
½ teaspoon baking soda
1½ cups mashed ripe banana (about 4 medium bananas)
¾ cup sugar
⅓ cup nonfat buttermilk
¼ cup vegetable oil
1 egg yolk
2 teaspoons vanilla extract
3 egg whites
¼ teaspoon cream of tartar
1 tablespoon powdered sugar

Coat a 13- x 9- x 2-inch baking dish with cooking spray; dust with 1 tablespoon cake flour, and set aside. Combine remaining 2½ cups flour, baking powder, and soda in a large bowl, stirring well. Set aside.

Position knife blade in food processor bowl; add banana and next 5 ingredients. Cover and process until smooth. Add banana mixture to flour mixture; stir gently until almost smooth. Set aside.

Beat egg whites and cream of tartar at high speed of an electric mixer just until stiff peaks form. Fold one-third of beaten egg white into batter. Gently fold in remaining egg white.

Spoon batter into prepared pan. Bake at 350° for 30 minutes or until cake springs back when lightly touched in center. Remove from oven, and let cool completely on a wire rack. Sift powdered sugar over cooled cake. Yield: 12 servings.

Per Serving:

Calories 217	Carbohydrate 39.0g	Fiber 0.9g
Fat 5.4g	Cholesterol 18mg	Calcium 50mg
Protein 3.5g	Sodium 75mg	Iron 1.9mg

Exchanges: 2 Starch, 1 Fat

Prune Spice Cake

Prep time: 12 minutes   Cook time: 20 minutes

1 cup sifted cake flour
½ teaspoon baking powder
¼ teaspoon baking soda
½ teaspoon ground cinnamon
¼ teaspoon ground nutmeg
¼ teaspoon ground cloves
½ cup firmly packed brown sugar
3 tablespoons reduced-calorie margarine, melted
2 egg whites
1½ teaspoons vanilla extract
½ teaspoon grated orange rind
½ cup nonfat buttermilk
¼ cup finely chopped prunes
Vegetable cooking spray
1 teaspoon powdered sugar

Combine first 6 ingredients in a medium bowl; stir well.

Combine brown sugar and next 4 ingredients in a large mixing bowl; beat at medium speed of an electric mixer until blended. Add flour mixture to sugar mixture alternately with buttermilk, beginning and ending with flour mixture; mix well after each addition. Stir in prunes.

Spread batter into an 8-inch square baking pan coated with cooking spray. Bake at 350° for 20 to 25 minutes or until a wooden pick inserted in center comes out clean. Let cool in pan on a wire rack. Sift powdered sugar over cooled cake. Yield: 9 servings.

Per Serving:

Calories 137	Carbohydrate 26.6g	Fiber 0.6g
Fat 2.7g	Cholesterol 0mg	Calcium 45mg
Protein 2.4g	Sodium 92mg	Iron 1.3mg

Exchanges: 1 Starch, ½ Fruit

Strawberry Snack Cake

Prep time: 12 minutes   Cook time: 25 minutes

1½   cups all-purpose flour
2   teaspoons baking powder
⅛   teaspoon salt
½   cup sugar
½   cup strawberry low-fat yogurt
¼   cup skim milk
3   tablespoons margarine, melted
1   egg, lightly beaten
½   teaspoon vanilla extract
⅔   cup sliced strawberries, slightly mashed
     Vegetable cooking spray
1   teaspoon powdered sugar

Combine first 4 ingredients in a large bowl, stirring well; make a well in center of mixture. Combine yogurt and next 4 ingredients; add to dry ingredients, stirring just until dry ingredients are moistened. Gently fold in mashed strawberries.

Spoon batter into an 8-inch square baking pan coated with cooking spray. Bake at 350° for 25 to 30 minutes or until a wooden pick inserted in center comes out clean. Cool in pan 10 minutes on a wire rack. Sift powdered sugar over cake just before serving. Yield: 9 servings.

Per Serving:

Calories 183	Carbohydrate 31.3g	Fiber 0.9g
Fat 4.8g	Cholesterol 25mg	Calcium 95mg
Protein 3.7g	Sodium 95mg	Iron 1.2mg

Exchanges: 2 Starch, 1 Fat

Chocolate-Almond Marbled Pound Cake

Prep time: 22 minutes   Cook time: 1 hour, 10 minutes

¼   cup stick margarine, softened
3   tablespoons shortening
1⅓   cups sugar
3   egg whites
1   cup nonfat buttermilk
½   teaspoon baking soda
2¼   cups sifted cake flour
⅛   teaspoon salt
¾   teaspoon almond extract
1   (1-ounce) square semisweet chocolate, melted
     Baking spray with flour

Beat margarine and shortening at medium speed of an electric mixer until creamy; gradually add sugar, beating at high speed until light and fluffy (about 5 minutes). Add egg whites, one at a time, beating after each addition.

Combine buttermilk and soda, and set aside. Combine flour and salt; with mixer at low speed, add flour mixture to margarine mixture alternately with buttermilk mixture, beginning and ending with flour mixture. Spoon 2 cups batter into a separate bowl, and stir in almond extract.

Stir chocolate into remaining batter. Spoon almond batter alternately with chocolate batter into a 9- x 5- x 3-inch loafpan coated with baking spray. Using the tip of a knife, swirl batters together to create a marbled effect. Bake at 325° for 1 hour and 10 minutes or until a wooden pick inserted in center comes out clean. Cool in pan 10 minutes on a wire rack; remove from pan, and let cool completely on wire rack. Yield: 16 servings.

Per Serving:

Calories 174	Carbohydrate 29.0g	Fiber 0.0g
Fat 5.6g	Cholesterol 1mg	Calcium 22mg
Protein 2.4g	Sodium 60mg	Iron 1.1mg

Exchanges: 1½ Starch, 1 Fat

Chocolate-Espresso Angel Food Cake

Prep time: 20 minutes   Cook time: 50 minutes

1¼   cups sifted cake flour
1¼   cups sugar, divided
⅓   cup unsweetened cocoa
1   teaspoon ground cinnamon
12   egg whites
1   teaspoon cream of tartar
1   tablespoon instant espresso powder
2   tablespoons warm water
1   teaspoon vanilla extract
1   tablespoon powdered sugar

Sift flour, ¾ cup sugar, cocoa, and cinnamon together 3 times; set aside.

Beat egg whites and cream of tartar in an extra large bowl at high speed of an electric mixer until foamy. Gradually add remaining ½ cup sugar, 2 tablespoons at a time, beating until soft peaks form. Sift flour mixture over egg white mixture, 2 tablespoons at a time; fold in gently after each addition. Combine espresso powder and water. Fold espresso mixture and vanilla into batter.

Spoon batter into an ungreased 10-inch tube pan; spread evenly with a spatula. Break large air pockets by cutting through batter with a knife.

Bake at 350° for 50 minutes or until cake springs back when lightly touched. Remove cake from oven; invert pan, and cool completely. Loosen cake from sides of pan, using a narrow metal spatula; remove from pan. Sift powdered sugar over cooled cake. Yield: 12 servings.

Per Serving:

Calories 154	Carbohydrate 32.3g	Fiber 0.1g
Fat 0.4g	Cholesterol 0mg	Calcium 10mg
Protein 5.1g	Sodium 54mg	Iron 1.4mg

Exchange: 2 Starch

Orange-Coconut Angel Food Cake

Prep time: 30 minutes   Cook time: 30 minutes
Chill time: 15 minutes

1   (16-ounce) package angel food cake mix
1   cup water
⅓   cup freshly squeezed orange juice
2   teaspoons orange extract, divided
1   (3-ounce) package French vanilla instant pudding mix
1¾   cups skim milk
1   tablespoon grated orange rind
2   cups flaked coconut, divided
3¼   cups reduced-calorie frozen whipped topping, thawed and divided

Prepare cake mix according to package directions, using 1 cup water and ⅓ cup orange juice instead of liquid called for on package directions. Fold 1 teaspoon orange extract into batter. Spoon batter into an ungreased 10-inch tube pan, spreading evenly with a spatula. Break large air pockets by cutting through batter with a knife. Bake at 375° on lowest oven rack for 30 minutes or until cake springs back when lightly touched.

Remove cake from oven; invert pan, and cool completely. Loosen cake from sides of pan, using a narrow metal spatula; remove from pan. Slice cake horizontally into 4 equal layers, using a serrated knife; set aside.

Prepare instant pudding mix according to package directions, using 1¾ cups skim milk instead of liquid called for on package directions. Stir in remaining 1 teaspoon orange extract and orange rind. Fold in 1 cup coconut and ¾ cup whipped topping. Chill at least 15 minutes.

Place bottom cake layer on a serving plate; spread top of layer with one-third of pudding mixture. Repeat procedure with remaining cake layers and pudding mixture, ending with top cake layer.

Spread remaining 2½ cups whipped topping on top, sides, and inside hole of cake; sprinkle with remaining 1 cup coconut. Store in refrigerator. Yield: 16 servings.

Per Serving:

Calories 213	Carbohydrate 35.5g	Fiber 0.6g
Fat 5.7g	Cholesterol 1mg	Calcium 45mg
Protein 4.1g	Sodium 306mg	Iron 0.2mg

Exchanges: 2½ Starch, ½ Fat

Orange-Coconut Angel Food Cake

Hawaiian Ice Box Cake

Prep time: 25 minutes   Cook time: 35 minutes
Chill time: 1 hour

1   (18.5-ounce) package 94% fat-free yellow
       cake mix
1⅓ cups water
3   egg whites
       Vegetable cooking spray
2   cups skim milk
1   (3.4-ounce) package banana cream instant
       pudding mix
1   (15-ounce) can unsweetened crushed
       pineapple, drained
2   cups reduced-calorie frozen whipped
       topping, thawed
¼   cup shredded coconut, toasted

Combine first 3 ingredients in a large mixing bowl; beat at low speed of an electric mixer 30 seconds. Increase speed to medium, and beat 2 minutes. Pour batter into a 13- x 9- x 2-inch baking pan coated with cooking spray. Bake at 350° for 35 minutes or until cake springs back when lightly touched in center. Remove from oven. Let cool in pan on a wire rack.

Combine milk and pudding mix in a medium bowl; beat at low speed 2 minutes or until thickened. Cover and chill 5 minutes.

Stir pineapple into pudding. Pierce 48 holes in top of cake, using the handle of a wooden spoon. Spread pudding mixture over cake; spread whipped topping over pudding mixture. Sprinkle topping with shredded coconut. Chill 1 hour. Yield: 16 servings.

Per Serving:

Calories 203	Carbohydrate 39.1g	Fiber 0.3g
Fat 3.5g	Cholesterol 1mg	Calcium 78mg
Protein 4.4g	Sodium 440mg	Iron 0.7mg

Exchanges: 2 Starch, ½ Fat

Grand Marnier Cheesecake

Prep time: 15 minutes   Cook time: 55 minutes
Chill time: 8 hours

     Vegetable cooking spray
½   cup plus 2 tablespoons chocolate wafer
       cookie crumbs (11 cookies), divided
2   (8-ounce) cartons light process cream
       cheese, softened
⅔   cup sugar
¾   cup fat-free egg substitute
1   cup nonfat sour cream
3   tablespoons Grand Marnier or other orange-
       flavored liqueur
1   cup frozen reduced-calorie whipped topping,
       thawed

Coat bottom of an 8-inch springform pan with cooking spray; sprinkle ½ cup crumbs over bottom of pan.

Beat cream cheese at medium speed of an electric mixer until creamy; gradually add sugar, beating well. Add egg substitute; beat well. Add sour cream and Grand Marnier. Beat at low speed just until blended. Pour mixture into prepared pan.

Bake at 300° for 55 minutes. (Center will be soft but will firm when chilled.) Turn oven off; partially open oven door. Leave cheesecake in oven 20 minutes. Remove from oven, and run a knife around edge of pan to release sides. Let cheesecake cool on a wire rack. Cover and chill 8 hours.

Remove cake from pan. Spread whipped topping over top of cake. Sprinkle with remaining 2 tablespoons cookie crumbs. Yield: 12 servings.

Per Serving:

Calories 185	Carbohydrate 19.5g	Fiber 0.0g
Fat 8.6g	Cholesterol 25mg	Calcium 65mg
Protein 7.3g	Sodium 272mg	Iron 0.4mg

Exchanges: 1 Very Lean Meat, 1 Starch, 1 Fat

Easy Does It

The great thing about cheesecake (besides the taste) is that you can make it a day ahead, chill it, and forget about it until serving time.

Chocolate Drops

Prep time: 28 minutes   Cook time: 30 minutes

⅓ cup chopped almonds, toasted
¼ cup unsweetened cocoa
2 tablespoons all-purpose flour
2 egg whites
¼ teaspoon vanilla extract
⅛ teaspoon almond extract
   Dash of salt
1 cup sifted powdered sugar

Combine first 3 ingredients in a small bowl; stir well.

Beat egg whites in a small bowl at high speed of an electric mixer until foamy. Add flavorings and salt; beat until soft peaks form. Gradually add sugar, 1 tablespoon at a time, beating until stiff peaks form (2 to 4 minutes). Fold cocoa mixture into egg white mixture.

Drop mixture by rounded teaspoonfuls, 2 inches apart, onto cookie sheets lined with parchment paper. Bake at 325° for 15 minutes. Let cool on cookie sheets. Carefully remove cookies from parchment paper; store in an airtight container. Yield: 2 dozen.

Per Cookie:

Calories 38	Carbohydrate 6.3g	Fiber 0.2g
Fat 1.1g	Cholesterol 0mg	Calcium 6mg
Protein 1.0g	Sodium 11mg	Iron 0.3mg

Exchange: ½ Starch

Whip in Shape

To whip egg whites into perfectly stiff peaks, use a small glass or stainless steel bowl. Gradually add sugar, 1 tablespoon at a time, until the peaks stand straight up without curling over when you lift the beaters.

Thumbprint Cookies

Prep time: 25 minutes   Cook time: 40 minutes

1 (17.5-ounce) package chocolate chip
      cookie mix
1 cup regular oats, uncooked
⅓ cup water
1 teaspoon vanilla extract
1 egg white
   Vegetable cooking spray
¼ cup plus 2 teaspoons strawberry jam

Combine first 5 ingredients in a bowl; stir well. Drop dough by 2 level teaspoonfuls 1 inch apart onto cookie sheets coated with cooking spray.

Press center of each cookie with thumb, making an indentation; fill with ¼ teaspoon jam. Bake at 375° for 10 minutes or until golden. Cool on wire racks. Store in an airtight container. Yield: 4½ dozen.

Per Cookie:

Calories 55	Carbohydrate 8.5g	Fiber 0.2g
Fat 2.0g	Cholesterol 0mg	Calcium 1mg
Protein 0.8g	Sodium 34mg	Iron 0.2mg

Exchange: ½ Starch

Oatmeal-Chocolate Chip Cookies

Prep time: 15 minutes   Cook time: 25 minutes

¼ cup margarine, softened
½ cup firmly packed brown sugar
1 egg
2 tablespoons light corn syrup
½ teaspoon vanilla extract
1 cup all-purpose flour
¼ cup instant nonfat dry milk powder
¼ teaspoon baking soda
¼ teaspoon salt
¾ cup regular oats, uncooked
⅓ cup semisweet chocolate mini-morsels
¼ cup crispy rice cereal
   Vegetable cooking spray

Beat margarine at medium speed of an electric mixer until light and fluffy; gradually add brown sugar, and beat well. Add egg, corn syrup, and vanilla, beating well.

Combine flour and next 3 ingredients; gradually add flour mixture to margarine mixture, mixing well. Stir in oats, chocolate morsels, and cereal.

Drop dough by 2 rounded teaspoonfuls 2 inches apart onto cookie sheets coated with cooking spray. Bake at 350° for 8 to 10 minutes or until lightly browned. Cool on wire racks. Store in an airtight container. Yield: 3 dozen.

Per Cookie:

Calories 61	Carbohydrate 9.2g	Fiber 0.3g
Fat 2.3g	Cholesterol 6mg	Calcium 16mg
Protein 1.2g	Sodium 47mg	Iron 0.4mg

Exchange: ½ Starch

Butterscotch Bars

Prep time: 15 minutes   Stand time: 1 hour

3 tablespoons margarine
½ cup firmly packed brown sugar
2 cups miniature marshmallows
4 cups crisp rice cereal
2 cups whole wheat flake cereal
   Vegetable cooking spray

Melt margarine in a large saucepan over medium heat. Add sugar; stir well. Add marshmallows; cook until marshmallows melt, stirring constantly. Remove from heat; stir in cereals.

Press cereal mixture in bottom of a 13- x 9- x 2-inch pan coated with cooking spray. Let cool 1 hour. Cut into bars. Yield: 18 bars.

Per Bar:

Calories 92	Carbohydrate 18.1g	Fiber 0.3g
Fat 2.0g	Cholesterol 0mg	Calcium 12mg
Protein 0.8g	Sodium 112mg	Iron 0.8mg

Exchange: 1 Starch

Fig Bars

Prep time: 12 minutes   Cook time: 5 minutes
Chill time: 30 minutes

1½ cups chopped dried figs
1   tablespoon all-purpose flour
½   cup water
¾   cup unsweetened flaked coconut
½   cup reduced-calorie margarine
¼   cup sugar
1¾ cups quick-cooking oats, toasted
½   teaspoon vanilla extract
    Vegetable cooking spray

Combine figs and flour in a medium bowl; toss lightly to coat.

Bring water to a boil in a medium saucepan. Add fig mixture, coconut, margarine, and sugar to saucepan, stirring well. Cook, uncovered, over medium heat 5 to 7 minutes or until mixture is thickened, stirring often. Add oats and vanilla, stirring until oats are moistened.

Press mixture in bottom of a 9-inch square pan coated with cooking spray. Cover and chill thoroughly. Cut into bars. Yield: 2 dozen.

Per Bar:

Calories 101	Carbohydrate 15.0g	Fiber 2.9g
Fat 4.6g	Cholesterol 0mg	Calcium 22mg
Protein 1.5g	Sodium 39mg	Iron 0.6mg

Exchanges: 1 Starch, 1 Fat

Microwave Instructions

Combine figs and flour in a medium bowl; toss lightly to coat. Add coconut, margarine, and sugar to fig mixture, stirring well.

Place water in a 1-cup glass measure. Microwave at HIGH 2 to 3 minutes or until water boils. Pour over fig mixture, stirring well. Microwave, uncovered, at HIGH 2 to 3 minutes or until mixture is thickened, stirring after every minute. Add oats and vanilla, stirring until oats are moistened.

Press mixture in bottom of a 9-inch square pan coated with cooking spray. Cover and chill thoroughly. Cut into bars. Yield: 2 dozen.

Frosted Peppermint Brownies

Frosted Peppermint Brownies

Prep time: 20 minutes   Cook time: 25 minutes

¾ cup reduced-calorie stick margarine, softened
1⅓ cups sugar
8 egg whites
½ cup nonfat sour cream
⅓ cup evaporated skimmed milk
1 teaspoon peppermint extract
1⅓ cups all-purpose flour
⅔ cup unsweetened cocoa
1 teaspoon baking powder
½ teaspoon salt
   Vegetable cooking spray
   Creamy Chocolate Frosting
3 tablespoons crushed peppermint candies (about 6 candies)

Beat margarine at medium speed of an electric mixer until creamy; gradually add sugar, and beat well. Add egg whites, sour cream, evaporated milk, and peppermint extract; beat well.

Combine flour and next 3 ingredients in a small bowl; stir well. Add flour mixture to margarine mixture, mixing well. Pour batter into a 13- x 9- x 2-inch baking pan coated with cooking spray. Bake at 350° for 25 minutes or until a wooden pick inserted in center comes out clean. Cool in pan on a wire rack. Spread Creamy Chocolate Frosting over cooled brownies; sprinkle with crushed candies, and cut into squares. Yield: 2 dozen.

Creamy Chocolate Frosting

3 cups sifted powdered sugar
¼ cup unsweetened cocoa
¼ cup skim milk
2 teaspoons vanilla extract
¼ teaspoon salt

Combine all ingredients; stir until frosting is spreading consistency. Yield: 1 cup.

Per Brownie:

Calories 191	Carbohydrate 35.3g	Fiber 0.2g
Fat 4.2g	Cholesterol 0mg	Calcium 28mg
Protein 3.5g	Sodium 158mg	Iron 0.9mg

Exchange: 2 Starch

Strawberry-Oatmeal Squares

Prep time: 10 minutes   Cook time: 25 minutes

⅓ cup margarine, softened
⅔ cup firmly packed brown sugar
1 teaspoon vanilla extract
1 cup regular oats, uncooked
⅔ cup whole wheat flour
½ teaspoon baking soda
⅛ teaspoon salt
2 tablespoons sugar
1½ tablespoons cornstarch
1 (10-ounce) package frozen strawberries in light syrup, thawed
¼ teaspoon almond extract

Beat margarine at medium speed of an electric mixer until light and fluffy; gradually add brown sugar, and beat well. Add vanilla, beating well. Stir in oats and next 3 ingredients. Firmly press 2 cups oat mixture evenly into an 8-inch square baking pan; reserve remaining oat mixture. Bake at 375° for 5 minutes.

Combine sugar and cornstarch in a medium saucepan; stir in strawberries. Bring to a boil, stirring constantly, until thickened and bubbly. Remove from heat; stir in almond extract.

Spread strawberry mixture over prepared oatmeal crust; top with reserved oat mixture. Bake at 375° for 15 minutes. Remove from oven; let cool completely. Cut into squares. Yield: 16 squares.

Per Square:

Calories 128	Carbohydrate 21.9g	Fiber 1.3 g
Fat 4.2g	Cholesterol 0mg	Calcium 16mg
Protein 1.6g	Sodium 93mg	Iron 0.7mg

Exchange: 1½ Starch

Greek-Seasoned Chicken with Orzo (page 88)

Entrées

Taco Pie

Prep time: 15 minutes   Cook time: 22 minutes
Stand time: 5 minutes

¾   pound ground round
1½ teaspoons chili powder
1   clove garlic, minced
1   (15-ounce) can or 1½ cups kidney beans,
      rinsed and drained
½   cup sliced green onions (about 2 green
      onions)
2   tablespoons red wine vinegar
2   tablespoons tomato paste
5   (6-inch) corn tortillas
1¼ cups canned no-salt-added chicken broth
1   tablespoon plus 2 teaspoons instant-blending
      flour
½   teaspoon ground cumin
1   (4½-ounce) can chopped green chiles,
      undrained
    Vegetable cooking spray
¾   cup (3 ounces) shredded reduced-fat
      Cheddar cheese

Combine first 3 ingredients in a nonstick skillet. Cook over medium-high heat until browned, stirring well. Drain well. Return meat mixture to skillet. Stir in kidney beans, green onions, vinegar, and tomato paste.

Cut each tortilla into 6 wedges. Wrap tortillas in aluminum foil, and bake at 350° for 8 minutes.

Bring broth to a boil in a saucepan. Reduce heat, and simmer. Add flour and cumin; cook, stirring constantly, until slightly thickened. Remove from heat; stir in chiles. Set aside.

Coat a 9-inch pieplate with cooking spray; line with 14 tortilla wedges. Top with one-third of meat mixture. Spoon one-third of broth mixture over meat. Repeat layers twice, using 10 tortilla wedges on second layer, and 6 on third layer. Sprinkle with cheese. Bake at 375° for 10 minutes or until cheese melts. Let stand 5 minutes on a wire rack. Cut into wedges to serve. Yield: 6 servings.

Per Serving:

Calories 255	Carbohydrate 28.6g	Fiber 3.5g
Fat 6.1g	Cholesterol 43mg	Calcium 161mg
Protein 22.6g	Sodium 357mg	Iron 3.5mg

Exchanges: 2½ Lean Meat, 1½ Starch

Salisbury Steak

Prep time: 10 minutes   Cook time: 16 minutes

1   pound ground round
¼   cup finely chopped onion
3   tablespoons fine, dry breadcrumbs
1   egg white
2   tablespoons water
¼   teaspoon beef-flavored bouillon granules
¼   teaspoon pepper
½   teaspoon salt
    Vegetable cooking spray
1   teaspoon margarine
1   (8-ounce) package sliced fresh mushrooms
1   small onion, thinly sliced and separated into
      rings
1   (14¼-ounce) can no-salt-added beef broth
2   tablespoons low-sodium Worcestershire
      sauce
2   tablespoons water
1   tablespoon cornstarch

Combine first 8 ingredients in a bowl; stir well. Divide into 4 equal portions, shaping each into a ¾-inch-thick patty.

Coat a large nonstick skillet with cooking spray; place over medium-high heat until hot. Add patties; cook 5 minutes on each side. Drain and pat dry with paper towels. Set patties aside, and keep warm.

Wipe drippings from skillet. Coat skillet with cooking spray; add margarine. Place skillet over medium-high heat until margarine melts. Add mushrooms and onion; sauté until tender. Add broth and Worcestershire sauce; cook 5 minutes. Return patties to skillet. Cover, reduce heat, and simmer 10 minutes. Remove from liquid with a slotted spoon; place on a platter; set aside, and keep warm.

Combine water and cornstarch; stir well. Add cornstarch mixture to broth mixture in skillet. Bring to a boil; cook 1 minute, stirring constantly, or until thickened. Spoon over patties.
Yield: 4 servings.

Per Serving:

Calories 237	Carbohydrate 13.7g	Fiber 1.7g
Fat 6.3g	Cholesterol 65mg	Calcium 26mg
Protein 29.2g	Sodium 511mg	Iron 3.5mg

Exchanges: 3 Lean Meat, ½ Starch, 1 Vegetable

Salisbury Steak

Marinated Flank Steak

Prep time: 5 minutes   Marinate time: 8 hours
Cook time: 14 minutes

1   (1½-pound) lean flank steak
¼   cup water
¼   cup dry red wine
¼   cup low-sodium soy sauce
3   tablespoons lemon juice
1   tablespoon vegetable oil
2   teaspoons honey
1   clove garlic, crushed
1   teaspoon cracked pepper
1   teaspoon dried oregano
1   teaspoon dry mustard
¼   teaspoon salt
    Vegetable cooking spray

Trim fat from steak. Score steak diagonally across grain in a diamond design at 1-inch intervals on both sides. Place steak in a heavy-duty, zip-top plastic bag. Combine water and next 10 ingredients; pour over meat. Seal bag securely; marinate in refrigerator 8 hours, turning bag occasionally.

Remove steak from marinade, discarding marinade.

Coat grill rack with cooking spray; place on grill over medium-hot coals (350° to 400°). Place steak on rack; grill, covered, 7 minutes on each side or to desired degree of doneness. Slice steak diagonally across grain into thin slices.
Yield: 6 servings.

Per Serving:

Calories 230	Carbohydrate 1.6g	Fiber 0.1g
Fat 14.1g	Cholesterol 60mg	Calcium 9mg
Protein 21.7g	Sodium 250mg	Iron 2.3mg

Exchanges: 3 Lean Meat, 1 Fat

Infuse Flavor

Score the steak (make shallow cuts in a diamond pattern on the surface of the meat). Scoring allows the meat to absorb more of the flavors of the marinade and tenderizes this lean cut of beef.

Flank Steak with Horseradish Cream

Prep time: 8 minutes   Marinate time: 8 hours
Cook time: 12 minutes

1   small onion, quartered
¼   cup light olive oil vinaigrette
1   teaspoon dried Italian seasoning
1   (1-pound) lean flank steak
    Vegetable cooking spray
½   cup nonfat sour cream
2   tablespoons nonfat mayonnaise
1½ tablespoons prepared horseradish

Position knife blade in food processor bowl; add first 3 ingredients. Process until onion is minced.

Score steak on both sides; place in a large heavy-duty, zip-top plastic bag. Pour onion mixture over meat; seal bag, and shake until meat is well coated. Marinate in refrigerator 8 hours, turning bag occasionally.

Remove steak from marinade; discard marinade. Coat grill rack with cooking spray; place on grill over medium-hot coals (350° to 400°). Place meat on rack; grill, covered, 10 to 12 minutes or to desired degree of doneness. Let stand 5 minutes.

Combine sour cream, mayonnaise, and horseradish, stirring well. Cut meat diagonally across grain into thin slices; arrange on serving plates, and serve with horseradish mixture.
Yield: 4 servings.

Per Serving:

Calories 238	Carbohydrate 4.4g	Fiber 0.1g
Fat 12.9g	Cholesterol 60mg	Calcium 11mg
Protein 23.7g	Sodium 191mg	Iron 2.3mg

Exchanges: 3 Lean Meat, ½ Starch

Teriyaki Beef and Peppers

Prep time: 18 minutes   Cook time: 9 minutes

½ cup low-sodium teriyaki sauce
¼ cup unsweetened pineapple juice
1 tablespoon cornstarch
2 teaspoons minced garlic
1 (1-pound) lean flank steak
   Vegetable cooking spray
1 tablespoon vegetable oil
1 medium-size sweet red pepper, seeded and
   cut into thin strips
1 medium-size sweet yellow pepper, seeded
   and cut into thin strips
1 medium-size green pepper, seeded and cut
   into thin strips
2 cups cooked long-grain rice (cooked without
   salt or fat)

Combine first 4 ingredients; set aside.
Partially freeze steak; trim fat from steak.
Slice steak diagonally across grain into ¼-inch-wide strips.

Coat a wok or large nonstick skillet with cooking spray; drizzle oil around top of wok, coating sides. Heat at medium-high (375°) until hot. Add steak, and stir-fry 2 minutes or until lightly browned. Add peppers to wok; stir-fry 4 minutes. Add teriyaki mixture to steak and peppers; stir-fry 3 minutes or until thickened. Serve over rice. Yield: 4 servings.

Per Serving:

Calories 391	Carbohydrate 39.0g	Fiber 1.9g
Fat 13.5g	Cholesterol 57mg	Calcium 26mg
Protein 26.6g	Sodium 726mg	Iron 4.3mg

Exchanges: 3 Lean Meat, 2 Starch, ½ Fat

Orange Beef Stir-Fry

SuperQuick

Prep time: 10 minutes   Cook time: 15 minutes

1   (1-pound) lean flank steak
1   (11-ounce) can mandarin oranges in light
      syrup, undrained
½   cup low-sugar orange marmalade
3   tablespoons hoisin sauce
      Vegetable cooking spray
2   teaspoons sesame oil, divided
2   (6-ounce) packages frozen snow peas
¼   teaspoon salt
2   cups cooked long-grain rice (cooked without
      salt or fat)
      Dried crushed red pepper (optional)

Trim fat from steak. Slice steak diagonally
across grain into thin strips; set aside.

Drain oranges, reserving 2 tablespoons juice.
Set oranges aside. Discard remaining juice.
Combine reserved 2 tablespoons juice, marmalade,
and hoisin sauce in a small bowl; set aside.

Coat a wok or large nonstick skillet with
cooking spray; drizzle 1 teaspoon oil around top of
wok, coating sides. Heat at medium-high (375°)
until hot. Add steak strips, and stir-fry 6 minutes.
Remove steak strips from wok; drain and pat dry
with paper towels.

Drizzle remaining 1 teaspoon oil around top
of wok, coating sides. Add snow peas; stir-fry 4
minutes. Add steak strips and salt.

Stir in marmalade mixture and oranges. Bring
to a boil, and stir-fry 1 minute or until thoroughly
heated. Serve over rice. Sprinkle with red pepper,
if desired. Yield: 4 servings.

Per Serving:

Calories 456	Carbohydrate 50.2g	Fiber 3.1g
Fat 15.5g	Cholesterol 60mg	Calcium 66mg
Protein 27.2g	Sodium 472mg	Iron 4.8mg

Exchanges: 3 Lean Meat, 1 Starch, 1 Vegetable, 1 Fruit, ½ Fat

Slice It Nice

Make it easy to slice thin, even pieces of meat
by partially freezing the meat 15 to 20 minutes or
until firm but not hard.

Beef Burgundy with Noodles

Prep time: 15 minutes   Cook time: 46 minutes

1   (1-pound) lean boneless top round steak
2   tablespoons all-purpose flour
⅛   teaspoon freshly ground pepper
      Vegetable cooking spray
1   cup finely chopped onion
½   teaspoon salt
¼   teaspoon pepper
¼   teaspoon dried oregano
⅛   teaspoon dried thyme
1   bay leaf
2   cloves garlic, minced
1   cup canned no-salt-added beef broth
½   cup dry red wine
1   cup sliced fresh mushrooms
¼   cup water
1   tablespoon cornstarch
3   cups hot cooked noodles (cooked without
      salt or fat)

Trim fat from steak; slice diagonally across
grain into 2- x ¾-inch strips.

Combine flour and pepper in a heavy-duty,
zip-top plastic bag; add steak. Seal bag securely,
and shake until steak is well coated.

Coat a Dutch oven with cooking spray; place
over medium-high heat until hot. Add steak; cook
until browned, stirring occasionally. Stir in onion
and next 8 ingredients. Bring to a boil; cover,
reduce heat, and simmer 40 minutes, stirring occasionally. Add mushrooms; cook 5 minutes.
Combine water and cornstarch; gradually stir into
beef mixture. Bring to a boil; boil 1 minute, stirring
constantly. Remove and discard bay leaf. Serve
steak mixture over noodles. Yield: 4 servings.

Per Serving:

Calories 386	Carbohydrate 40.8g	Fiber 4.0g
Fat 6.7g	Cholesterol 104mg	Calcium 36mg
Protein 33.3g	Sodium 368mg	Iron 5.3mg

Exchanges: 4 Lean Meat, 1 Starch, ½ Vegetable

Baked Sweet-and-Sour Steak

Prep time: 20 minutes   Cook time: 1 hour

2   (1-pound) lean boneless top round steaks
    Vegetable cooking spray
1   (16-ounce) package frozen pepper stir-fry
⅓   cup firmly packed brown sugar
⅓   cup cider vinegar
⅓   cup ketchup
½   teaspoon salt
½   teaspoon pepper
2   tablespoons cornstarch
¼   cup water
1   (15¼-ounce) can pineapple chunks in juice,
    drained

Trim fat from steak. Place 1 steak between 2 sheets of heavy-duty plastic wrap, and flatten to ¼-inch thickness, using a meat mallet or rolling pin. Cut steak into 4 pieces. Repeat procedure with remaining steak.

Coat a large nonstick skillet with cooking spray; place over medium-high heat until hot. Add 4 steak pieces, and cook 1½ minutes on each side or until browned. Place in a 13- x 9- x 2-inch baking dish coated with cooking spray. Repeat procedure with remaining meat.

Top meat with frozen vegetables. Combine brown sugar and next 4 ingredients in a small bowl, stirring mixture well. Pour brown sugar mixture over vegetables. Cover and bake at 350° for 40 minutes.

Combine cornstarch and water, stirring until smooth. Add to meat and vegetables, stirring well. Add pineapple, and bake, uncovered, 20 additional minutes. Yield: 8 servings.

Per Serving:

Calories 243	Carbohydrate 21.9g	Fiber 2.0g
Fat 4.9g	Cholesterol 65mg	Calcium 18mg
Protein 26.9g	Sodium 337mg	Iron 2.9mg

Exchanges: 3 Very Lean Meat, 1½ Starch

Save Those Juices

Spoon the delicious juices in the baking dish over some steamed rice for a flavorful side dish.

Beef Stroganoff

Prep time: 12 minutes   Cook time: 23 minutes

1   pound lean boneless top sirloin steak
    Vegetable cooking spray
1   (8-ounce) package sliced fresh mushrooms
1   small onion, cut in half and sliced
2   cloves garlic, crushed
½   cup water
¼   cup dry red wine
1   tablespoon all-purpose flour
1   teaspoon dry mustard
1   teaspoon beef-flavored bouillon granules
½   teaspoon dried thyme
¼   teaspoon pepper
½   cup low-fat sour cream
3   cups cooked medium egg noodles (cooked
    without salt or fat)
2   tablespoons sliced green onions

Trim fat from steak; cut steak diagonally across grain into ¼-inch-thick slices. Coat a large nonstick skillet with cooking spray. Place over medium-high heat until hot. Add steak, mushrooms, onion, and garlic. Cook until meat is browned on all sides, stirring often.

Combine water and next 6 ingredients in a small bowl; stir well with a wire whisk. Add to beef mixture. Bring to a boil; cover, reduce heat, and simmer 10 minutes or until steak is tender. Uncover and cook 5 additional minutes or until slightly thickened. Remove from heat; stir in sour cream. Serve over noodles, and sprinkle with green onions. Yield: 6 servings.

Per Serving:

Calories 272	Carbohydrate 26.1g	Fiber 2.8g
Fat 7.9g	Cholesterol 80mg	Calcium 50mg
Protein 21.9g	Sodium 219mg	Iron 4.2mg

Exchanges: 3 Lean Meat, 1 Starch, 1 Vegetable

Beef Tenderloin with Mustard Sauce

Prep time: 5 minutes   Cook time: 34 minutes
Stand time: 10 minutes

1 (2-pound) beef tenderloin, trimmed
   Vegetable cooking spray
¼ cup dry red wine
¼ teaspoon salt
¼ teaspoon pepper
1 (8-ounce) carton nonfat sour cream
¾ cup skim milk
2 tablespoons stone-ground or coarse-grained
      mustard
¼ teaspoon salt
¼ teaspoon pepper

Place tenderloin on a rack in a roasting pan coated with cooking spray. Insert meat thermometer into thickest portion of tenderloin. Combine wine, ¼ teaspoon salt, and ¼ teaspoon pepper; brush over tenderloin. Bake at 425° for 30 to 45 minutes or until meat thermometer registers 140° (rare) or 160° (medium), basting often with wine mixture. Let stand 10 minutes.

Combine sour cream and remaining 4 ingredients in a small saucepan. Cook over low heat until thoroughly heated, stirring often. Slice meat, and serve with sauce. Yield: 8 servings.

Per Serving:

Calories 212	Carbohydrate 3.5g	Fiber 0.0g
Fat 8.2g	Cholesterol 72mg	Calcium 36mg
Protein 26.8g	Sodium 344mg	Iron 3.1mg

Exchanges: 3 Lean Meat, ½ Starch

Robust Mustard

A stone-ground or finely ground mustard such as Dijon imparts an intense flavor and a smooth consistency to this sauce. A coarsely ground mustard adds a milder flavor punch and not as smooth a consistency. But both types act as a natural thickening agent in the sauce.

Honey-Orange Roast

Prep time: 13 minutes   Cook time: 1 hour, 50 minutes

1 (2½-pound) lean boneless sirloin roast
8 cloves garlic, halved
¼ teaspoon salt
1 teaspoon coarsely ground pepper
   Vegetable cooking spray
1 cup unsweetened orange juice
½ cup low-sugar orange marmalade
2 tablespoons honey
1 tablespoon low-sodium soy sauce
1 teaspoon dried rosemary, crushed

Trim fat from roast. Make 16 slits halfway through roast; insert 1 garlic clove half in each slit. Sprinkle roast with salt and pepper. Coat a large skillet with cooking spray; place over medium-high heat until hot. Add roast, and cook 5 to 6 minutes on each side or until browned on all sides.

Combine orange juice and remaining 4 ingredients. Pour juice mixture over roast; bring to a boil. Cover, reduce heat, and simmer 1½ hours or until roast is tender. Remove roast from skillet; set aside, and keep warm.

Skim fat from pan juices. Bring juices to a boil; cook over medium heat 20 minutes or until mixture is reduced by half, stirring occasionally. Cut roast into thin slices; serve with juices. Yield: 8 servings.

Per Serving:

Calories 213	Carbohydrate 9.9g	Fiber 0.2g
Fat 6.5g	Cholesterol 79mg	Calcium 29mg
Protein 27.5g	Sodium 185mg	Iron 3.2mg

Exchanges: 3 Lean Meat, ½ Starch

Mellow Out

Inserting pieces of garlic in the roast gives the meat a mellow garlic flavor.

French-Style Beef Roast

Prep time: 10 minutes   Cook time: 3 hours
Stand time: 10 minutes

1   (3-pound) boneless rump roast
3   large cloves garlic, quartered
2   bay leaves
4   cups canned no-salt-added beef broth
1   teaspoon dried thyme
1   teaspoon pepper
½   teaspoon salt
7   medium carrots, scraped and cut into 2-inch pieces
4   stalks celery, cut into 2-inch pieces
1   pound fresh turnips, peeled and quartered
¾   pound small onions, quartered

Trim fat from roast. Place roast and next 6 ingredients in a large Dutch oven. Bring to a boil; cover, reduce heat, and simmer 2 hours.

Add carrot and remaining 3 ingredients; cover and simmer 1 hour or until vegetables are tender.

Remove and discard bay leaves. Transfer roast to a serving platter; cover and let stand 10 minutes. Arrange vegetables around roast. Pour cooking liquid through a wire-mesh strainer into a bowl, and serve with roast and vegetables.
Yield: 10 servings.

Per Serving:

Calories 227	Carbohydrate 11.9g	Fiber 3.2g
Fat 5.4g	Cholesterol 73mg	Calcium 46mg
Protein 30.6g	Sodium 243mg	Iron 3.4mg

Exchanges: 3 Lean Meat, 2 Vegetable

Apple Veal Chops

Prep time: 8 minutes   Cook time: 27 minutes

4   (6-ounce) lean veal loin chops (½ inch thick)
¼   cup all-purpose flour, divided
½   teaspoon dried marjoram
½   teaspoon salt
     Olive oil-flavored vegetable cooking spray
1   tablespoon olive oil
½   cup chopped onion
½   cup canned no-salt-added chicken broth
¼   cup unsweetened apple juice
1   small Granny Smith apple, cored and sliced
1   small Rome apple, cored and sliced

Trim fat from chops. Combine 3 tablespoons flour, marjoram, and salt; dredge veal shanks in flour mixture.

Coat a large nonstick skillet with cooking spray; add oil. Place over medium-high heat until hot. Add veal, and cook 2 minutes on each side or until browned. Remove veal from skillet; drain. Wipe drippings from skillet with a paper towel, if necessary.

Coat skillet with cooking spray; place over medium-high heat until hot. Add onion; sauté until tender. Add remaining 1 tablespoon flour; cook, stirring constantly, 1 minute. Add broth and apple juice, stirring well. Return veal to skillet; top with apple slices. Bring to a boil; cover, reduce heat, and simmer 20 minutes or until veal is tender.
Yield: 4 servings.

Per Serving:

Calories 257	Carbohydrate 21.5g	Fiber 3.1g
Fat 8.0g	Cholesterol 91mg	Calcium 33mg
Protein 24.3g	Sodium 414mg	Iron 1.5mg

Exchanges: 3 Lean Meat, ½ Starch, 1 Fruit

Veal Marsala

Prep time: 20 minutes   Cook time: 15 minutes

3   ounces fettuccine, uncooked
6   ounces veal cutlets (¼ inch thick)
2   tablespoons all-purpose flour
    Olive oil-flavored vegetable cooking spray
⅓   cup Marsala
1   cup sliced fresh mushrooms
⅔   cup canned no-salt-added chicken broth
½   cup sweet red pepper strips
½   medium onion, sliced and separated into rings
1   teaspoon lemon juice
¼   teaspoon salt
¼   teaspoon pepper

Cook fettuccine according to package directions, omitting salt and fat; drain. Set aside, and keep warm.

Place cutlets between 2 sheets of heavy-duty plastic wrap; flatten to ⅛-inch thickness, using a meat mallet or rolling pin. Cut veal into 1-inch pieces.

Combine veal and flour in a heavy-duty, zip-top plastic bag. Seal bag, and shake until veal is coated.

Coat a large nonstick skillet with cooking spray; place over medium-high heat until hot. Add veal, and cook until browned on all sides. Transfer veal to a 1-quart casserole coated with cooking spray; set aside.

Add wine to skillet; bring to a boil, scraping browned particles that cling to bottom of skillet. Pour wine over veal; set aside.

Coat skillet with cooking spray; place over medium-high heat until hot. Add mushrooms and remaining 6 ingredients; cook, stirring constantly, until vegetables are tender. Spoon vegetables over veal. Bake, uncovered, at 400° for 15 to 20 minutes or until mixture is bubbly.

To serve, place ½ cup cooked pasta on each individual serving plate; spoon veal mixture evenly over pasta. Yield: 2 servings.

Per Serving:

Calories 364	Carbohydrate 45.2g	Fiber 5.3g
Fat 4.5g	Cholesterol 71mg	Calcium 59mg
Protein 24.5g	Sodium 379mg	Iron 3.6mg

Exchanges: 3 Lean Meat, 1 Starch, 2 Vegetable

Grilled Ginger Lamb Chops

Prep time: 5 minutes   Marinate time: 8 hours
Cook time: 21 minutes

8   (4-ounce) lean lamb loin chops (1 inch thick)
½   cup dry red wine
2   tablespoons peeled, minced gingerroot
2   tablespoons low-sodium soy sauce
1   tablespoon honey
1   teaspoon onion powder
¼   teaspoon pepper
2   cloves garlic, minced
    Vegetable cooking spray
1½ teaspoons cornstarch
¼   cup canned no-salt-added beef broth, divided

Trim fat from chops. Place chops in a heavy-duty, zip-top plastic bag. Combine wine and next 6 ingredients; stir well. Pour marinade over chops. Seal bag securely; marinate in refrigerator 8 hours, turning bag occasionally.

Remove chops from marinade, straining and reserving ½ cup marinade. Coat grill rack with cooking spray; place on grill over medium-hot coals (350° to 400°). Place chops on rack; grill, uncovered, 8 to 10 minutes on each side or to desired degree of doneness. Transfer chops to a serving platter, and keep warm.

Dissolve cornstarch in 1 tablespoon beef broth; add remaining 3 tablespoons broth, stirring well. Combine reserved ½ cup marinade and beef broth mixture in a small saucepan, stirring until smooth. Bring to a boil, and cook, stirring constantly, 1 minute. Spoon broth mixture evenly over chops. Yield: 4 servings.

Per Serving:

Calories 236	Carbohydrate 6.9g	Fiber 0.1g
Fat 8.5g	Cholesterol 81mg	Calcium 24mg
Protein 25.8g	Sodium 271mg	Iron 2.1mg

Exchanges: 3 Lean Meat, ½ Starch

Ginger Grilled Lamb Chops

Lamb Chops with Herbs

SuperQuick

Prep time: 5 minutes   Cook time: 20 minutes

4 (4-ounce) lean lamb loin chops
¼ teaspoon freshly ground pepper
1 tablespoon minced fresh chives
1 tablespoon minced fresh parsley
1 tablespoon chopped fresh rosemary
   Vegetable cooking spray

Trim fat from chops; sprinkle chops with pepper. Combine chives, parsley, and rosemary; press herb mixture evenly onto both sides of chops.

Coat a large nonstick skillet with cooking spray; place over medium-high heat until hot. Add chops, and cook 10 minutes on each side or to desired degree of doneness. Yield: 2 servings.

Per Serving:

Calories 194	Carbohydrate 0.8g	Fiber 0.4g
Fat 9.1g	Cholesterol 81mg	Calcium 30mg
Protein 25.7g	Sodium 73mg	Iron 2.1mg

Exchange: 3 Lean Meat

Lamb Steaks with Artichokes and Mushrooms

Prep time: 10 minutes   Cook time: 25 minutes

¼ teaspoon salt
¼ teaspoon pepper
6 (5-ounce) lean lamb sirloin steaks (¾ inch thick)
   Butter-flavored vegetable cooking spray
1½ cups fresh mushrooms, halved
1½ cups canned no-salt-added beef broth
1 tablespoon plus 1 teaspoon cornstarch
2 tablespoons dry sherry
1 large clove garlic, minced
1 (14-ounce) can quartered artichoke hearts, drained

Combine salt and pepper. Sprinkle meat with half of salt mixture. Set remaining salt mixture aside.

Coat a large nonstick skillet with cooking spray. Place over medium-high heat until hot. Add steaks to skillet, and cook 4 to 5 minutes on each side or to desired degree of doneness. Transfer steaks to a serving platter; set aside, and keep warm. Wipe drippings from skillet with a paper towel. Coat skillet with cooking spray. Place over medium-high heat until hot.

Add mushrooms to skillet. Sauté 5 minutes or until tender; remove mushrooms from skillet. Set aside, and keep warm.

Combine remaining salt mixture, broth, and next 3 ingredients in a medium bowl, stirring well. Add broth mixture to skillet. Cook over medium heat, stirring constantly, until thickened. Return mushrooms to skillet; add artichokes. Cook until thoroughly heated.

Spoon mushrooms and artichokes over lamb steaks, using a slotted spoon. Pour broth mixture over lamb and vegetables. Serve immediately. Yield: 6 servings.

Per Serving:

Calories 217	Carbohydrate 8.4g	Fiber 1.4g
Fat 8.2g	Cholesterol 78mg	Calcium 29mg
Protein 26.2g	Sodium 299mg	Iron 2.8mg

Exchanges: 3 Lean Meat, ½ Starch

Pork Chops with Orange-Mustard Sauce

SuperQuick
Prep time: 5 minutes   Cook time: 11 minutes

8 (2-ounce) lean boneless center-cut loin pork chops (¼ inch thick)
2 tablespoons all-purpose flour
½ teaspoon salt
⅛ teaspoon pepper
 Vegetable cooking spray
1 teaspoon olive oil
½ cup frozen orange juice concentrate, thawed
2 tablespoons lemon juice
2 tablespoons minced green onions
1 tablespoon Dijon mustard
1 teaspoon brown sugar
1 teaspoon minced fresh cilantro
¼ teaspoon curry powder
 Dash of ground red pepper

Trim fat from chops. Combine flour, salt, and pepper; dredge chops in flour mixture.

Coat a large nonstick skillet with cooking spray, and add oil. Place over medium heat until hot. Add chops; cook 3 minutes on each side or until browned. Add orange juice concentrate and lemon juice; cook over medium heat 4 minutes or until pork chops are tender. Transfer chops to a serving platter. Set aside, and keep warm.

Add green onions and remaining 5 ingredients to orange juice mixture; cook over medium heat, uncovered, 1 minute or until thickened, stirring often. Spoon sauce over pork chops.
Yield: 4 servings.

Per Serving:

Calories 229	Carbohydrate 8.1g	Fiber 0.3g
Fat 9.6g	Cholesterol 71mg	Calcium 14mg
Protein 25.7g	Sodium 481mg	Iron 1.3mg

Exchanges: 3 Lean Meat, ½ Starch

Hoisin Pork Medaillons

SuperQuick
Prep time: 10 minutes   Cook time: 8 minutes

1 (1-pound) pork tenderloin
 Vegetable cooking spray
1 teaspoon dark sesame oil
⅛ teaspoon dried crushed red pepper
1 clove garlic, minced
2 tablespoons water
2 tablespoons dry sherry
1 tablespoon hoisin sauce
1 teaspoon dried cilantro
2 cups hot cooked long-grain rice (cooked without salt or fat)
¼ cup sliced green onions

Slice pork diagonally across grain into ½-inch-thick slices. Coat a large nonstick skillet with cooking spray; add sesame oil. Place skillet over medium-high heat until hot. Add red pepper and garlic; sauté 1 minute. Add pork medaillons, and cook 4 to 5 minutes on each side or until browned. Transfer to a serving platter, and keep warm. Wipe drippings from skillet with a paper towel.

Add water and next 3 ingredients to skillet; stir well. Cook over medium heat 1 minute or until slightly thickened, stirring constantly.

To serve, place ½ cup cooked rice on each of 4 individual plates; place medaillons over rice. Spoon sauce evenly over each serving. Sprinkle each serving with 1 tablespoon green onions.
Yield: 4 servings.

Per Serving:

Calories 348	Carbohydrate 28.0g	Fiber 0.7g
Fat 13.2g	Cholesterol 77mg	Calcium 25mg
Protein 24.9g	Sodium 194mg	Iron 2.0mg

Exchanges: 3 Medium-Fat Meat, 1½ Starch

Sweet and Spicy Hoisin

Flavorful oriental ingredients such as sesame oil and hoisin sauce, a thick, sweet, spicy sauce, are available in most supermarkets. A simple substitute for hoisin sauce is equal parts of brown sugar and reduced-sodium soy sauce along with a dash of garlic powder.

Pork Curry

Prep time: 5 minutes   Cook time: 25 minutes

2   (¾-pound) pork tenderloins
2   teaspoons curry powder
1   teaspoon garlic powder
    Vegetable cooking spray
1¼ cups unsweetened orange juice, divided
¾   cup thinly sliced green onions
1   medium-size sweet red pepper, cut into thin
       strips
1½ teaspoons cornstarch
¼   cup plus 2 tablespoons raisins
1   teaspoon curry powder
½   teaspoon ground cumin
½   teaspoon salt

Trim fat from tenderloins; combine 2 tea-spoons curry powder and garlic powder, and rub over tenderloins.

Coat grill rack with cooking spray, and place on grill over medium-hot coals (350° to 400°). Insert meat thermometer into thickest part of pork, if desired. Place tenderloins on rack. Grill, covered, 20 minutes or until meat thermometer registers 160°, turning occasionally. Let stand 10 minutes.

Combine 2 tablespoons orange juice, green onions, and red pepper in a medium skillet; stir well. Cook over medium-high heat, stirring con-stantly, 2 minutes or until vegetables are tender.

Combine cornstarch and remaining 1 cup plus 2 tablespoons orange juice, stirring until smooth. Add cornstarch mixture to vegetable mixture in skillet; stir well. Add raisins and remaining 3 ingre-dients. Bring to a boil; reduce heat, and simmer, stirring constantly, 1 minute. Set aside.

Slice pork diagonally across grain into ¼-inch-thick slices. Serve with curry sauce.
Yield: 6 servings.

Per Serving:

Calories 211	Carbohydrate 16.6g	Fiber 1.7g
Fat 4.6g	Cholesterol 79mg	Calcium 34mg
Protein 25.8g	Sodium 258mg	Iron 2.5mg

Exchanges: 3 Very Lean Meat, 1½ Vegetable, ½ Fruit

Pork Chow Mein

Prep time: 25 minutes   Cook time: 11 minutes

1   (1-pound) lean boneless pork loin roast
1   cup canned no-salt-added chicken broth
¼   cup low-sodium soy sauce
1½ tablespoons cornstarch
1   teaspoon ground ginger
⅛   teaspoon dried crushed red pepper
    Vegetable cooking spray
1   clove garlic, minced
1   cup thinly sliced carrot
1   cup thinly sliced celery
1   cup chopped onion
1   cup coarsely chopped cabbage
1   cup chopped fresh spinach
4   cups cooked long-grain rice (cooked without
    salt or fat)

Trim fat from pork. Partially freeze pork; slice diagonally across grain into 2- x ¼-inch strips. Combine broth and next 4 ingredients; set aside.

Coat a wok or nonstick skillet with cooking spray; place over medium-high heat (375°) until hot. Add pork and garlic; stir-fry 5 minutes or until browned. Add carrot and next 4 ingredients; stir-fry 3 minutes. Add broth mixture; cover and cook 3 minutes or until vegetables are crisp-tender, stirring occasionally. Serve over rice. Yield: 4 servings.

Per Serving:		
Calories 458	Carbohydrate 59.4g	Fiber 3.8g
Fat 9.6g	Cholesterol 68mg	Calcium 73mg
Protein 29.4g	Sodium 540mg	Iron 3.5mg

Exchanges: 3 Lean Meat, 2 Starch, 2 Vegetable

Roasted Pork with Cinnamon Apples

Prep time: 15 minutes   Cook time: 1 hour, 30 minutes

½   cup honey, divided
2   tablespoons Dijon mustard
1   tablespoon low-sodium soy sauce
1   (1½-pound) lean boneless pork loin roast
    Vegetable cooking spray
1   tablespoon cider vinegar
¼   teaspoon ground cinnamon
⅛   teaspoon salt
1   (20-ounce) can unsweetened sliced apples,
    undrained

Combine ¼ cup honey, mustard, and soy sauce; stir well, and set aside.

Trim fat from roast; place roast on a rack in a roasting pan coated with cooking spray. Insert meat thermometer into thickest part of roast, if desired. Cover and bake at 325° for 1 hour. Uncover and brush with half of honey mixture; bake, uncovered, 15 minutes. Brush with remaining honey mixture; bake 15 additional minutes or until meat thermometer registers 160°. Set aside, and keep warm.

Combine remaining ¼ cup honey, vinegar, cinnamon, and salt in a large nonstick skillet; bring to a boil. Add apples; cook over medium heat 7 minutes or until apples are tender.

Slice roast, and arrange on a serving platter; serve roast with apple mixture. Yield: 6 servings.

Per Serving:		
Calories 324	Carbohydrate 31.8g	Fiber 1.4g
Fat 11.7g	Cholesterol 73mg	Calcium 10mg
Protein 21.9g	Sodium 333mg	Iron 1.1mg

Exchanges: 3 Lean Meat, 1 Starch, 1 Fruit

Singled Out

Be sure to buy a single loin roast because it cooks quicker than a double loin roast. A double loin roast will be tied together with a net or butcher string.

Barbecued Pork Loin Roast

Prep time: 15 minutes   Marinate time: 8 hours
Cook time: 40 minutes

1   (2¼-pound) boneless pork loin roast, trimmed
1   cup finely chopped onion
1   cup plus 2 tablespoons reduced-calorie ketchup
2   cloves garlic, minced
1½ tablespoons honey
2¼ teaspoons unsweetened cocoa
2¼ teaspoons brown sugar
1   tablespoon lemon juice
2¼ teaspoons liquid smoke
¼   teaspoon pepper
⅛   teaspoon ground mace
    Vegetable cooking spray

Butterfly roast by making a lengthwise cut down center of roast, cutting to within ½ inch of other side. Place roast in a shallow dish; set aside.

Combine onion and next 9 ingredients; spread half of marinade mixture over both sides of roast, reserving remaining marinade. Cover roast, and marinate in refrigerator 8 hours. Chill reserved marinade in refrigerator.

Coat a grill rack with cooking spray; place on grill over medium-hot coals (350° to 400°). Remove roast from marinade, discarding marinade in dish. Insert meat thermometer into thickest part of roast, if desired. Place roast on rack, and grill, uncovered, 30 minutes or until meat thermometer registers 160°, turning once. Remove roast from grill; cover with aluminum foil, and keep warm.

Cook reserved marinade in a heavy saucepan over medium-low heat 10 minutes or until mixture reaches desired consistency, stirring often. Cut roast into thin slices, and serve with sauce. Yield: 8 servings.

Per Serving:

Calories 238	Carbohydrate 8.8g	Fiber 0.3g
Fat 9.1g	Cholesterol 83mg	Calcium 11mg
Protein 27.6g	Sodium 75mg	Iron 0.9mg

Exchanges: 3½ Lean Meat, ½ Starch

Hawaiian Ham Kabobs

Prep time: 18 minutes   Marinate time: 15 minutes
Cook time: 10 minutes

1   (15¼-ounce) can pineapple chunks in juice, undrained
¼   cup low-sodium soy sauce
1   tablespoon brown sugar
1   tablespoon balsamic vinegar
1   tablespoon honey
2   teaspoons peeled, grated gingerroot
1   teaspoon Dijon mustard
¼   teaspoon pepper
1   pound reduced-fat, low-salt cooked ham, cut into 1-inch cubes
2   medium-size green peppers, cut into 1-inch pieces
2   medium-size sweet red peppers, cut into 1-inch pieces
    Vegetable cooking spray

Drain pineapple chunks, reserving juice. Set pineapple aside.

Combine juice, soy sauce, and next 6 ingredients in a shallow dish; stir well. Add ham and pineapple to juice mixture; stir gently to coat. Cover and marinate in refrigerator at least 15 minutes, stirring occasionally.

Remove ham and pineapple from marinade, reserving marinade. Place marinade in a small saucepan. Bring to a boil; reduce heat, and simmer 10 minutes or until the consistency of syrup.

Thread ham, pineapple, and peppers alternately onto 12 (10-inch) skewers. Coat grill rack with cooking spray; place on grill over medium-hot coals (350° to 400°). Place kabobs on rack; grill, uncovered, 10 minutes, turning and basting often with marinade. Yield: 6 servings.

Per Serving:

Calories 173	Carbohydrate 19.8g	Fiber 2.1g
Fat 4.1g	Cholesterol 37mg	Calcium 18mg
Protein 14.0g	Sodium 873mg	Iron 0.9mg

Exchanges: 2 Lean Meat, ½ Starch, ½ Vegetable, ½ Fruit

Chicken Jambalaya

Prep time: 10 minutes   Cook time: 35 minutes

　 Vegetable cooking spray
2 teaspoons vegetable oil
¾ cup coarsely chopped lean cooked ham
　　 (about ¼ pound)
¾ cup chopped green pepper
½ cup chopped onion
½ cup chopped celery
2 cloves garlic, minced
2 cups canned low-sodium chicken broth
1 (14½-ounce) can no-salt-added stewed
　　 tomatoes, undrained and chopped
2 cups chopped cooked chicken
⅔ cup long-grain rice, uncooked
1 bay leaf
1 teaspoon dried basil
½ teaspoon dried thyme
½ teaspoon chili powder
½ teaspoon hot sauce
¼ teaspoon salt
¼ teaspoon pepper

　　Coat a Dutch oven with cooking spray; add oil. Place over medium heat until hot. Add ham, green pepper, onion, celery, and garlic; sauté 5 minutes. Stir in chicken broth and remaining ingredients. Bring to a boil; cover, reduce heat, and simmer 15 minutes. Uncover and cook 15 additional minutes or until liquid is absorbed and rice is tender, stirring occasionally. Remove and discard bay leaf. Yield: 4(1½-cup) servings.

Per Serving:

Calories 365	Carbohydrate 35.8g	Fiber 2.4g
Fat 10.4g	Cholesterol 77mg	Calcium 81mg
Protein 31.2g	Sodium 624mg	Iron 4.5mg

Exchanges: 3 Lean Meat, 2 Starch, 1 Vegetable

What's Jambalaya?

　　Jambalaya is a hearty classic Cajun dish—Louisiana country food—that combines rice with almost any type of meat, poultry, or shellfish, and the culinary "holy trinity" of onions, green peppers, and celery.

Honey-Baked Drumsticks

Prep time: 5 minutes   Cook time: 35 minutes

½ cup regular oats, uncooked
2 tablespoons grated Parmesan cheese
⅛ teaspoon salt
¼ teaspoon paprika
¼ teaspoon pepper
　 Dash of garlic powder
8 chicken drumsticks, skinned (about 1¾
　　 pounds)
2 tablespoons honey

　　Combine first 6 ingredients in container of an electric blender or food processor; cover and process until mixture resembles coarse meal.
　　Brush chicken drumsticks lightly with honey; dredge in oat mixture. Place drumsticks on a rack in a roasting pan. Bake at 400° for 15 minutes. Turn drumsticks, and bake 20 additional minutes or until chicken is tender and golden. Transfer drumsticks to a large serving platter.
Yield: 4 servings.

Per Serving:

Calories 242	Carbohydrate 15.8g	Fiber 1.1g
Fat 6.0g	Cholesterol 104mg	Calcium 56mg
Protein 30.1g	Sodium 235mg	Iron 1.9mg

Exchanges: 4 Very Lean Meat, 1 Starch, ½ Fat

Chicken with Garlic and Spinach

Prep time: 15 minutes   Cook time: 35 minutes

½   pound fresh spinach
1   tablespoon olive oil
3   chicken breast halves (about 1½ pounds), skinned
3   chicken thighs (about ¾ pound), skinned
3   chicken drumsticks (about ½ pound), skinned
¾   cup diagonally sliced carrot
10 cloves garlic, halved
½   cup canned no-salt-added chicken broth
¼   teaspoon salt
¼   teaspoon pepper

Remove stems from spinach; wash leaves thoroughly, and pat dry. Tear into bite-size pieces; set spinach aside.

Heat oil in a large nonstick skillet over medium heat until hot. Add chicken pieces, and cook 5 minutes on each side or until browned; add carrot and garlic. Cover, reduce heat, and cook 20 minutes, turning chicken once. Remove chicken and carrot from skillet with a slotted spoon; set aside, and keep warm.

Cover and cook garlic 3 additional minutes. Add broth, salt, and pepper; bring to a boil. Cook, uncovered, 3 minutes or until reduced to ¼ cup. Place mixture in container of an electric blender or food processor; cover and process 30 seconds or until smooth, stopping once to scrape down sides. Set aside.

Place a large Dutch oven over medium heat, and add spinach; cover and cook 3 minutes. (Do not add water.) Drain well.

Place spinach on a serving platter. Arrange chicken and carrot on top of spinach; drizzle with garlic mixture. Yield: 6 servings.

Per Serving:

Calories 185	Carbohydrate 4.6g	Fiber 2.0g
Fat 5.5g	Cholesterol 86mg	Calcium 64mg
Protein 28.0g	Sodium 228mg	Iron 2.3mg

Exchanges: 3 Very Lean Meat, 1 Vegetable, ½ Fat

Chicken à la King

SuperQuick

Prep time: 15 minutes   Cook time: 10 minutes

6   slices whole wheat bread
1   tablespoon reduced-calorie margarine
3   (4-ounce) skinned, boned chicken breast halves, cut into bite-size pieces
¼   cup chopped onion
¼   cup sliced fresh mushrooms
¼   cup all-purpose flour
2   cups skim milk
¼   cup frozen English peas, thawed
1   (2-ounce) jar diced pimiento, drained
½   teaspoon salt
¼   teaspoon pepper
¼   teaspoon paprika

Trim crust from bread slices. Toast bread slices; cut each slice into 4 triangles, and set aside.

Melt margarine in a large nonstick skillet over medium heat. Add chicken and onion; cook, stirring constantly, 5 minutes or until chicken is browned. Add mushrooms to chicken mixture; cook, stirring constantly, 1 minute. Stir in flour, and cook, stirring constantly, 1 minute. Gradually add milk and next 4 ingredients; cook over medium heat, stirring constantly, until mixture is thickened and bubbly.

To serve, arrange 6 toast triangles on each individual serving plate. Spoon chicken mixture evenly over each serving; sprinkle with paprika. Yield: 4 servings.

Per Serving:

Calories 234	Carbohydrate 22.6g	Fiber 1.4g
Fat 3.8g	Cholesterol 52mg	Calcium 182mg
Protein 27.2g	Sodium 530mg	Iron 2.1mg

Exchanges: 3 Very Lean Meat, 1 Starch, 1 Vegetable

Crispy Oven-Fried Chicken

Prep time: 8 minutes   Cook time: 1 hour

¼ cup plus 2 tablespoons fat-free egg substitute
1 tablespoon water
1 cup crispy rice cereal, crushed
⅓ cup toasted wheat germ
1 tablespoon instant minced onion
1 teaspoon salt-free herb seasoning blend
¼ teaspoon garlic powder
¼ teaspoon salt
¼ teaspoon pepper
4 (6-ounce) skinned chicken breast halves
¼ cup all-purpose flour
Vegetable cooking spray

Combine egg substitute and water in a shallow dish; stir well. Combine cereal and next 6 ingredients in a shallow dish; stir well.

Place chicken and flour in a large heavy-duty, zip-top plastic bag; seal bag, and shake until chicken is coated.

Dip chicken in egg substitute mixture; dredge in cereal mixture. Place chicken on rack of a broiler pan coated with cooking spray. Bake, uncovered, at 350° for 1 hour or until chicken is done. Yield: 4 servings.

Per Serving:

Calories 237	Carbohydrate 19.6g	Fiber 1.8g
Fat 2.6g	Cholesterol 66mg	Calcium 30mg
Protein 32.2g	Sodium 311mg	Iron 2.5mg

Exchanges: 4 Very Lean Meat, 1 Starch

Sesame-Ginger Chicken

SuperQuick
Prep time: 10 minutes   Cook time: 8 minutes

1 tablespoon sesame seeds, toasted
2 tablespoons honey
2 tablespoons reduced-sodium soy sauce
2 teaspoons peeled, grated gingerroot
4 (4-ounce) skinned, boned chicken breast halves
Vegetable cooking spray

Combine first 4 ingredients in a small bowl; stir well, and set aside.

Place chicken between 2 sheets of heavy-duty plastic wrap, and flatten to ¼-inch thickness, using a meat mallet or rolling pin.

Coat grill rack with cooking spray; place on grill over medium-hot coals (350° to 400°). Place chicken on rack; grill, uncovered, 4 minutes on each side or until done, basting often with soy sauce mixture. Transfer chicken to a serving platter. Yield: 4 servings.

Per Serving:

Calories 196	Carbohydrate 10.4g	Fiber 0.1g
Fat 4.5g	Cholesterol 72mg	Calcium 19mg
Protein 27.6g	Sodium 365mg	Iron 1.3mg

Exchanges: 3 Very Lean Meat, ½ Starch, ½ Fat

Lime Chicken with Black Bean Sauce

Prep time: 20 minutes   Marinate time: 8 hours
Cook time: 16 minutes

3   tablespoons fresh lime juice
1½   tablespoons vegetable oil
¼   teaspoon ground red pepper
4   cloves garlic, crushed
4   (4-ounce) skinned, boned chicken breast
     halves
     Vegetable cooking spray
1   cup drained canned black beans
½   cup unsweetened orange juice
2   tablespoons balsamic vinegar
¼   teaspoon salt
⅛   teaspoon freshly ground black pepper
2   cloves garlic, crushed
½   cup diced sweet red pepper
1   tablespoon chopped purple onion

Combine first 4 ingredients in a large heavy-duty, zip-top plastic bag. Add chicken; seal bag, and marinate in refrigerator 8 hours, turning bag occasionally.

Remove chicken from bag, reserving marinade. Place marinade in a saucepan; bring to a boil. Remove from heat.

Coat grill rack with cooking spray; place on grill over medium-hot coals (350° to 400°). Place chicken on rack; grill 7 minutes on each side or until chicken is done, basting occasionally with reserved marinade. Set chicken aside; keep warm.

Position knife blade in food processor bowl; add beans and next 5 ingredients. Process until smooth. Cook in a small saucepan over medium heat until heated.

Coat a small nonstick skillet with cooking spray. Place over medium-high heat until hot. Add sweet red pepper and onion; sauté until crisp-tender. Set aside.

Spoon sauce evenly onto each of 4 serving plates. Place chicken on sauce; top each with 2 tablespoons sweet red pepper mixture.
Yield: 4 servings.

Per Serving:

Calories 292	Carbohydrate 21.0g	Fiber 2.9g
Fat 8.9g	Cholesterol 72mg	Calcium 43mg
Protein 32.1g	Sodium 312mg	Iron 2.4mg

Exchanges: 4 Very Lean Meat, 1½ Starch, 1 Fat

Oven-Barbecued Chicken and Beans

Prep time: 14 minutes   Cook time: 45 minutes

⅓   cup reduced-calorie ketchup
3   tablespoons honey
1   tablespoon prepared mustard
1   tablespoon cider vinegar
2   (16-ounce) cans vegetarian baked beans
     Vegetable cooking spray
6   (4-ounce) skinned, boned chicken breast
     halves
1   medium onion, thinly sliced

Combine first 4 ingredients in a small bowl, stirring well; set aside.

Place beans in an 11- x 7- x 1½-inch baking dish coated with cooking spray. Arrange chicken over beans. Set aside.

Coat a large nonstick skillet with cooking spray; place over medium-high heat until hot. Add onion, and sauté until tender. Spoon onion over chicken. Pour ketchup mixture over onion. Bake, uncovered, at 350° for 45 minutes or until chicken is done. Yield: 6 servings.

Per Serving:

Calories 333	Carbohydrate 41.3g	Fiber 7.7g
Fat 1.8g	Cholesterol 66mg	Calcium 23mg
Protein 33.8g	Sodium 753mg	Iron 1.0mg

Exchanges: 3 Very Lean Meat, 2 Starch

Quick Cleanup

You won't have to fire up the grill for this dish because you bake the chicken in the barbecue sauce with the beans.

Chicken Cordon Bleu

Prep time: 15 minutes   Cook time: 20 minutes

4   (4-ounce) skinned, boned chicken breast
    halves
3   tablespoons chopped fresh parsley
1   teaspoon dried Italian seasoning, divided
4   (1-ounce) slices reduced-fat, low-salt cooked
    ham
4   (1-ounce) slices part-skim mozzarella cheese
1   tablespoon nonfat mayonnaise
1   teaspoon warm water
⅓   cup soft breadcrumbs
    Vegetable cooking spray
    Fresh oregano sprigs (optional)

Place chicken between 2 sheets of heavy-duty plastic wrap, and flatten to ¼-inch thickness, using a meat mallet or rolling pin. Sprinkle chicken with chopped parsley and ¼ teaspoon Italian seasoning. Place 1 slice ham and 1 slice cheese on each piece of chicken. Roll up, tucking ends under; secure rolls with wooden picks.

Combine mayonnaise and water; brush over entire surface of chicken rolls. Combine breadcrumbs and remaining ¾ teaspoon Italian seasoning; dredge rolls in breadcrumb mixture.

Place rolls, seam side down, on a baking sheet coated with cooking spray. Bake at 425° for 20 minutes or until chicken is done. Remove wooden picks before serving. Garnish with fresh oregano sprigs, if desired. Yield: 4 servings.

Per Serving:

Calories 248	Carbohydrate 4.5g	Fiber 0.3g
Fat 7.7g	Cholesterol 96mg	Calcium 211mg
Protein 38.6g	Sodium 493mg	Iron 1.5mg

Exchanges: 5 Very Lean Meat, ½ Starch, ½ Fat

Greek-Seasoned Chicken with Orzo

Prep time: 8 minutes   Cook time: 1 hour, 5 minutes

 Vegetable cooking spray
1 (3-pound) broiler-fryer, cut up and skinned
2 tablespoons lemon juice
2 tablespoons reduced-calorie margarine, melted
1 teaspoon Greek-style seasoning
¾ teaspoon paprika
1 cup orzo, uncooked
¼ cup sliced pitted ripe olives
1½ tablespoons chopped fresh chives
1 tablespoon reduced-calorie margarine
¾ teaspoon Greek-style seasoning

Coat a 13- x 9- x 2-inch baking dish with cooking spray. Place chicken pieces in dish. Combine lemon juice, 2 tablespoons margarine, 1 teaspoon Greek seasoning, and paprika; stir well. Pour mixture evenly over chicken pieces.

Cover and bake at 350° for 30 minutes. Uncover and bake 35 additional minutes or until chicken is done, basting often with pan juices.

Cook orzo according to package directions, omitting salt and fat; drain. Combine orzo, olives, chives, 1 tablespoon margarine, and ¾ teaspoon Greek seasoning; toss gently.

Serve chicken over orzo. Spoon any remaining pan juices over chicken. Yield: 6 servings.

Per Serving:

Calories 300	Carbohydrate 27.4g	Fiber 1.1g
Fat 8.2g	Cholesterol 76mg	Calcium 26mg
Protein 27.9g	Sodium 866mg	Iron 2.6mg

Exchanges: 3 Lean Meat, 1½ Starch

Make It Quick

Keep preparation time to a minimum by asking your butcher to cut up and skin the broiler-fryer while you finish shopping.

Thai Chicken Barbecue

*Prep time: 5 minutes   Marinate time: 4 hours
Cook time: 20 minutes*

¼ cup firmly packed brown sugar
¼ cup low-sodium soy sauce
1 tablespoon fresh lime juice
3 cloves garlic, minced
½ teaspoon dried crushed red pepper
¼ to ½ teaspoon curry powder
1 (3-pound) broiler-fryer, cut up and skinned
 Vegetable cooking spray
 Lime wedges (optional)

Combine first 6 ingredients in an extra large heavy-duty, zip-top plastic bag; add chicken. Seal bag, and marinate in refrigerator at least 4 hours, turning bag occasionally.

Remove chicken from marinade, reserving marinade. Place marinade in a small saucepan; bring to a boil. Remove from heat.

Coat grill rack with cooking spray; place on grill over medium-hot coals (350° to 400°). Place chicken on rack, and grill, uncovered, 20 to 25 minutes or until chicken is done, turning and basting often with marinade. Transfer to a large serving platter. Garnish with lime wedges, if desired. Yield: 6 servings.

Per Serving:

Calories 198	Carbohydrate 9.8g	Fiber 0.1g
Fat 6.1g	Cholesterol 73mg	Calcium 24mg
Protein 23.7g	Sodium 334mg	Iron 1.2mg

Exchanges: 3 Lean Meat, ½ Starch

Thai Chicken Barbecue

Savory Turkey Loaf

Prep time: 10 minutes   Cook time: 1 hour

1   cup soft reduced-calorie whole wheat
      breadcrumbs
¼   cup sliced green onions
¼   cup fat-free egg substitute
1   tablespoon minced fresh parsley
½   teaspoon salt
¼   teaspoon poultry seasoning
¼   teaspoon pepper
1   pound freshly ground raw turkey
      Vegetable cooking spray
¼   cup cranberry-orange relish

Combine first 7 ingredients in a large bowl,
stirring well. Add turkey; stir well. Shape turkey
mixture into a 6- x 4-inch loaf; place on a rack in a
roasting pan coated with cooking spray. Bake at
350° for 1 hour. Transfer meat loaf to a serving
platter. Serve with cranberry-orange relish.
Yield: 4 servings.

Per Serving:

Calories 209	Carbohydrate 13.9g	Fiber 2.5g
Fat 4.2g	Cholesterol 74mg	Calcium 43mg
Protein 27.9g	Sodium 479mg	Iron 2.7mg

Exchanges: 3½ Very Lean Meat, 1 Starch

Keep It Clean

To simplify cleanup, line the roasting pan
with heavy-duty aluminum foil.

Turkey Noodle Casserole

Prep time: 13 minutes   Cook time: 42 minutes

6   ounces wide egg noodles, uncooked
      Vegetable cooking spray
1   pound freshly ground raw turkey breast
½   cup sliced fresh mushrooms
¼   cup chopped onion
2   (8-ounce) cans no-salt-added tomato sauce
½   teaspoon salt
¼   teaspoon pepper
¼   teaspoon garlic powder
¼   teaspoon dried oregano
1   cup part-skim ricotta cheese
3   tablespoons skim milk
½   (8-ounce) package Neufchâtel cheese,
      softened
2   teaspoons poppy seeds

Cook noodles according to package directions, omitting salt and fat; drain well, and set
aside.

Coat a large nonstick skillet with cooking
spray; place over medium-high heat until hot. Add
turkey, mushrooms, and onion; cook until turkey is
browned and onion is tender, stirring until turkey
crumbles. Drain, if necessary.

Add tomato sauce and next 4 ingredients to
turkey mixture in skillet. Bring to a boil; reduce
heat, and simmer, uncovered, 3 minutes, stirring
occasionally.

Combine ricotta cheese and milk in container
of an electric blender; cover and process until
smooth, stopping once to scrape down sides.
Transfer cheese mixture to a large bowl; stir in
Neufchâtel and poppy seeds, stirring well. Add
noodles, tossing to coat.

Layer two-thirds of noodle mixture in an
11- x 7- x 1½-inch baking dish coated with cooking spray. Spread turkey mixture over noodle mixture. Top with remaining one-third noodle mixture.
Cover and bake at 400° for 20 to 25 minutes or
until thoroughly heated. Serve immediately.
Yield: 6 servings.

Per Serving:

Calories 342	Carbohydrate 30.4g	Fiber 1.5g
Fat 10.8g	Cholesterol 100mg	Calcium 170mg
Protein 29.7g	Sodium 397mg	Iron 2.6mg

Exchanges: 3 Very Lean Meat, 1 Starch, 1 Vegetable, 1 Fat

Turkey Cutlets in Lemon-Caper Sauce

SuperQuick
Prep time: 5 minutes   Cook time: 10 minutes

1   tablespoon lemon juice
2   (4-ounce) turkey breast cutlets
1½ tablespoons all-purpose flour
1½ teaspoons paprika
¼   teaspoon ground white pepper
⅛   teaspoon salt
    Vegetable cooking spray
½   teaspoon olive oil
1   tablespoon margarine
1   tablespoon all-purpose flour
½   cup canned no-salt-added chicken broth
1   tablespoon lemon juice
1   tablespoon capers
1   teaspoon chopped fresh parsley

Drizzle 1 tablespoon lemon juice over cutlets; set aside. Combine 1½ tablespoons flour, paprika, pepper, and salt. Dredge cutlets in flour mixture. Coat a large nonstick skillet with cooking spray; add oil. Place over medium-high heat until hot. Add cutlets, and sauté 2 minutes on each side. Transfer to a serving platter, and keep warm.

Melt margarine in a small heavy saucepan over low heat; add 1 tablespoon flour, stirring until smooth. Cook 1 minute, stirring constantly. Gradually add broth and 1 tablespoon lemon juice; cook over medium heat, stirring constantly, until mixture is thickened and bubbly. Remove from heat, and stir in capers. Spoon sauce over cutlets, and sprinkle with parsley. Serve warm.
Yield: 2 servings.

Per Serving:

Calories 249	Carbohydrate 10.9g	Fiber 0.7g
Fat 9.6g	Cholesterol 68mg	Calcium 23mg
Protein 28.9g	Sodium 640mg	Iron 2.6mg

Exchanges: 4 Very Lean Meat, ½ Starch, 1 Fat

The Scoop on Capers

No, it's not a huge piece of black pepper, it's a caper. A caper is a sun-dried, pickled (that's why it tastes so salty) flower bud native to the Mediterranean. You'll see them most often used in sauces, meats, and vegetable recipes.

Turkey Cutlets à la Grecque

SuperQuick
Prep time: 5 minutes   Cook time: 18 minutes

6   dried tomatoes (packed without oil)
¾   cup boiling water
1½ pounds turkey breast cutlets
¾   teaspoon freshly ground pepper
¼   teaspoon salt
    Olive oil-flavored vegetable cooking spray
¾   cup dry white wine
¾   cup canned no-salt-added chicken broth
1   tablespoon plus 1 teaspoon cornstarch
2   tablespoons sliced ripe olives
¼   teaspoon dried oregano

Combine tomato and boiling water in a small bowl. Let stand 10 minutes. Drain; cut tomato into thin slices, and set aside.

Sprinkle turkey with pepper and salt. Coat a large nonstick skillet with cooking spray. Place over medium-high heat until hot. Add half of cutlets; cook 3 minutes on each side or until done. Transfer to a platter, and keep warm. Repeat procedure with remaining cutlets.

Combine wine, chicken broth, and cornstarch in a small bowl, stirring until smooth. Add reserved tomato slices, olives, and oregano. Pour wine mixture into skillet. Bring to a boil. Cook, stirring constantly, 1 minute or until wine mixture is thickened and bubbly. Pour wine mixture over turkey.
Yield: 6 servings.

Per Serving:

Calories 156	Carbohydrate 3.9g	Fiber 0.5g
Fat 3.2g	Cholesterol 59mg	Calcium 25mg
Protein 25.8g	Sodium 225mg	Iron 1.5mg

Exchanges: 3 Very Lean Meat, 1 Vegetable

A Taste of Greece

The term "à la Grecque" means in the Greek style. Oregano, tomatoes, and olives are typical ingredients of Greek cuisine.

Red Beans and Rice

Prep time: 12 minutes   Cook time: 25 minutes

Vegetable cooking spray
2 teaspoons olive oil
6 ounces smoked turkey sausage
1¼ cups chopped onion
1 teaspoon minced garlic
1½ cups long-grain rice, uncooked
½ teaspoon dried thyme
½ teaspoon ground red pepper
¼ teaspoon salt
3 bay leaves
2 (15-ounce) cans reduced-sodium kidney beans, drained
2 (14¼-ounce) cans no-salt-added beef broth
1½ cups seeded, chopped tomato
3 tablespoons sliced green onions

Coat a Dutch oven with cooking spray; add oil. Place over medium-high heat until hot. Add sausage, onion, and garlic; sauté 5 minutes or until onion is tender. Add rice and next 4 ingredients; sauté 30 seconds. Stir in beans and beef broth. Bring to a boil; cover, reduce heat, and simmer 20 minutes or until liquid is absorbed and rice is tender. Remove and discard bay leaves.

To serve, spoon into 4 individual bowls, and top evenly with tomato and green onions. Yield: 4 servings.

Per Serving:

Calories 411	Carbohydrate 55.3g	Fiber 16.6g
Fat 11.6g	Cholesterol 0mg	Calcium 81mg
Protein 21.5g	Sodium 503mg	Iron 2.1mg

Exchanges: 3 Lean Meat, 2½ Starch

Baked Catfish Fillets

Prep time: 18 minutes   Cook time: 25 minutes

½ cup pineapple tidbits in juice, drained
½ cup chopped sweet red pepper
⅓ cup chopped green pepper
⅓ cup chopped sweet yellow or orange pepper
1 tablespoon cider vinegar
1 tablespoon unsweetened pineapple juice
1 teaspoon sugar
1 teaspoon peeled, minced gingerroot
⅛ to ¼ teaspoon dried crushed red pepper
6 (4-ounce) farm-raised catfish fillets
Vegetable cooking spray
2 tablespoons reduced-calorie margarine, melted
1 tablespoon lemon juice
¼ teaspoon ground ginger
¼ teaspoon curry powder
¼ teaspoon dried crushed red pepper

Combine first 9 ingredients in a small bowl; stir well. Cover and chill at least 30 minutes.

Place catfish fillets on rack of a broiler pan coated with cooking spray.

Combine margarine and remaining 4 ingredients; stir well. Brush fillets with margarine mixture.

Bake at 400° for 25 to 30 minutes or until fish flakes easily when tested with a fork. Transfer fillets to a serving platter. Top with pineapple relish. Yield: 6 servings.

Per Serving:

Calories 173	Carbohydrate 4.9g	Fiber 0.7g
Fat 7.6g	Cholesterol 66mg	Calcium 52mg
Protein 21.1g	Sodium 110mg	Iron 1.6mg

Exchanges: 2 Lean Meat, 1 Vegetable

Flounder Athenian

Prep time: 15 minutes   Cook time: 4 minutes
Stand time: 2 minutes

1 (10-ounce) package frozen chopped spinach,
   thawed
2 tablespoons lemon juice, divided
¾ cup crumbled feta cheese
½ teaspoon dried dillweed
⅛ teaspoon pepper
4 (4-ounce) flounder fillets
2 tablespoons dry white wine
1 tablespoon chopped fresh parsley
¼ teaspoon paprika

Drain spinach; press between paper towels to remove excess moisture. Combine spinach, 1 tablespoon lemon juice, feta cheese, dillweed, and pepper, stirring well.

Spoon spinach mixture evenly onto center of each fillet; roll up each fillet, jellyroll fashion, beginning at narrow end. Place rolls, seam side down, around the edges of a 9-inch glass pieplate.

Combine remaining 1 tablespoon lemon juice, wine, parsley, and paprika; drizzle over flounder. Cover with heavy-duty plastic wrap, and vent. Microwave at HIGH 4 to 5 minutes or until fish flakes easily when tested with a fork, rotating a half-turn after 2 minutes. Let stand, covered, 2 minutes. Yield: 4 servings.

Per Serving:

Calories 184	Carbohydrate 4.6g	Fiber 2.3g
Fat 6.1g	Cholesterol 73mg	Calcium 208mg
Protein 26.6g	Sodium 383mg	Iron 2.2mg

Exchanges: 3½ Very Lean Meat, ½ Vegetable, ½ Fat

Crispy Orange Roughy

Prep time: 10 minutes   Cook time: 10 minutes

2 egg whites, lightly beaten
2 tablespoons water
½ cup cornmeal
¼ cup grated Parmesan cheese
½ teaspoon dried oregano
½ teaspoon dried parsley flakes
½ teaspoon salt
¼ teaspoon pepper
6 (4-ounce) orange roughy fillets (about ½
   inch thick)
3 tablespoons all-purpose flour
   Vegetable cooking spray
1 tablespoon vegetable oil

Combine egg whites and water in a shallow dish. Combine cornmeal and next 5 ingredients in a medium bowl; stir well.

Sprinkle each side of fillets with flour. Dip fillets into egg white mixture, and dredge in cornmeal mixture.

Coat a large nonstick skillet with cooking spray; add oil. Place over medium-high heat until hot. Add fillets, and cook 4 to 5 minutes on each side or until golden and fish flakes easily when tested with a fork. Yield: 6 servings.

Per Serving:

Calories 171	Carbohydrate 11.2g	Fiber 1.3g
Fat 4.6g	Cholesterol 25mg	Calcium 50mg
Protein 20.4g	Sodium 350mg	Iron 0.9mg

Exchanges: 3 Very Lean Meat, ½ Starch, 1 Fat

Sounds Fishy

Don't have the fish listed? No problem. If you have grouper or any other firm white fish on hand, substitute it for the orange roughy.

Oven-Blackened Red Snapper

Oven-Blackened Red Snapper

SuperQuick

Prep time: 15 minutes   Cook time: 10 minutes

Vegetable cooking spray
1 tablespoon olive oil
¼ cup minced onion
2 cloves garlic, minced
1½ teaspoons paprika
¼ teaspoon ground white pepper
¼ teaspoon ground red pepper
¼ teaspoon black pepper
¼ teaspoon dried oregano
4 (4-ounce) skinned red snapper fillets
Fresh oregano sprigs (optional)
Broiled cloves garlic (optional)

Coat a large nonstick skillet with cooking spray; add oil. Place over medium-high heat until hot. Add onion and 2 cloves garlic; cook, stirring constantly, until tender. Stir in paprika and next 4 ingredients. Remove skillet from heat; let cool.

Spread spice mixture on both sides of fillets. Place fillets on rack of a broiler pan coated with cooking spray. Broil 3 inches from heat (with electric oven door partially opened) 10 minutes or until fish is lightly charred and flakes easily when tested with a fork. Transfer fish to serving plates. If desired, garnish with fresh oregano sprigs and broiled garlic. Yield: 4 servings.

Per Serving:

Calories 153	Carbohydrate 1.9g	Fiber 0.4g
Fat 5.2g	Cholesterol 42mg	Calcium 44mg
Protein 23.7g	Sodium 51mg	Iron 0.6mg

Exchanges: 3 Very Lean Meat, 1 Fat

No Smoking Allowed

Don't worry about smoking up your kitchen with this blackening technique. The snapper broils in the oven until charred, which blackens the fish without the smoke. And if you want to broil a few garlic cloves for a garnish, add them to the broiler rack while the fish broils, and turn the cloves once.

Grilled Salmon with Honey-Mustard Sauce

SuperQuick

Prep time: 4 minutes   Cook time: 11 minutes

4 (4-ounce) salmon steaks (½ inch thick)
1 tablespoon lemon juice
Vegetable cooking spray
¼ cup Dijon mustard
3 tablespoons honey
2 tablespoons plain low-fat yogurt

Brush salmon steaks with lemon juice. Coat grill rack with cooking spray; place on grill over medium-hot coals (350° to 400°). Place salmon on rack; grill, uncovered, 5 to 6 minutes on each side or until fish flakes easily when tested with a fork.

Combine Dijon mustard, honey, and yogurt in a 2-cup glass measure. Microwave at HIGH 1 minute or until hot. Spoon sauce over steaks. Yield: 4 servings.

Per Serving:

Calories 265	Carbohydrate 14.9g	Fiber 0.0g
Fat 11.0g	Cholesterol 78mg	Calcium 20mg
Protein 24.6g	Sodium 509mg	Iron 0.6mg

Exchanges: 3 Lean Meat, 1 Starch, ½ Fat

Swordfish Santa Fe

Prep time: 10 minutes   Marinate time: 30 minutes
Cook time: 6 minutes

⅓ cup lime juice
⅓ cup beer
2 cloves garlic, minced
1 teaspoon vegetable oil
1 tablespoon ground cumin
1 tablespoon Dijon mustard
¼ teaspoon salt
6 (4-ounce) swordfish steaks (½ inch thick)
Vegetable cooking spray
Salsa Fresca

Place first 7 ingredients in a large heavy-duty, zip-top plastic bag. Add swordfish steaks; seal bag, and shake gently until steaks are well coated. Marinate in refrigerator 30 minutes, turning bag occasionally.

Remove steaks from marinade, reserving marinade. Place marinade in a small saucepan. Bring to a boil; remove from heat.

Coat grill rack with cooking spray. Place on grill over medium-hot coals (350° to 400°). Place steaks on rack; grill, covered, 3 to 4 minutes on each side or until fish flakes easily when tested with a fork, basting occasionally with marinade.

Transfer steaks to a serving platter; top evenly with Salsa Fresca. Yield: 6 servings.

Salsa Fresca

1 cup coarsely chopped tomato
⅓ cup chopped onion
¼ cup chopped green pepper
1½ tablespoons lime juice
3 tablespoons chopped fresh cilantro or parsley
1 teaspoon seeded, chopped jalapeño pepper
1 clove garlic, minced
2 tablespoons spicy vegetable juice
⅛ teaspoon ground cumin

Combine all ingredients. Cover and chill 30 minutes. Yield: 1¾ cups.

Per Serving:

Calories 169	Carbohydrate 6.2g	Fiber 0.9g
Fat 5.8g	Cholesterol 43mg	Calcium 27mg
Protein 22.5g	Sodium 287mg	Iron 2.0mg

Exchanges: 3 Very Lean Meat, 1 Vegetable, ½ Fat

Trout Fillets with Capers

SuperQuick

Prep time: 5 minutes   Cook time: 4 minutes
Stand time: 3 minutes

½   cup all-purpose flour
½   teaspoon paprika
¼   teaspoon pepper
4   (4-ounce) trout fillets
   Vegetable cooking spray
¼   cup fresh lemon juice
¼   cup drained capers

Combine first 3 ingredients in a shallow dish; dredge fillets in flour mixture.

Coat a large nonstick skillet with cooking spray; place over medium heat until hot. Place fillets in skillet, skin side down; cook 3 minutes. Turn fillets, and cook 1 additional minute.

Add lemon juice and capers to skillet; cover and remove from heat. Let stand 3 to 5 minutes or until fish flakes easily when tested with a fork.

Transfer fillets to a serving plate; spoon sauce evenly over fillets. Serve immediately.
Yield: 4 servings.

Per Serving:

Calories 201	Carbohydrate 6.6g	Fiber 0.2g
Fat 8.0g	Cholesterol 66mg	Calcium 52mg
Protein 24.7g	Sodium 729mg	Iron 2.1mg

Exchanges: 3 Lean Meat, ½ Starch

A Sticking Situation

Give your skillet a thick coating of cooking spray for this recipe. Otherwise, the trout fillets will stick and fall apart when turned.

Linguine with Red Clam Sauce

Prep time: 7 minutes   Cook time: 20 minutes

   Vegetable cooking spray
¼   cup chopped onion
1   clove garlic, minced
1   (14½-ounce) can no-salt-added whole tomatoes, undrained and chopped
1   (8-ounce) can no-salt-added tomato sauce
¼   cup dry white wine
1   teaspoon dried basil
⅛   teaspoon dried crushed red pepper
2   (6-ounce) cans minced clams, drained
8   ounces linguine, uncooked
¼   cup freshly grated Parmesan cheese

Coat a large nonstick skillet with cooking spray; place over medium-high heat until hot. Add onion and garlic, and sauté until tender. Add chopped tomato and next 4 ingredients. Bring to a boil; reduce heat, and simmer, uncovered, 10 minutes. Add clams, and cook 2 additional minutes.

Cook pasta according to package directions, omitting salt and fat; drain well. Place pasta in a serving bowl; top with clam mixture. Sprinkle with cheese. Yield: 4 (2-cup) servings.

Per Serving:

Calories 401	Carbohydrate 58.5g	Fiber 2.6g
Fat 4.2g	Cholesterol 49mg	Calcium 196mg
Protein 28.7g	Sodium 224mg	Iron 21.7mg

Exchanges: 3 Very Lean Meat, 2½ Starch, 1 Vegetable

Crab Mornay

SuperQuick
Prep time: 10 minutes   Cook time: 2 minutes

½ cup dry white wine
¼ cup water
1 teaspoon chicken-flavored bouillon granules
   Dash of white pepper
1 cup sliced fresh mushrooms
2 tablespoons sliced green onions
¼ cup skim milk
1 tablespoon cornstarch
½ cup (2 ounces) shredded reduced-fat
   Jarlsberg cheese
⅔ pound fresh lump crabmeat, drained
1 (2-ounce) jar chopped pimiento, drained

Combine first 4 ingredients in a small saucepan; bring to a boil. Add mushrooms and green onions. Cover, reduce heat, and simmer 1 minute or until mushrooms are tender.

Combine milk and cornstarch; add to mushroom mixture. Bring to a boil over medium heat; boil 1 minute, stirring constantly. Remove from heat; add cheese, and stir until melted. Stir in crabmeat and pimiento. Spoon into 4 (6-ounce) ramekins or custard cups. Broil 2 minutes or until hot and bubbly. Yield: 4 servings.

Per Serving:

Calories 149	Carbohydrate 5.7g	Fiber 0.4g
Fat 3.6g	Cholesterol 76mg	Calcium 266mg
Protein 21.7g	Sodium 566mg	Iron 1.2mg

Exchanges: 3 Very Lean Meat, ½ Starch

Crab Cakes

SuperQuick
Prep time: 15 minutes   Cook time: 6 minutes

2 (6-ounce) cans lump crabmeat, drained
½ cup finely chopped water chestnuts
¼ cup soft breadcrumbs
1 tablespoon plus 1 teaspoon dried parsley
   flakes
½ teaspoon pepper
½ teaspoon dark sesame oil
3 tablespoons reduced-calorie mayonnaise
   Vegetable cooking spray

Combine first 7 ingredients in a small bowl; stir well. Shape into 8 patties.

Coat a large nonstick skillet with cooking spray; place over medium-high heat until hot. Add crabmeat patties, and cook 6 to 8 minutes or until lightly browned on both sides, turning once. Transfer to a serving platter. Yield: 4 servings.

Per Serving:

Calories 129	Carbohydrate 6.6g	Fiber 0.3g
Fat 5.0g	Cholesterol 68mg	Calcium 72mg
Protein 13.7g	Sodium 283mg	Iron 1.1mg

Exchanges: 2 Lean Meat, ½ Starch

Appetizer Idea

To serve as an appetizer, divide the crabmeat mixture evenly into 16 small patties, and cook 3 to 4 minutes or until lightly browned on both sides, turning once. These smaller versions will have about 31 calories each.

Crab and Shrimp Étouffée

Prep time: 20 minutes   Cook time: 20 minutes

2 pounds unpeeled medium-size fresh shrimp
⅔ cup chopped onion
¼ cup chopped green pepper
¼ cup chopped celery
3 cloves garlic, minced
2 tablespoons reduced-calorie margarine, melted
1 cup canned no-salt-added chicken broth, divided
⅓ cup dry white wine
¼ cup chopped green onions
1 tablespoon no-salt-added tomato paste
2 tablespoons chopped fresh parsley
2 teaspoons low-sodium Worcestershire sauce
¼ teaspoon salt
¼ teaspoon pepper
⅛ teaspoon hot sauce
1½ tablespoons cornstarch
12 ounces fresh crabmeat, drained and flaked
5 cups cooked long-grain rice (cooked without salt or fat)

Peel shrimp and devein; set aside.

Cook ⅔ cup onion and next 4 ingredients in a large skillet over medium-high heat, stirring constantly, until tender. Stir in ⅔ cup chicken broth and next 8 ingredients. Add shrimp; cover, reduce heat, and simmer 5 minutes, stirring occasionally.

Combine cornstarch and remaining ⅓ cup chicken broth, stirring until smooth; add to shrimp mixture. Cook, stirring constantly, until mixture comes to a boil. Boil, stirring constantly, 1 minute. Stir in crabmeat. Cook until thoroughly heated, stirring often.

To serve, spoon 1 cup rice onto each individual serving plate. Spoon shrimp mixture evenly over rice. Yield: 5 servings.

Per Serving:

Calories 462	Carbohydrate 56.9g	Fiber 1.8g
Fat 6.1g	Cholesterol 220mg	Calcium 158mg
Protein 38.7g	Sodium 513mg	Iron 5.3mg

Exchanges: 3½ Lean Meat, 2½ Starch, 2 Vegetable

Scallop Vegetable Stir-Fry

SuperQuick
Prep time: 8 minutes   Cook time: 8 minutes

¾ cup canned low-sodium chicken broth
1½ tablespoons low-sodium soy sauce
1 tablespoon cornstarch
½ teaspoon light sesame oil
   Vegetable cooking spray
2 teaspoons vegetable oil
1¼ cups diagonally sliced carrot
1 cup sliced fresh mushrooms
1 (6-ounce) package frozen snow peas, thawed
½ cup diagonally sliced green onions
1 tablespoon peeled, minced gingerroot
½ pound bay scallops

Combine first 4 ingredients in a small bowl, stirring well. Set broth mixture aside.

Coat a large nonstick skillet or wok with cooking spray; add vegetable oil. Place over medium-high heat until hot. Add carrot; stir-fry 1 minute. Add mushrooms; stir-fry 1 minute. Add snow peas; stir-fry 1 minute. Remove vegetables from skillet; set aside, and keep warm. Wipe drippings from skillet with a paper towel.

Coat skillet with cooking spray. Add green onions and gingerroot; stir-fry 30 seconds. Add scallops; stir-fry 1 to 2 minutes or until scallops are white. Add reserved vegetables to skillet; stir well. Pour reserved broth mixture over vegetable mixture. Cook, stirring constantly, 1 minute or until slightly thickened and thoroughly heated. Transfer to a serving platter. Yield: 2 servings.

Per Serving:

Calories 274	Carbohydrate 26.3g	Fiber 5.6g
Fat 8.0g	Cholesterol 37mg	Calcium 106mg
Protein 24.9g	Sodium 696mg	Iron 4.0mg

Exchanges: 3 Very Lean Meat, 1½ Starch, 1 Fat

Purchasing Power

When buying fresh bay scallops, count on about 100 to the pound. Since they are highly perishable, cook scallops within 2 days of purchase. Before cooking, always wash scallops well to remove sand and grit.

Italian Scallop Kabobs

Prep time: 20 minutes   Cook time: 9 minutes

36 sea scallops (about 1 pound)
1   (5-ounce) package lean, smoked sliced ham,
      cut into 36 (½-inch-wide) strips
    Vegetable cooking spray
2   cloves garlic, minced
¼   cup lemon juice
2   tablespoons minced fresh parsley
¾   teaspoon dried oregano

Wrap each scallop with a strip of ham; thread 6 scallops onto each of 6 (12-inch) skewers. Set aside.

Coat a small nonstick skillet with cooking spray; place over medium heat until hot. Add garlic; sauté until browned. Remove from heat, and stir in lemon juice, parsley, and oregano.

Coat grill rack with cooking spray; place on grill over medium-hot coals (350° to 400°). Place kabobs on rack, and grill 9 to 10 minutes or until scallops are white, turning and basting often with lemon juice mixture. Yield: 6 servings.

Per Serving:

Calories 103	Carbohydrate 3.4g	Fiber 0.1g
Fat 1.9g	Cholesterol 36mg	Calcium 27mg
Protein 17.4g	Sodium 460mg	Iron 0.6mg

Exchange: 3 Very Lean Meat

Shrimp Jambalaya

Prep time: 20 minutes   Cook time: 35 minutes

1   pound unpeeled medium-size fresh shrimp
    Vegetable cooking spray
¼   pound smoked turkey sausage, cubed
1   cup frozen chopped onion, celery, pepper,
      and parsley blend
1   (14¼-ounce) can no-salt-added chicken
      broth
1   (14½-ounce) can Cajun-style stewed
      tomatoes, undrained
1   tablespoon salt-free Creole seasoning blend
¾   cup long-grain rice, uncooked

Peel and devein shrimp; set aside.

Coat a large nonstick skillet with cooking spray; place over medium-high heat until hot. Add sausage and frozen vegetable blend; sauté until vegetables are tender. Stir in broth, tomato, and Creole seasoning blend. Bring to a boil; stir in rice. Cover, reduce heat, and simmer 25 minutes.

Add shrimp to rice mixture; bring to a boil. Cover; reduce heat, and simmer 10 minutes or until liquid is absorbed and shrimp turn pink. Yield: 4 servings.

Per Serving:

Calories 343	Carbohydrate 40.2g	Fiber 2.5g
Fat 7.8g	Cholesterol 144mg	Calcium 91mg
Protein 25.8g	Sodium 761mg	Iron 4.5mg

Exchanges: 3 Lean Meat, 2 Starch, 1 Vegetable

A Tip for All Seasons

Keep a package of frozen Seasoning Blend in your freezer—it's a mix of chopped onion, celery, green peppers, and parsley available in the frozen vegetable section of your local supermarket. Add it anytime a recipe calls for chopped onion and peppers.

Meatless Main Dishes

Cuban Black Beans (page 107)

Vegetable Omelet For One

SuperQuick

Prep time: 8 minutes   Cook time: 5 minutes

¼   cup julienne-sliced carrot
¼   cup julienne-sliced zucchini
3   tablespoons part-skim ricotta cheese
1½   teaspoons chopped fresh or frozen chives
1½   teaspoons chopped fresh dill
½   cup fat-free egg substitute
2   teaspoons water
⅛   teaspoon salt
    Vegetable cooking spray

Arrange carrot and zucchini in a steamer basket over boiling water. Cover and steam 2 to 3 minutes or until crisp-tender. Drain well. Combine vegetable mixture, ricotta cheese, chives, and dill; set aside.

Combine egg substitute, water, and salt. Coat a 6-inch omelet pan or nonstick skillet with cooking spray; place over medium heat until hot.

Pour egg substitute mixture into skillet. As mixture starts to cook, gently lift edges of omelet with a spatula, and tilt pan so uncooked portion flows underneath. Spoon vegetable mixture over half of omelet. Fold omelet in half; transfer to a serving plate. Yield: 1 serving.

Per Serving:

Calories 150	Carbohydrate 9.0g	Fiber 1.3g
Fat 4.4g	Cholesterol 14mg	Calcium 190mg
Protein 18.1g	Sodium 533mg	Iron 2.9mg

Exchanges: 2 Very Lean Meat, 1 Vegetable, ½ Fat

Artichoke Quiche

Prep time: 10 minutes   Cook time: 55 minutes

2   cups cooked long-grain rice (cooked without salt or fat)
¾   cup (3 ounces) shredded reduced-fat extra sharp Cheddar cheese, divided
¾   cup fat-free egg substitute, divided
1   teaspoon dried dillweed
½   teaspoon salt
1   small clove garlic, crushed
    Vegetable cooking spray
1   (14-ounce) can quartered artichoke hearts, drained
¾   cup skim milk
¼   cup sliced green onions
1   tablespoon Dijon mustard
¼   teaspoon ground white pepper
    Green onion strips (optional)

Combine rice, ¼ cup cheese, ¼ cup fat-free egg substitute, dillweed, salt, and garlic; press into a 9-inch pieplate coated with cooking spray. Bake at 350° for 5 minutes. Set aside.

Arrange artichoke quarters on bottom of rice crust; sprinkle evenly with remaining ½ cup cheese. Combine remaining ½ cup fat-free egg substitute, skim milk, and next 3 ingredients; pour over cheese. Bake at 350° for 50 minutes or until set. Let stand 5 minutes; cut into wedges. Garnish with green onion strips, if desired. Serve immediately. Yield: 6 servings.

Per Serving:

Calories 169	Carbohydrate 23.1g	Fiber 0.4g
Fat 3.5g	Cholesterol 11mg	Calcium 78mg
Protein 10.4g	Sodium 490mg	Iron 1.8mg

Exchanges: 1½ Very Lean Meat, 1½ Starch

Rice Is Nice

This artichoke-studded quiche has an unusual crust. Rice and cheese bake into a thick crust that's crispy on the bottom and tender inside.

Artichoke Quiche

Southwestern Eggs

Prep time: 18 minutes   Cook time: 10 minutes

1   cup drained canned black beans
⅔   cup chopped tomato
1   tablespoon sliced green onions
1   teaspoon chili powder
2   eggs
32   baked low-fat tortilla chips
2   tablespoons mild salsa
2   tablespoons low-fat sour cream
1   tablespoon finely chopped fresh cilantro

Combine first 4 ingredients in a saucepan. Cook, uncovered, over medium heat 5 minutes, until thoroughly heated, stirring occasionally. Set aside, and keep warm.

Add water to a small skillet to depth of 2 inches. Bring to a boil; reduce heat, and maintain at a light simmer. Break eggs, one at a time, into a saucer; slip eggs, one at a time, into water, holding saucer as close as possible to surface of water. Simmer 7 to 9 minutes or to desired degree of doneness. Remove eggs with a slotted spoon.

To serve, arrange 16 chips around edge of each individual serving plate; place ¾ cup bean mixture on each plate. Top each serving with an egg. Spoon 1 tablespoon salsa, 1 tablespoon sour cream, and 1½ teaspoons cilantro over each serving. Serve immediately. Yield: 2 servings.

Per Serving:

Calories 450	Carbohydrate 36.3g	Fiber 9.7g
Fat 10.1g	Cholesterol 227mg	Calcium 88mg
Protein 20.3g	Sodium 586mg	Iron 3.7mg

Exchanges: 2 Lean Meat, 2 Starch, 1 Vegetable, ½ Fat

Curried Vegetable Fried Rice

SuperQuick
Prep time: 10 minutes   Cook time: 10 minutes

1   cup coarsely chopped fresh cauliflower flowerets
½   cup diced carrot
2   teaspoons curry powder
1   teaspoon chili powder
½   teaspoon salt
⅛   teaspoon ground red pepper
1   tablespoon water
2   teaspoons vegetable oil
¼   cup finely chopped onion
1   clove garlic, minced
4   cups cooked long-grain rice (cooked without salt or fat)
½   cup frozen green peas, thawed
¼   cup raisins
1   (8-ounce) carton fat-free egg substitute
½   cup chopped almonds, toasted

Cook cauliflower and carrot in boiling water 3 minutes. Drain and rinse under cold water; set aside.

Combine curry powder and next 4 ingredients; stir well. Heat oil in a large nonstick skillet over medium heat. Add curry powder mixture, onion, and garlic; sauté 3 minutes. Add cauliflower, carrot, rice, peas, and raisins; sauté 2 minutes or until heated. Add egg substitute; cook 1 minute or until egg is done, stirring constantly. Add almonds; toss well. Yield: 6 servings.

Per Serving:

Calories 291	Carbohydrate 46.3g	Fiber 4.2g
Fat 7.6g	Cholesterol 0mg	Calcium 77mg
Protein 10.4g	Sodium 281mg	Iron 3.1mg

Exchanges: 2½ Starch, 1 Vegetable, 1 Fat

Stuffed Peppers

Prep time: 15 minutes   Cook time: 45 minutes

⅔ cup boiling water
⅔ cup bulgur (cracked wheat), uncooked
6 small green peppers
  Vegetable cooking spray
½ cup diced carrot
½ cup diced onion
½ cup diced celery
1 egg, lightly beaten
½ cup raisins
⅓ cup pine nuts, toasted
¼ cup part-skim ricotta cheese
¼ cup lemon juice
¼ teaspoon salt
½ teaspoon dried mint flakes
½ cup canned vegetable broth
4½ cups cooked long-grain rice (cooked without salt or fat)

Pour ⅔ cup boiling water over bulgur in a large bowl; cover and let stand 15 minutes or until bulgur is tender and water is absorbed.

Cut tops off peppers, and reserve tops; remove and discard seeds and membranes. Cook peppers and tops in a small amount of boiling water 10 minutes. Drain and set aside.

Coat a nonstick skillet with cooking spray; place over medium heat until hot. Add carrot, onion, and celery; sauté until crisp-tender. Add bulgur mixture, egg, and next 6 ingredients; stir well. Spoon mixture evenly into peppers. Cover with reserved tops. Place peppers in a shallow baking dish. Pour broth over peppers. Bake at 350° for 30 minutes or until thoroughly heated.

To serve, place ¾ cup cooked rice on each of 6 individual serving plates; place 1 pepper with top over each serving. Yield: 6 servings.

Per Serving:

Calories 351	Carbohydrate 66.5g	Fiber 6.4g
Fat 6.6g	Cholesterol 38mg	Calcium 59mg
Protein 10.5g	Sodium 195mg	Iron 3.9mg

Exchanges: 1 Lean Meat, 3 Starch, 2 Vegetable, ½ Fruit

Curried Lentils and Rice

Prep time: 12 minutes   Cook time: 25 minutes

1 tablespoon olive oil
10 shallots, minced
2 cloves garlic, minced
8 cups canned low-sodium chicken broth
1 pound dried lentils
½ cup sliced green onions
1 tablespoon plus 2 teaspoons chili powder
1 tablespoon ground coriander
2 teaspoons ground turmeric
⅓ cup lime juice
¼ teaspoon salt
5 cups cooked long-grain rice (cooked without salt or fat)

Heat olive oil in a Dutch oven over medium-high heat until hot. Add shallot and garlic; sauté until shallot is tender.

Add chicken broth and next 5 ingredients, stirring well. Bring to a boil; cover, reduce heat, and simmer 25 minutes or until lentils are tender. Stir in lime juice and salt.

Place ½ cup cooked rice in each individual serving bowl, and spoon 1 cup lentil mixture over each serving. Yield: 10 servings.

Per Serving:

Calories 315	Carbohydrate 55.6g	Fiber 6.3g
Fat 3.4g	Cholesterol 0mg	Calcium 47mg
Protein 17.1g	Sodium 140mg	Iron 6.5mg

Exchanges: 1 Lean Meat, 3 Starch

Nutty Rice and Cheese Casserole

Prep time: 18 minutes   Cook time: 25 minutes

1   (8-ounce) carton plain nonfat yogurt
1   tablespoon all-purpose flour
1½ cups 1% low-fat cottage cheese
1   egg white
½   teaspoon hot sauce
4   cups cooked instant brown rice (cooked
      without salt or fat)
½   cup sliced green onions
½   cup grated Parmesan cheese, divided
¼   cup slivered almonds, toasted and chopped
3   tablespoons minced fresh parsley
    Vegetable cooking spray

Combine yogurt and flour in a medium bowl; stir until smooth. Add cottage cheese, egg white, and hot sauce, stirring well. Stir in brown rice, green onions, ¼ cup Parmesan cheese, almonds, and parsley; spoon mixture into a 2-quart casserole coated with cooking spray.

Sprinkle casserole with remaining ¼ cup Parmesan cheese. Bake, uncovered, at 350° for 25 minutes or until thoroughly heated.
Yield: 6 servings.

Per Serving:

Calories 271	Carbohydrate 37.1g	Fiber 3.0g
Fat 6.0g	Cholesterol 8mg	Calcium 234mg
Protein 17.0g	Sodium 403mg	Iron 1.2mg

Exchanges: 2 Lean Meat, 2 Starch

Chinese Vegetable Stir-Fry

*Prep time: 5 minutes   Marinate time: 2 hours
Cook time: 12 minutes*

¼   cup fresh lemon juice
¼   cup low-sodium soy sauce
1   tablespoon peeled, grated gingerroot
1   teaspoon sugar
2   cloves garlic, minced
1   (10½-ounce) package firm low-fat tofu,
      drained and cubed
1   cup chopped onion
1½ tablespoons vegetable oil
2   cups shredded Chinese cabbage
1   cup fresh bean sprouts
1   cup diced sweet red pepper
1   cup sliced fresh mushrooms
¼   cup sliced green onions
2   teaspoons cornstarch
3¾ cups cooked instant brown rice (cooked
      without salt or fat)

Combine first 5 ingredients in a bowl. Add tofu and onion. Cover and marinate in refrigerator 2 to 3 hours. Drain, reserving marinade.

Drizzle oil around top of wok, coating sides. Heat at medium (350°) until hot. Add tofu mixture; stir-fry 5 minutes or until tofu starts to brown and onion is tender. Remove from wok; set aside, and keep warm.

Add cabbage and next 4 ingredients to wok; stir-fry 2 to 3 minutes or until vegetables are crisp-tender.

Combine reserved marinade and cornstarch, stirring well. Add marinade mixture to vegetables; stir-fry 3 minutes or until thickened. Add tofu mixture, and stir-fry 30 seconds or until thoroughly heated. To serve, spoon ¾ cup rice onto each individual serving plate. Top with vegetable mixture.
Yield: 5 servings.

Per Serving:

Calories 276	Carbohydrate 45.0g	Fiber 4.4g
Fat 6.5g	Cholesterol 0mg	Calcium 71mg
Protein 16.4g	Sodium 390mg	Iron 2.1mg

Exchanges: 2 Very Lean Meat, 2 Starch, 1 Vegetable, 1 Fat

Sesame Broccoli Stir-Fry

SuperQuick

Prep time: 12 minutes   Cook: 9 minutes

Vegetable cooking spray
- 1 tablespoon dark sesame oil
- 1 (10½-ounce) package firm low-fat tofu, drained and cubed
- 4 cups fresh broccoli flowerets
- 1½ cups diced sweet red pepper
- ¼ cup low-sodium soy sauce
- 3 cups cooked instant brown rice (cooked without salt and fat)
- 1½ tablespoons sesame seeds, toasted

Coat a wok or large nonstick skillet with cooking spray; drizzle oil around top of wok, coating sides. Heat at medium-high (375°) until hot. Add tofu; stir-fry 5 to 6 minutes or until tofu starts to brown. Remove tofu from wok; set aside, and keep warm.

Add broccoli, red pepper, and soy sauce to wok; stir-fry 3 minutes or until vegetables are crisp-tender. Add tofu, and stir-fry 30 seconds or until thoroughly heated. To serve, spoon ¾ cup rice onto each individual serving plate. Top evenly with broccoli mixture. Sprinkle with sesame seeds. Yield: 4 servings.

Per Serving:

Calories 302	Carbohydrate 42.1g	Fiber 6.6g
Fat 9.6g	Cholesterol 0mg	Calcium 79mg
Protein 21.4g	Sodium 484mg	Iron 2.5mg

Exchanges: 2½ Very Lean Meat, 1½ Starch, 2 Vegetable, 1 Fat

Quick Tip

To keep prep time under 15 minutes, cook the instant brown rice while you chop the vegetables for the stir-fry.

Cuban Black Beans

Prep time: 6 minutes   Cook time: 35 minutes

Vegetable cooking spray
- 1 tablespoon olive oil
- 1 cup chopped onion
- ¾ cup chopped green pepper
- 2 cups no-salt-added tomato juice
- 3 (15-ounce) cans black beans, drained
- 1 (14½-ounce) can no-salt-added whole tomatoes, undrained and chopped
- 1 (8-ounce) can no-salt-added tomato sauce
- 1 (4-ounce) jar diced pimiento, drained
- 1 teaspoon pepper
- ½ teaspoon garlic powder
- ¼ teaspoon salt
- 8 cups cooked instant brown rice (cooked without salt or fat)
- 1 cup (4 ounces) shredded Monterey Jack cheese

Coat a large Dutch oven with cooking spray; add oil. Place over medium-high heat until hot. Add onion and green pepper; sauté until tender. Add tomato juice and next 7 ingredients; bring to a boil. Cover, reduce heat, and simmer 20 to 25 minutes or until vegetables are tender.

Place 1 cup rice in each individual bowl. Spoon 1 cup bean mixture over rice, and top each serving with 2 tablespoons cheese. Yield: 8 servings.

Per Serving:

Calories 472	Carbohydrate 81.2g	Fiber 8.5g
Fat 8.7g	Cholesterol 11mg	Calcium 179mg
Protein 19.9g	Sodium 378mg	Iron 3.9mg

Exchanges: 1 Medium-Fat Meat, 3 Starch, 2 Vegetable, 1 Fat

Black Bean Burritos

SuperQuick

Prep time: 10 minutes   Cook time: 9 minutes

1	(15-ounce) can black beans, drained
¼	cup finely chopped onion
¼	cup finely chopped green pepper
¼	cup finely chopped sweet red pepper
1	large clove garlic, minced
1	tablespoon chili powder
1	tablespoon vegetable oil
¼	teaspoon dried oregano
¼	teaspoon ground cumin
⅛	teaspoon salt
1	(4½-ounce) can chopped green chiles, drained
8	(6-inch) flour tortillas
1	cup (4 ounces) shredded reduced-fat Monterey Jack cheese
¼	cup nonfat sour cream
½	cup no-salt-added salsa

Place beans in a 1½ quart baking dish; mash to desired consistency. Add onion and next 8 ingredients; stir well. Cover with wax paper, and microwave at HIGH 5 to 6 minutes or until vegetables are tender, stirring every 2 minutes. Stir in green chiles.

Lightly brush 1 side of each tortilla with water. Stack 4 tortillas, and wrap in wax paper. Microwave at HIGH 30 seconds. Repeat procedure with remaining tortillas.

Spread ¼ cup bean mixture down center of each tortilla; top each with 2 tablespoons cheese. Roll up tortillas. Place tortillas in an 11- x 7- x 1½-inch baking dish. Cover with 2 damp paper towels, and microwave at HIGH 3 to 4 minutes or until thoroughly heated, rotating a half-turn after 1½ minutes. Top each with 1 tablespoon sour cream and 2 tablespoons salsa. Yield: 4 servings.

Per Serving:

Calories 475	Carbohydrate 63.7g	Fiber 6.6g
Fat 14.8g	Cholesterol 19mg	Calcium 368mg
Protein 23.0g	Sodium 907mg	Iron 4.8mg

Exchanges: 3 Lean Meat, 2 Starch, 1 Fat

Black Bean Casserole

Prep time: 35 minutes   Cook time: 35 minutes

¾ cup no-salt-added salsa
1 (14½-ounce) can no-salt-added whole
    tomatoes, drained and chopped
1 (10-ounce) package frozen chopped onion,
    celery, and pepper blend, thawed
1 (15-ounce) can black beans, drained
¼ teaspoon salt
3 (8-inch) flour tortillas
    Vegetable cooking spray
1 cup (4 ounces) shredded reduced-fat
    Monterey Jack cheese

Combine first 3 ingredients in a large
saucepan. Bring to a boil over medium-high heat.
Cover, reduce heat, and simmer 10 minutes. Stir in
beans and salt; cook 5 additional minutes.

Place 1 tortilla in bottom of a 9-inch deep-dish
pieplate coated with cooking spray. Spoon one-
third of bean mixture over tortilla. Repeat layers
with remaining 2 tortillas and bean mixture.

Cover and bake at 350° for 30 minutes.
Uncover and sprinkle with cheese. Bake, uncov-
ered, 5 additional minutes or until cheese melts.
Yield: 4 servings.

Per Serving:

Calories 336	Carbohydrate 46.3g	Fiber 4.3g
Fat 8.5g	Cholesterol 19mg	Calcium 337mg
Protein 18.9g	Sodium 821mg	Iron 3.2mg

Exchanges: 1 Medium-Fat Meat, 2 Starch, 2 Vegetable

A Flavor Kick

For extra flavor, top each serving with 2
tablespoons of salsa and 1 tablespoon of nonfat
sour cream. The toppings will add about 20 calories and virtually no fat.

Vegetarian Dutch Baby

Prep time: 18 minutes   Cook time: 17 minutes

    Vegetable cooking spray
1 cup sliced fresh mushrooms
½ cup thinly sliced and quartered yellow
    squash
½ cup thinly sliced and quartered zucchini
½ (16-ounce) package slaw mix
¾ cup drained canned black beans
½ teaspoon dried basil
¼ teaspoon dried thyme
¼ teaspoon onion powder
¼ teaspoon garlic powder
⅛ teaspoon salt
⅛ teaspoon pepper
1 tablespoon reduced-calorie margarine
½ cup all-purpose flour
½ cup skim milk
2 eggs, lightly beaten
½ cup (2 ounces) shredded provolone cheese

Coat a large nonstick skillet with cooking
spray; place over medium-high heat until hot. Add
mushrooms and next 3 ingredients; sauté 5 to 7
minutes or until vegetables are tender, stirring
often. Stir in black beans and next 6 ingredients.
Set aside, and keep warm.

Coat a 9-inch pieplate with cooking spray;
add margarine. Place in 425° oven 1 minute or
until margarine melts. Combine flour, milk, and
eggs in a medium bowl; stir well with a wire whisk.
Pour mixture into prepared pieplate (do not stir).

Bake at 425° for 15 to 20 minutes or until
puffed and browned. Spoon vegetable mixture into
shell; sprinkle with cheese. Bake 1 to 2 additional
minutes or until cheese melts. Serve immediately.
Yield: 4 servings.

Per Serving:

Calories 232	Carbohydrate 25.7g	Fiber 3.6g
Fat 8.9g	Cholesterol 121mg	Calcium 206mg
Protein13.4g	Sodium 358mg	Iron 2.6mg

Exchanges: 1 High-Fat Meat, 1 Starch, 3 Vegetable

Spicy Bean Enchiladas

Prep time: 22 minutes   Cook time: 25 minutes

¾ cup chopped green onions
2½ teaspoons chili powder, divided
1 teaspoon ground cumin
¼ teaspoon dried oregano
2 (8-ounce) cans no-salt-added tomato sauce
1 (4½-ounce) can chopped green chiles, undrained
1 (15-ounce) can pinto beans, undrained
¾ teaspoon salt
¼ teaspoon pepper
2 large cloves garlic, minced
1 bay leaf
8 (6-inch) corn tortillas
 Vegetable cooking spray
1 cup (4 ounces) shredded reduced-fat sharp Cheddar cheese
½ cup nonfat sour cream

Combine green onions, 2 teaspoons chili powder, and next 4 ingredients in a medium skillet. Bring to a boil; reduce heat, and simmer, uncovered, 5 minutes, stirring occasionally. Reserve ½ cup sauce mixture. Set remaining tomato sauce mixture aside.

Combine reserved ½ cup sauce mixture, remaining ½ teaspoon chili powder, beans, and next 4 ingredients in a medium saucepan. Bring to a boil; cover, reduce heat, and simmer 10 minutes, stirring often. Remove and discard bay leaf. Mash beans.

Dip each tortilla into tomato sauce mixture to soften; spread about ¼ cup bean mixture over tortilla. Roll up tortillas, and place, seam side down, in an 11- x 7- x 1½-inch baking dish coated with cooking spray.

Pour remaining sauce mixture over enchiladas. Cover and bake at 350° for 20 minutes. Top with cheese, and bake, uncovered, 5 additional minutes or until cheese melts. Top each enchilada with 1 tablespoon sour cream. Serve immediately. Yield: 4 servings.

Per Serving:

Calories 374	Carbohydrate 57.2g	Fiber 15.2g
Fat 8.1g	Cholesterol 19mg	Calcium 403mg
Protein 19.9g	Sodium 1086mg	Iron 2.9mg

Exchanges: 2 Lean Meat, 3 Starch, 1 Vegetable

Corn and Rice Burritos

SuperQuick

Prep time: 15 minutes   Cook: 5 minutes

1 (4.4-ounce) package Spanish rice and sauce mix
1½ cups drained canned no-salt-added pinto beans
1 cup frozen whole-kernel corn, thawed
¾ cup chopped tomato
8 (6-inch) flour tortillas
1 cup (4 ounces) shredded Monterey Jack cheese with peppers
½ cup plus 2 tablespoons nonfat sour cream

Cook rice according to package directions, omitting fat. Add beans, corn, and tomato; stir well. Cook over low heat until thoroughly heated.

Wrap tortillas in heavy-duty aluminum foil. Bake at 350° for 5 minutes or until thoroughly heated. Spoon rice mixture evenly down center of each tortilla. Top each with 2 tablespoons cheese and 1 tablespoon sour cream. Roll up, and serve immediately. Yield: 8 servings.

Per Serving:

Calories 263	Carbohydrate 38.9g	Fiber 3.1g
Fat 6.7g	Cholesterol 11mg	Calcium 147mg
Protein 11.6g	Sodium 442mg	Iron 2.0mg

Exchanges: ½ High-Fat Meat, 2½ Starch

Nuke It

If you don't want to heat up your oven, warm the tortillas wrapped in paper towels in the microwave at HIGH about 20 seconds.

Mexican Vegetables in Pastry Bowl

Prep time: 16 minutes   Cook time: 11 minutes

Vegetable cooking spray
¾ cup sliced green onions
¼ cup chopped green pepper
1 clove garlic, minced
1 (15-ounce) can pinto beans, drained
¾ cup frozen whole-kernel corn
1 medium tomato, seeded and chopped
¼ cup chunky picante sauce
1 tablespoon lime juice
1 tablespoon minced fresh cilantro
½ cup skim milk
¼ cup all-purpose flour
¼ cup yellow cornmeal
⅛ teaspoon chili powder
2 eggs, beaten
¼ cup (1 ounce) shredded reduced-fat
    Monterey Jack cheese
¼ cup (1 ounce) shredded reduced-fat
    Cheddar cheese

Coat a large nonstick skillet with cooking spray; place over medium-high heat until hot. Add green onions, green pepper, and garlic; sauté 3 to 4 minutes or until tender, stirring often. Stir in beans and next 5 ingredients; cook until thoroughly heated. Remove from heat; set aside, and keep warm.

Combine milk and next 4 ingredients in a medium bowl; stir well with a wire whisk. Pour mixture into a 9-inch pieplate coated with cooking spray. (Do not stir.) Bake at 475° for 10 minutes or until puffed and browned.

Spoon bean mixture into shell; sprinkle with cheeses. Bake 1 to 2 additional minutes or until cheese melts. Serve immediately. Yield: 4 servings.

Per Serving:

Calories 297	Carbohydrate 43.9g	Fiber 5.2g
Fat 6.3g	Cholesterol 120mg	Calcium 222mg
Protein 17.5g	Sodium 509mg	Iron 3.7mg

Exchanges: 2 Lean Meat, 2 Starch, 2 Vegetable

A Cool Tip

Freeze semi-soft cheeses, such as Monterey Jack, 10 to 15 minutes to make the cheese easier to shred.

Creole Black-Eyed Peas and Polenta

Prep time: 13 minutes   Cook time: 43 minutes

1 (16-ounce) package frozen black-eyed peas
2 cups water
2 (16-ounce) packages refrigerated polenta
Vegetable cooking spray
1¼ cups chopped green pepper
1¼ cups chopped onion
2 cloves garlic, minced
2 (14½-ounce) cans no-salt-added stewed
    tomatoes, undrained and chopped
1 tablespoon low-sodium Worcestershire
    sauce
½ teaspoon hot sauce
¼ teaspoon salt
¼ teaspoon ground red pepper
¼ teaspoon black pepper

Combine peas and water in a medium saucepan. Bring to a boil; cover, reduce heat, and simmer 20 minutes or until peas are tender. Drain and set aside.

Slice each package of polenta into 6 equal slices. Coat a nonstick skillet with cooking spray; place over medium-high heat until hot. Add polenta slices, and cook 1 to 2 minutes on each side or until thoroughly heated. Remove slices from skillet; cover and keep warm.

Coat skillet with cooking spray; place over medium-high heat until hot. Add green pepper, onion, and garlic; sauté until tender. Stir in peas, tomato, and remaining 5 ingredients. Bring to a boil; reduce heat, and simmer, uncovered, 10 minutes, stirring occasionally.

To serve, arrange 2 slices polenta on each of 6 plates; top each serving with 1 cup pea mixture. Yield: 6 servings.

Per Serving:

Calories 273	Carbohydrate 54.1g	Fiber 5.9g
Fat 0.9g	Cholesterol 0mg	Calcium 69mg
Protein 11.6g	Sodium 407mg	Iron 3.1mg

Exchanges: 1½ Very Lean Meat, 2 Starch, 2 Vegetable

Roasted Peppers and Feta Pizza

Prep time: 12 minutes   Cook time: 26 minutes

1   large sweet red pepper
1   large sweet yellow pepper
1   teaspoon reduced-calorie margarine
½   cup sliced onion
½   teaspoon sugar
1   clove garlic, minced
¾   cup pizza sauce
1   (1-pound) Italian cheese-flavored pizza crust
      (such as Boboli)
1   (4-ounce) package reduced-fat feta cheese

Cut peppers in half lengthwise; remove and discard seeds and membranes. Place peppers, skin side up, on a baking sheet, and flatten with palm of hand. Broil 5½ inches from heat (with electric oven door partially opened) 15 to 20 minutes or until charred. Place in ice water until cool; peel and discard skins. Coarsely chop peppers, and press between paper towels to remove excess moisture.

Melt margarine in a nonstick skillet over medium-high heat; add onion and sugar. Sauté 3 to 4 minutes or until golden, stirring in garlic during last 30 seconds of cooking time.

Spread pizza sauce over pizza crust to within ¾ inch of edge; top with pepper and onion mixture. Sprinkle with cheese.

Place pizza directly on oven rack. Bake at 450° for 8 minutes or until crust is golden. Yield: 4 servings.

Per Serving:

Calories 292	Carbohydrate 37.3g	Fiber 1.6g
Fat 9.2g	Cholesterol 16mg	Calcium 6mg
Protein 15.0g	Sodium 848mg	Iron 0.5mg

Exchanges: 1 Lean Meat, 2 Starch, 2 Vegetable, 1 Fat

Caramelized Onion Pizza

Prep time: 15 minutes   Cook time: 18 minutes

2   tablespoons reduced-calorie margarine
2   cups thinly sliced yellow onion (about 2 medium)
1   tablespoon sugar
1¼ cups lite ricotta cheese
2   teaspoons Italian seasoning, divided
¾   cup (3 ounces) shredded part-skim mozzarella cheese
¼   cup grated Parmesan cheese
⅛   teaspoon pepper
1   (11-ounce) can refrigerated French bread dough
    Vegetable cooking spray
1   large unpeeled tomato, seeded and thinly sliced
¼   cup chopped fresh parsley

Melt margarine in a skillet over medium-high heat. Add sliced onion and sugar; sauté 5 minutes or until onion is deep golden. Set aside.

Combine ricotta cheese, 1 teaspoon Italian seasoning, and next 3 ingredients; stir well.

Unroll bread dough, and pat into a 13- x 9- x 2-inch baking pan coated with cooking spray. Spread ricotta cheese mixture evenly over dough; top with tomato. Sprinkle with remaining 1 teaspoon Italian seasoning and parsley. Bake at 450° for 13 minutes. Top with onion mixture, and bake 5 additional minutes. Yield: 6 servings.

Per Serving:

Calories 273	Carbohydrate 33.4g	Fiber 1.3g
Fat 9.5g	Cholesterol 19mg	Calcium 235mg
Protein 15.7g	Sodium 480mg	Iron 1.0mg

Exchanges: 1 High-Fat Meat, 2 Starch, 1 Vegetable

Spaghetti Squash with Garden Vegetables

Prep time: 12 minutes   Stand time: 10 minutes
Cook time: 37 minutes

1   (3-pound) spaghetti squash
¾   cup grated Parmesan cheese
     Vegetable cooking spray
2   teaspoons olive oil
1½   cups diagonally sliced carrot
¾   cup diagonally sliced celery
1½   cups shredded cabbage
1   small zucchini, cut into very thin strips
1   (16-ounce) can kidney beans, drained
1   (14½-ounce) can no-salt-added whole tomatoes, drained and chopped
⅓   cup dry white wine
1   teaspoon dried thyme
1   teaspoon dried parsley flakes
½   teaspoon garlic powder
⅛   teaspoon pepper

Pierce squash 6 to 8 times with a fork. Place squash on a layer of paper towels in microwave oven. Microwave, uncovered, at HIGH 15 to 18 minutes or until squash is soft to the touch, turning squash over every 5 minutes. Let stand 5 minutes. Cut squash in half lengthwise; remove and discard seeds. Using a fork, remove 3 cups spaghetti-like strands from squash, reserving remaining squash for another use.

Combine squash strands and Parmesan cheese in a medium bowl, tossing gently. Set aside, and keep warm. Coat a 2-quart baking dish with cooking spray; add oil, carrot, and celery. Cover with heavy-duty plastic wrap, and vent; microwave at HIGH 6 minutes. Add cabbage and zucchini; stir well. Microwave, covered, at HIGH 6 minutes. Stir in beans and remaining 6 ingredients. Microwave, covered, at HIGH 10 to 12 minutes or until vegetables are tender. Let stand 5 minutes.

To serve, place ½ cup spaghetti squash mixture on each of 6 serving plates, and top evenly with vegetable mixture. Yield: 6 servings.

Per Serving:

Calories 182	Carbohydrate 23.6g	Fiber 7.9g
Fat 5.2g	Cholesterol 8mg	Calcium 217mg
Protein 9.7g	Sodium 495mg	Iron 2.2mg

Exchanges: 1 Starch, 2 Vegetable, 1 Fat

Baked Macaroni and Cheese

Prep time: 5 minutes   Cook time: 55 minutes

2   cups elbow macaroni, uncooked
1   tablespoon reduced-calorie margarine
¼   cup all-purpose flour
½   teaspoon dry mustard
⅛   teaspoon ground red pepper
3   cups skim milk
1   cup (4 ounces) shredded reduced-fat sharp
      Cheddar cheese
2   tablespoons grated Parmesan cheese
½   teaspoon salt
⅛   teaspoon black pepper
      Vegetable cooking spray
¼   teaspoon paprika
1   tablespoon fine, dry breadcrumbs

Cook pasta according to package directions, omitting salt and fat; drain and set aside.

Melt margarine in a large heavy saucepan over low heat; add flour, mustard, and red pepper. Cook, stirring constantly with a wire whisk, 1 minute. Gradually add milk, stir well. Cook over medium heat, stirring constantly, 10 minutes or until slightly thickened and bubbly; remove from heat. Add Cheddar cheese and next 3 ingredients, stirring until cheese melts.

Stir in macaroni; spoon into a 2-quart baking dish coated with cooking spray. Combine paprika and breadcrumbs in a bowl; sprinkle over macaroni mixture. Cover and bake at 400° for 30 minutes. Uncover and bake 5 additional minutes. Yield: 4 servings.

Per Serving:

Calories 426	Carbohydrate 59.9g	Fiber 1.7g
Fat 9.6g	Cholesterol 25mg	Calcium 531mg
Protein 24.0g	Sodium 691mg	Iron 2.9mg

Exchanges: 2 Medium-Fat Meat, 2½ Starch, ½ Skim Milk

Horseradish Cheese Bake

Prep time: 23 minutes   Cook time: 20 minutes

¼   cup plus 2 tablespoons all-purpose flour
3   cups skim milk, divided
1   tablespoon plus 1 teaspoon horseradish
      mustard (or 1 tablespoon Dijon mustard
      plus 1 teaspoon prepared horseradish)
2   tablespoons reduced-calorie margarine
1   cup (4 ounces) shredded reduced-fat sharp
      Cheddar cheese, divided
½   cup (2 ounces) shredded Gruyère or Swiss
      cheese
½   teaspoon salt
¼   teaspoon freshly ground pepper
5   cups cooked penne pasta (short tubular
      pasta), cooked without salt or fat
      Vegetable cooking spray

Combine flour, 1 cup milk, and mustard, stirring until smooth. Melt margarine in a large heavy saucepan over medium heat. Add flour mixture to margarine; cook, stirring constantly with a wire whisk, 1 minute.

Gradually add remaining 2 cups milk, stirring constantly. Cook, stirring constantly, 10 to 15 additional minutes or until thickened and bubbly. Remove from heat.

Add ½ cup Cheddar cheese and next 3 ingredients to milk mixture, stirring until cheese melts. Stir in pasta.

Spoon mixture into an 11- x 7- x 1½-inch baking dish coated with cooking spray. Sprinkle with remaining ½ cup Cheddar cheese. Cover and bake at 350° for 20 minutes. Let stand, covered, 5 minutes before serving. Yield: 6 servings.

Per Serving:

Calories 342	Carbohydrate 43.3g	Fiber 1.9g
Fat 10.2g	Cholesterol 26mg	Calcium 423mg
Protein 18.4g	Sodium 502mg	Iron 2.0mg

Exchanges: 1 Medium-Fat Meat, 2 Starch, 1 Fat, ½ Skim Milk

Mama Mia Pasta

SuperQuick
Prep time: 5 minutes   Cook time: 18 minutes

4   ounces wagon wheel pasta, uncooked
4   cloves garlic, minced
1   cup finely chopped onion
2   teaspoons olive oil
1   (14½-ounce) can no-salt-added whole
       tomatoes, undrained and chopped
1   tablespoon no-salt-added tomato paste
2   teaspoons sugar
1   teaspoon dried oregano
1   teaspoon dried basil
⅛   teaspoon salt
¼   teaspoon freshly ground pepper
3   tablespoons freshly grated Parmesan cheese
½   cup (2 ounces) shredded part-skim
       mozzarella cheese, divided

Cook pasta according to package directions, omitting salt and fat; drain and set aside.

Cook garlic and onion in olive oil in a large skillet over medium heat until tender. Add tomato and next 6 ingredients; cook 5 minutes. Add Parmesan cheese and ¼ cup mozzarella, stirring until cheese melts. Stir in pasta.

Transfer mixture to a serving bowl, and sprinkle with remaining ¼ cup mozzarella. Serve immediately. Yield: 2 servings.

Per Serving:

Calories 450	Carbohydrate 65.6g	Fiber 3.4g
Fat 12.1g	Cholesterol 21mg	Calcium 387mg
Protein 19.7g	Sodium 426mg	Iron 2.0mg

Exchanges: 1 Lean Meat, 2½ Starch, 2 Vegetable, 2 Fat

From Mama's Kitchen

If you don't want to open a can of tomato paste for only 1 tablespoon, omit paste and sugar, and substitute 1½ tablespoons reduced-sodium ketchup.

Mediterranean Casserole

Prep time: 20 minutes   Cook time: 15 minutes

8   ounces penne pasta (short tubular pasta),
       uncooked
    Olive oil-flavored vegetable cooking spray
½   cup crumbled feta cheese, divided
1   tablespoon olive oil
4   cups peeled, cubed eggplant
1   cup chopped purple onion
1   (14½-ounce) can no-salt-added whole
       tomatoes, undrained and chopped
¼   cup chopped ripe olives
¼   teaspoon salt
¼   teaspoon pepper

Cook pasta according to package directions, omitting salt and fat; drain. Place cooked pasta in an 11- x 7- x 1½-inch baking dish coated with cooking spray. Sprinkle with ¼ cup feta cheese; set aside.

Place oil in a large nonstick skillet. Heat over medium-high heat until hot. Add eggplant and onion; sauté 5 minutes or until tender.

Stir in tomato and remaining 3 ingredients. Cover, reduce heat, and simmer 5 minutes, stirring occasionally. Pour eggplant mixture over pasta; sprinkle with remaining ¼ cup cheese.

Bake at 350° for 15 minutes or until thoroughly heated and cheese melts. Yield: 4 servings.

Per Serving:

Calories 359	Carbohydrate 56.3g	Fiber 4.2g
Fat 9.9g	Cholesterol 18mg	Calcium 190mg
Protein 12.3g	Sodium 475mg	Iron 3.6mg

Exchanges: 1 Medium-Fat Meat, 2 Starch, 2 Vegetable, 1 Fat

Great Greek Flavor

Substitute dark, almond-shaped kalamata olives for the ripe olives for a more distinct flavor. You can find kalamata olives at an ethnic market or in the pickle and relish section of your local supermarket.

Penne Pasta with Fresh Tomatoes and Basil

Prep time: 11 minutes   Cook time: 15 minutes

5 ripe plum tomatoes, chopped
½ cup chopped fresh basil
¼ cup halved ripe olives
1 clove garlic, minced
1½ tablespoons olive oil
1 tablespoon balsamic vinegar
¼ teaspoon salt
⅛ teaspoon coarsely ground pepper
6 ounces penne pasta, uncooked
¼ cup crumbled feta cheese
 Fresh basil sprig (optional)

Combine first 8 ingredients in a medium bowl; toss well. Cover and let stand 15 minutes.

Cook pasta according to package directions, omitting salt and fat; drain well. Add pasta to tomato mixture; toss gently. Transfer to a serving dish, and sprinkle with feta cheese. Garnish with fresh basil sprig, if desired. Yield: 3 servings.

Per Serving:

Calories 345	Carbohydrate 49.5g	Fiber 3.2g
Fat 12.1g	Cholesterol 12mg	Calcium 106mg
Protein 10.5g	Sodium 453mg	Iron 3.2mg

Exchanges: 2½ Starch, 2 Vegetable, 2 Fat

Less Is More

Plum tomatoes are flavorful oblong-shaped tomatoes. They have more pulp (less juice and seeds) and usually are sweeter than round red tomatoes. Plum tomatoes are often used in sauces and salads.

Pesto Stuffed Shells

Prep time: 35 minutes   Cook time: 40 minutes

Vegetable cooking spray
1¾ cups finely chopped sweet red pepper
½ cup chopped onion
2 cloves garlic, minced
1 (14½-ounce) can no-salt-added whole
    tomatoes, undrained
1 (8-ounce) can no-salt-added tomato sauce
½ teaspoon dried Italian seasoning
¼ teaspoon salt
¼ teaspoon ground white pepper
12 jumbo pasta shells, uncooked
½ pound firm tofu
1¼ cups part-skim ricotta cheese
¼ cup grated Parmesan cheese
½ cup minced fresh basil
½ cup minced fresh parsley

Coat a nonstick skillet with cooking spray;
place over medium-high heat until hot. Add red
pepper, onion, and garlic; sauté until tender.

Place pepper mixture and tomato in container
of an electric blender or food processor; cover and
process until smooth. Transfer to a saucepan. Add
tomato sauce and next 3 ingredients; stir. Bring to
a boil; reduce heat, and simmer 20 minutes.

Spread ½ cup sauce mixture in an 11- x 7- x
1½-inch baking dish coated with cooking spray.

Cook pasta according to package directions,
omitting salt and fat; drain and set aside.

Wrap tofu in paper towels; press lightly to
remove excess moisture. Remove towels; crumble
tofu. Position knife blade in food processor bowl;
add tofu, ricotta cheese, and remaining 3 ingredients. Process 1 minute.

Spoon mixture into shells; place in baking
dish. Top with remaining sauce mixture. Cover and
bake at 400° for 40 minutes. Yield: 6 servings.

Per Serving:

Calories 268	Carbohydrate 35.3g	Fiber 3.1g
Fat 7.7g	Cholesterol 19mg	Calcium 276mg
Protein 15.7g	Sodium 251mg	Iron 4.7mg

Exchanges: 1 High-Fat Meat, 2 Starch

Mushroom Marinara

SuperQuick
Prep time: 5 minutes   Cook time: 18 minutes

Vegetable cooking spray
1 teaspoon olive oil
2 cups sliced fresh mushrooms
1 (14½-ounce) can no-salt-added whole
    tomatoes, undrained and coarsely
    chopped
¼ cup no-salt-added tomato paste
1 tablespoon dried parsley flakes
1 tablespoon dry red wine
½ teaspoon dried oregano
½ teaspoon dried basil
½ teaspoon dried thyme
¼ teaspoon pepper
⅛ teaspoon garlic powder
⅛ teaspoon salt
3 ounces angel hair pasta, uncooked
2 teaspoons grated Parmesan cheese

Coat a medium saucepan with cooking spray;
add olive oil. Place saucepan over medium-high
heat until hot. Add sliced mushrooms, and sauté
until tender.

Add tomato and next 9 ingredients; stir well.
Bring mixture to a boil; reduce heat, and simmer,
uncovered, 5 to 10 minutes or until slightly thickened, stirring occasionally.

Cook angel hair pasta according to package
directions, omitting salt and fat. Drain.

Divide pasta evenly between 2 individual
serving plates; top evenly with mushroom mixture.
Sprinkle each serving with 1 teaspoon Parmesan
cheese. Yield: 2 servings.

Per Serving:

Calories 276	Carbohydrate 50.6g	Fiber 3.6g
Fat 4.1g	Cholesterol 1mg	Calcium 128mg
Protein 10.6g	Sodium 220mg	Iron 4.8mg

Exchanges: 2 Starch, 2½ Vegetable, ½ Fat

Linguine with Asparagus and Goat Cheese

SuperQuick
Prep time: 10 minutes   Cook time: 15 minutes

½ pound fresh asparagus
8 ounces linguine, uncooked
½ cup canned no-salt-added chicken broth
¼ cup dry white wine
¼ cup chopped shallot
¼ teaspoon pepper
¾ (8-ounce) package Neufchâtel cheese, softened
2 ounces goat cheese, crumbled
2 tablespoons fresh lemon juice
½ cup thinly sliced sweet red pepper

Snap off tough ends of asparagus. Remove scales from stalks with a vegetable peeler, if desired. Cut asparagus into 1-inch pieces; set aside.

Cook pasta according to package directions, omitting salt and fat. Drain and set aside.

Combine broth and next 3 ingredients in a saucepan; bring to a boil over medium-high heat. Add asparagus. Reduce heat, and simmer, uncovered, 5 minutes. Add cheeses and lemon juice; cook over low heat, stirring constantly, until cheese melts.

Place pasta in a serving bowl. Add asparagus mixture and red pepper; toss gently. Serve immediately. Yield: 3 servings.

Per Serving:

Calories 520	Carbohydrate 65.4g	Fiber 3.5g
Fat 19.2g	Cholesterol 60mg	Calcium 152mg
Protein 11.2g	Sodium 467mg	Iron 1.1mg

Exchanges: 2 Medium-Fat Meat, 2½ Starch, 2 Vegetable, 1 Fat

For Goat Cheese Aficionados

If you're a fan of goat cheese, you'll love the tangy flavor it adds to this elegant pasta entrée. A smaller serving makes a complementary side dish for a simple beef or chicken entrée.

Eggplant Linguine

SuperQuick
Prep time: 15 minutes   Cook time: 10 minutes

8 ounces linguine, uncooked
   Vegetable cooking spray
3 cups cubed eggplant (about 1 small eggplant)
½ cup sliced fresh mushrooms
½ cup dry red wine
¼ cup dried tomato tidbits
1½ teaspoons sugar
1 (26-ounce) jar low-fat tomato-and-herb spaghetti sauce
¼ teaspoon chopped fresh parsley
¼ cup grated Parmesan cheese

Cook pasta according to package directions, omitting salt and fat. Drain and set aside.

Coat a nonstick skillet with cooking spray; place over medium-high heat until hot. Add eggplant and mushrooms; cook 3 minutes, stirring occasionally. Add wine; cook 2 minutes. Add tomato tidbits, sugar, and sauce; reduce heat, and simmer 5 minutes. Spoon sauce over pasta; sprinkle with parsley and cheese. Yield: 4 servings.

Per Serving:

Calories 395	Carbohydrate 72.7g	Fiber 5.7g
Fat 3.8g	Cholesterol 4mg	Calcium 126mg
Protein 15.5g	Sodium 985mg	Iron 3.1mg

Exchanges: 1 Lean Meat, 3 Starch, 2 Vegetable

Four-Cheese Vegetable Lasagna

Prep time: 25 minutes   Cook time: 35 minutes

 1 **(10-ounce) package frozen chopped spinach, thawed**
 1 **(16-ounce) package frozen broccoli, sweet red pepper, onion, and mushroom blend, thawed**
1½ **cups 1% low-fat cottage cheese**
 1 **cup (4 ounces) shredded part-skim mozzarella cheese**
 ½ **cup (2 ounces) shredded reduced-fat Swiss cheese**
 3 **cloves garlic, crushed**
 ½ **cup all-purpose flour**
 3 **cups 1% low-fat milk**
 ½ **cup freshly grated Parmesan cheese, divided**
 ½ **teaspoon salt**
 ¼ **teaspoon ground red pepper**
    Vegetable cooking spray
12 **cooked lasagna noodles (cooked without salt or fat)**

Drain spinach, and press gently between paper towels to remove excess moisture. Combine spinach and broccoli blend; set aside.

Combine cottage cheese and next 3 ingredients; set aside.

Place flour in a medium saucepan. Gradually add milk, stirring with a wire whisk until mixture is blended. Bring to a boil over medium heat, and cook 5 minutes or until mixture is thickened, stirring constantly. Remove from heat, and add ¼ cup Parmesan cheese, salt, and red pepper; stir until cheese melts.

Coat a 13- x 9- x 2-inch baking dish with cooking spray. Spread ½ cup cheese sauce evenly in bottom of dish, and reserve an additional ½ cup cheese sauce. Arrange 4 lasagna noodles over cheese sauce; top with one-half cottage cheese mixture, one-half vegetable mixture, and one-half remaining cheese sauce. Repeat layers, ending with noodles. Top noodles with reserved ½ cup sauce and remaining ¼ cup Parmesan cheese. Cover and bake at 375° for 35 minutes. Let stand 5 minutes before serving. Yield: 8 servings.

Per Serving:

Calories 357	Carbohydrate 73.8g	Fiber 3.5g
Fat 7.1g	Cholesterol 21mg	Calcium 423mg
Protein 24.3g	Sodium 562mg	Iron 2.9mg

Exchanges: 3 Very Lean Meat, 2½ Starch, 2 Vegetable

Spinach-Bean Lasagna

Prep time: 10 minutes   Cook time: 1 hour, 15 minutes

2   (15-ounce) cans no-salt-added kidney beans,
        drained
1¾   cups water
1   (26-ounce) jar low-fat spaghetti sauce
1   (10-ounce) package frozen chopped spinach,
        thawed
1   (15-ounce) carton part-skim ricotta cheese
¼   cup fat-free egg substitute
     Vegetable cooking spray
10   lasagna noodles, uncooked
1   cup (4 ounces) shredded part-skim
        mozzarella cheese
¼   cup grated Parmesan cheese

Position knife blade in food processor bowl; add beans. Pulse 2 or 3 times; gradually add water, and pulse several times until beans are coarsely chopped, stopping once to scrape down sides.

Combine bean mixture and sauce in a saucepan; bring to a boil. Reduce heat, and simmer, uncovered, stirring occasionally, 10 minutes; set aside.

Place spinach between paper towels; press to remove excess moisture. Combine spinach, ricotta cheese, and egg substitute; set aside.

Coat a 13- x 9- x 2-inch baking dish with cooking spray, and spread a thin layer of sauce on bottom of dish. Arrange 5 uncooked noodles over sauce mixture. Spread half of spinach mixture over noodles; top with mozzarella cheese. Spoon half of remaining sauce mixture over cheese. Repeat layers with remaining noodles, spinach mixture, and sauce mixture.

Cover and bake at 350° for 50 minutes. Sprinkle with Parmesan cheese; bake, uncovered, 15 additional minutes. Yield: 8 servings.

Per Serving:

Calories 389	Carbohydrate 54.1g	Fiber 4.4g
Fat 8.1g	Cholesterol 27mg	Calcium 318mg
Protein 25.9g	Sodium 526mg	Iron 2.4mg

Exchanges: 2 Lean Meat, 2½ Starch, 2 Vegetable

No Cooking Required

There's no need to precook the noodles for this recipe. They will soften as the lasagna cooks.

Ravioli with Red Pepper Sauce

Prep time: 15 minutes   Cook time: 20 minutes

1   (9-ounce) package fresh four-cheese ravioli,
        uncooked
1   (½-ounce) package dried wild mushrooms
½   cup dry sherry
2   cups fat-free chunky spaghetti sauce with
        mushrooms and sweet peppers
     Olive oil-flavored vegetable cooking spray
1   large sweet red pepper, cut into thin strips
1½   tablespoons pine nuts, toasted
2   tablespoons chopped fresh basil

Cook ravioli according to package directions, omitting salt and fat; drain. Place ravioli in a bowl; set aside, and keep warm.

Rinse mushrooms thoroughly. Combine mushrooms and sherry in a small saucepan. Bring to a boil; reduce heat, and simmer 3 minutes. Remove from heat; cover and let stand 15 minutes. Drain mushrooms, reserving liquid. Chop mushrooms; set aside. Position knife blade in food processor bowl; add sauce and reserved mushroom liquid. Process until smooth.

Coat a large nonstick skillet with cooking spray; place over medium-high heat until hot. Add chopped mushrooms and pepper strips; sauté 2 minutes or until tender. Add spaghetti sauce mixture. Bring to a boil; reduce heat, and simmer, uncovered, 10 minutes. Pour sauce over ravioli; toss lightly.

To serve, spoon onto individual serving plates. Sprinkle with pine nuts; top with basil.
Yield: 4 servings.

Per Serving:

Calories 313	Carbohydrate 38.5g	Fiber 3.6g
Fat 12.5g	Cholesterol 64mg	Calcium 158mg
Protein 13.0g	Sodium 660mg	Iron 2.6mg

Exchanges: 1 High-Fat Meat, 1 Starch, 1½ Vegetable, 1 Fat

Salads and Dressings

Mexicali Coleslaw (page 129)

Kiwifruit-Grapefruit Salad

Prep time: 25 minutes

1½ cups torn Boston lettuce
1½ cups torn red leaf lettuce
1 (½-pound) jicama, peeled and cut into very thin strips
1½ cups sliced celery
1 large pink grapefruit, peeled and sectioned
2 medium kiwifruit, peeled and sliced
1 small purple onion, thinly sliced
¼ cup sliced green onions
½ cup unsweetened grapefruit juice
2 tablespoons lime juice
¼ teaspoon salt
¼ teaspoon pepper
1½ tablespoons vegetable oil

Combine first 8 ingredients in a large bowl, and toss well. Combine grapefruit juice and remaining 4 ingredients in a small bowl; stir with a wire whisk to combine. Pour over lettuce mixture, tossing gently. Yield: 8 (1-cup) servings.

Per Serving:

Calories 75	Carbohydrate 12.0g	Fiber 1.9g
Fat 2.9g	Cholesterol 0mg	Calcium 34mg
Protein 1.4g	Sodium 96mg	Iron 0.9mg

Exchanges: 1 Vegetable, ½ Fruit, ½ Fat

Peculiar Produce

Jicama, a large bulbous root vegetable, has a thin brown skin and white crunchy flesh. Often referred to as the Mexican potato, jicama has a sweet, nutty flavor, and is good raw or cooked. Store jicama in the refrigerator, and peel before using.

Orange-Avocado Salad

SuperQuick
Prep time: 22 minutes

2 tablespoons unsweetened orange juice
2 tablespoons red wine vinegar
2 teaspoons olive oil
¼ teaspoon grated orange rind
⅛ teaspoon salt
⅛ teaspoon pepper
2 cups torn fresh watercress
1 cup torn fresh spinach
2 oranges, peeled and sectioned
1 small avocado, peeled and thinly sliced

Combine first 6 ingredients in a small bowl, stirring well with a wire whisk.
Combine watercress and spinach. Pour orange juice mixture over greens; toss gently.
Place watercress mixture evenly onto 6 individual salad plates. Arrange orange sections and avocado slices evenly over each salad.
Yield: 6 servings.

Per Serving:

Calories 60	Carbohydrate 5.1g	Fiber 1.9g
Fat 4.5g	Cholesterol 0mg	Calcium 33mg
Protein 1.1g	Sodium 63mg	Iron 0.5mg

Exchanges: 1 Vegetable, 1 Fat

Wilted Spinach and Fruit Salad

SuperQuick
Prep time: 5 minutes   Cook time: 12 minutes

1 (15¼-ounce) can pineapple chunks in juice
1 (11-ounce) can mandarin oranges in light
   syrup
¼ cup ginger liqueur
2 tablespoons low-sodium soy sauce
2 teaspoons dark sesame oil
5 cups shredded fresh spinach
1 (8-ounce) can sliced water chestnuts,
   drained

Drain fruits, reserving ¼ cup liquid from each can; set fruit aside.

Combine reserved fruit liquid, liqueur, soy sauce, and sesame oil in a small saucepan. Bring to a boil; reduce heat, and simmer 12 to 15 minutes or until thickened.

Combine spinach and water chestnuts in a large bowl; toss gently. Pour soy mixture over spinach mixture, tossing well. Top with reserved fruit. Serve immediately. Yield: 6 (1-cup) servings.

Per Serving:

Calories 143	Carbohydrate 27.6g	Fiber 1.6g
Fat 3.4g	Cholesterol 0mg	Calcium 26mg
Protein 1.2g	Sodium 175mg	Iron 1.0mg

Exchanges: 1 Vegetable, 1½ Fruit, ½ Fat

A Savvy Substitute

If you don't have ginger liqueur, use an equal amount of Grand Marnier or other orange-flavored liqueur.

Frozen Fruit Cups

Prep time: 15 minutes   Freeze time: 1 hour

1 (12-ounce) carton 1% low-fat cottage cheese
1 (8-ounce) carton strawberry low-fat yogurt
¼ cup reduced-calorie mayonnaise
1 tablespoon honey
1¼ cups sliced fresh strawberries
1 (15¼-ounce) can pineapple tidbits in juice,
   drained
2 medium-size ripe bananas, peeled and sliced
   Curly leaf lettuce leaves (optional)

Combine first 4 ingredients in container of an electric blender or food processor. Cover and process until smooth, stopping twice to scrape down sides.

Combine strawberries, pineapple, and banana in a large bowl. Fold cottage cheese mixture into fruit mixture. Spoon mixture evenly into 12 muffin cups lined with foil liners. Cover and freeze at least 1 hour.

Remove from muffin cups; peel off foil liners. To serve, place fruit cups on lettuce-lined salad plates, if desired. Yield: 12 servings.

Per Serving:

Calories 88	Carbohydrate 13.7g	Fiber 1.1g
Fat 2.0g	Cholesterol 4mg	Calcium 50mg
Protein 4.7g	Sodium 163mg	Iron 0.3mg

Exchanges: ½ Fruit, ½ Skim Milk

Thawing Out

This is a great recipe to keep on hand for quick meals. Pull individual servings from the freezer for an instant cool, refreshing salad. Take salads out of the freezer about 30 minutes before serving so they can thaw slightly.

Mixed Greens with Tarragon Dressing

Prep time: 20 minutes   Cook time: 5 minutes

½ cup light process cream cheese
2 tablespoons freeze-dried chives
2 tablespoons skim milk
1 teaspoon dried tarragon
  Olive oil-flavored vegetable cooking spray
¼ teaspoon olive oil
¼ teaspoon garlic powder
2 (1-ounce) slices whole wheat bread, cut into
  ½-inch cubes
8 cups torn leaf lettuce
2 cups torn curly endive
  Dash of coarsely ground pepper

Combine first 4 ingredients in container of an electric blender; cover and process until smooth. Transfer to a small bowl; cover and chill.

Coat a small nonstick skillet with cooking spray; add olive oil. Place over medium heat until hot; add garlic powder and bread cubes. Cook 5 minutes or until bread is lightly browned, stirring often. Set aside.

Combine leaf lettuce and curly endive in a large bowl; add bread cubes, and sprinkle with pepper. Arrange lettuce mixture on each serving plate. Drizzle cream cheese mixture over each salad. Yield: 10 (1-cup) servings.

Per Serving:

Calories 49	Carbohydrate 5.2g	Fiber 0.9g
Fat 2.3g	Cholesterol 7mg	Calcium 54mg
Protein 2.5g	Sodium 100mg	Iron 0.7mg

Exchanges: 1 Vegetable, ½ Fat

Mixed Greens and Walnut Salad

SuperQuick
Prep time: 15 minutes   Cook time: 5 minutes

3 heads Belgian endive
2 cups torn Boston lettuce
2 cups torn curly leaf lettuce
2 cups torn iceberg lettuce
¼ cup red wine vinegar
3 tablespoons water
2 teaspoons olive oil
½ teaspoon dry mustard
¼ teaspoon salt
¼ teaspoon pepper
6 walnut halves, toasted and coarsely chopped

Peel leaves from core of Belgian endive. Wash leaves, and pat dry with paper towels. Line a medium platter with leaves; set aside.

Combine Boston lettuce, curly leaf lettuce, and iceberg lettuce in a large bowl; toss well. Arrange lettuce mixture in center of endive-lined platter.

Combine vinegar and next 5 ingredients in a small saucepan. Bring to a boil. Remove from heat, and add walnuts. Spoon vinegar mixture evenly over salad, and serve immediately.
Yield: 6 (1-cup) servings.

Per Serving:

Calories 75	Carbohydrate 4.3g	Fiber 0.8g
Fat 6.1g	Cholesterol 0mg	Calcium 14mg
Protein 2.1g	Sodium 106mg	Iron 0.7mg

Exchanges: 1 Vegetable, 1 Fat

Greek Salad

SuperQuick
Prep time: 15 minutes

4 cups torn romaine lettuce
2 medium tomatoes, cut into wedges
1 small cucumber, sliced
1 small purple onion, thinly sliced
1 small green pepper, seeded and cut into
    strips
⅓ cup sliced ripe olives
½ cup crumbled feta cheese with peppercorns
¼ cup red wine vinegar
1 tablespoon lemon juice
2 teaspoons olive oil
½ teaspoon dried oregano
¼ teaspoon pepper

Combine first 7 ingredients in a large bowl. Combine vinegar and remaining 4 ingredients in a small bowl; stir well. Pour vinegar mixture over lettuce mixture, tossing well; serve immediately. Yield: 8 (1¼-cup) servings.

Per Serving:

Calories 63	Carbohydrate 6.5g	Fiber 1.8g
Fat 3.7g	Cholesterol 6mg	Calcium 57mg
Protein 2.2g	Sodium 144mg	Iron 1.0mg

Exchanges: 1 Vegetable, ½ Fat

Marinated Bean Salad

Prep time: 12 minutes   Chill time: 3 hours

1 (16-ounce) can no-salt-added green beans, drained
1 (16-ounce) can yellow wax beans, drained
1 (10-ounce) package frozen English peas, thawed
1 cup chopped green pepper
1 cup thinly sliced purple onion
1 (2-ounce) jar diced pimiento, drained
1 teaspoon minced garlic
¾ cup white vinegar
1 teaspoon vegetable oil
½ teaspoon salt
½ teaspoon pepper
½ cup sugar
   Curly leaf lettuce leaves (optional)

Combine first 7 ingredients in a large bowl; set aside.

Combine vinegar, oil, salt, and pepper in a small saucepan; bring to a boil. Remove from heat; stir in sugar. Pour dressing over vegetables; toss gently. Cover and chill at least 3 hours, stirring occasionally. To serve, spoon bean salad onto individual lettuce-lined salad plates, if desired. Yield: 13 (½-cup) servings.

Per Serving:

Calories 66	Carbohydrate 14.5g	Fiber 1.7g
Fat 0.6g	Cholesterol 0mg	Calcium 21mg
Protein 1.8g	Sodium 171mg	Iron 1.0mg

Exchanges: ½ Starch, 1 Vegetable

Black and White Bean Salad

SuperQuick
Prep time: 22 minutes

1 (15.8-ounce) can Great Northern beans, rinsed and drained
1 (15-ounce) can black beans, rinsed and drained
1¼ cups peeled, seeded, and chopped tomato
¾ cup diced sweet red pepper
¾ cup diced sweet yellow pepper
¾ cup thinly sliced green onions
½ cup salsa
¼ cup red wine vinegar
2 tablespoons chopped fresh cilantro
¼ teaspoon salt
⅛ teaspoon freshly ground pepper
10 cups finely shredded romaine lettuce (about 1 head)

Combine beans and chopped tomato in a large bowl, stirring gently. Add red pepper, yellow pepper, and green onions; stir to combine. Set aside.

Combine salsa and next 4 ingredients; stir with a wire whisk until well blended. Pour over bean mixture, and toss gently.

Line a large serving bowl with shredded lettuce; top with bean mixture. Yield: 10 servings.

Per Serving:

Calories 80	Carbohydrate 14.9g	Fiber 3.5g
Fat 0.6g	Cholesterol 0mg	Calcium 56mg
Protein 5.2g	Sodium 147mg	Iron 2.2mg

Exchange: 1 Starch

Mozzarella and Plum Tomato Salad

SuperQuick
Prep time: 8 minutes

1   small head radicchio, separated into leaves
4   large plum tomatoes, cut into ¼-inch slices
2   ounces part-skim mozzarella cheese, cut into
     8 slices
2   tablespoons minced fresh basil
2   tablespoons balsamic vinegar
½   teaspoon olive oil
⅛   teaspoon freshly ground pepper

Place radicchio leaves on each individual salad plate. Arrange tomato slices and cheese over radicchio on each plate.

Combine basil and remaining 3 ingredients in a small bowl, stirring well. Drizzle vinegar mixture evenly over each serving; serve immediately. Yield: 4 servings.

Per Serving:

Calories 71	Carbohydrate 6.7g	Fiber 0.9g
Fat 3.2g	Cholesterol 8mg	Calcium 113mg
Protein 5.0g	Sodium 86mg	Iron 0.4mg

Exchanges: ½ Lean Meat, 1 Vegetable

What's Radicchio?
(rah-DEE-kee-o)

Radicchio is Italian chicory. The heads are small and round with white-ribbed red leaves and a bitter flavor. Look for it in the produce section along with the other lettuces.

Marinated Hearts of Palm Salad

Prep time: 20 minutes   Marinate time: 30 minutes

1   pound fresh asparagus spears
1   (14-ounce) can hearts of palm, drained and sliced
4   medium-size plum tomatoes, quartered lengthwise
½   cup fat-free balsamic vinaigrette
6   Boston lettuce leaves
¼   cup freshly grated Parmesan cheese
½   teaspoon freshly ground pepper

Snap off tough ends of asparagus. Remove scales from stalks with a vegetable peeler, if desired. Arrange asparagus in a steamer basket over boiling water. Cover and steam 7 minutes or until crisp-tender. Drain well.

Place asparagus, hearts of palm, and tomato in a shallow dish; add vinaigrette. Cover and marinate in refrigerator 30 minutes.

Drain vegetables, discarding vinaigrette. Arrange asparagus, hearts of palm, and tomato evenly on lettuce-lined salad plates. Sprinkle evenly with Parmesan cheese and pepper.
Yield: 6 servings.

Per Serving:

Calories 70	Carbohydrate 13.2g	Fiber 5.2g
Fat 1.0g	Cholesterol 1mg	Calcium 61mg
Protein 3.9g	Sodium 479mg	Iron 2.3mg

Exchange: 2 Vegetable

Broccoli-Corn Salad

Prep time: 5 minutes   Cook time: 5 minutes
Chill time: 30 minutes

2   (10-ounce) packages frozen broccoli flowerets
1   (15¼-ounce) can no-salt-added whole-kernel corn, drained
1   (4-ounce) jar diced pimiento, drained
¼   cup rice wine vinegar
1   tablespoon vegetable oil
¼   teaspoon salt
⅛   teaspoon pepper
⅛   teaspoon chili powder
⅛   teaspoon ground cumin
⅛   teaspoon dried oregano

Arrange broccoli in a steamer basket over boiling water. Cover and steam 5 to 6 minutes or until crisp-tender. Let cool.

Combine broccoli, corn, and pimiento in a large bowl. Combine vinegar and remaining 6 ingredients in a small bowl; stir well with a wire whisk. Pour vinegar mixture over broccoli mixture, and toss gently. Cover and chill.
Yield: 5 (1-cup) servings.

Per Serving:

Calories 118	Carbohydrate 17.9g	Fiber 3.3g
Fat 3.8g	Cholesterol 0mg	Calcium 67mg
Protein 4.9g	Sodium 153mg	Iron 1.6mg

Exchanges: ½ Starch, 1 Vegetable, 1 Fat

Calico Corn Salad

SuperQuick

Prep time: 8 minutes   Cook time: 3 minutes

2   (11-ounce) cans no-salt-added whole-kernel corn, drained
⅓   cup white wine
¾   cup chopped green pepper
½   cup chopped purple onion
1   (4-ounce) jar diced pimiento, drained
2   tablespoons chopped fresh cilantro
2   tablespoons rice wine vinegar
2   teaspoons lime juice
¼   teaspoon salt
¼   teaspoon garlic powder
¼   teaspoon ground red pepper
     Lettuce leaves (optional)

Combine corn and wine in a large nonstick skillet; place over medium-high heat, and cook 3 to 5 minutes or until liquid evaporates. Remove from heat; add green pepper and next 8 ingredients, stirring well. To serve, spoon mixture into a lettuce-lined bowl, if desired. Yield: 8 (½-cup) servings.

Per Serving:

Calories 64	Carbohydrate 11.5g	Fiber 0.7g
Fat 0.7g	Cholesterol 0mg	Calcium 6mg
Protein 1.6g	Sodium 80mg	Iron 0.7mg

Exchanges: ½ Starch, 1 Vegetable

Measuring Up

If no-salt-added corn is unavailable, substitute 2 cups frozen corn for an 11-ounce can.

Mexicali Coleslaw

Prep time: 15 minutes   Chill time: 30 minutes

1   small head savoy cabbage, untrimmed
½   cup coarsely shredded red cabbage
½   cup no-salt-added whole-kernel corn, drained
¼   cup seeded, chopped tomato
2   tablespoons chopped green pepper
2   tablespoons (½ ounce) shredded reduced-fat Cheddar cheese
2   teaspoons seeded and minced jalapeño pepper
2   tablespoons plain low-fat yogurt
2   tablespoons low-fat sour cream
¼   teaspoon chili powder
⅛   teaspoon ground cumin
⅛   teaspoon hot sauce

Remove 3 large outer leaves of savoy cabbage; set leaves aside. Coarsely shred inner leaves.

Combine shredded savoy cabbage, red cabbage, and next 5 ingredients in a medium bowl; toss well, and set aside.

Combine yogurt and remaining 4 ingredients in a small bowl, stirring well. Add yogurt mixture to shredded cabbage mixture, tossing gently. Cover and chill. Yield: 3 (1-cup) servings.

Per Serving:

Calories 84	Carbohydrate 13.1g	Fiber 1.3g
Fat 2.5g	Cholesterol 7mg	Calcium 95mg
Protein 4.2g	Sodium 74mg	Iron 0.7mg

Exchanges: 2 Vegetable, ½ Fat

Warm Potato Salad

SuperQuick

Prep time: 10 minutes   Cook time: 10 minutes

2 cups cubed red potatoes
2 tablespoons finely chopped purple onion
1 tablespoon plus 1 teaspoon white wine vinegar
1 tablespoon freeze-dried chives
1 teaspoon olive oil
½ teaspoon sugar
¼ teaspoon salt
¼ teaspoon pepper

Place potato in a medium saucepan; add water to cover. Bring to a boil; cover, reduce heat, and simmer 10 minutes or until potato is tender. Drain and transfer to a bowl. Add chopped onion.

Combine vinegar and remaining 5 ingredients; stir well. Add to potato mixture; toss gently to coat. Serve warm. Yield: 4 (½-cup) servings.

Per Serving:

Calories 82	Carbohydrate 16.4g	Fiber 1.5g
Fat 1.2g	Cholesterol 0mg	Calcium 8mg
Protein 1.8g	Sodium 152mg	Iron 0.7mg

Exchange: 1 Starch

Pesto Potato Salad

Prep time: 15 minutes   Cook time: 21 minutes

½ cup dried tomatoes (packed without oil)
½ cup hot water
2 pounds small round red potatoes
  Olive oil-flavored vegetable cooking spray
2 cloves garlic, minced
½ cup sliced green onions
⅓ cup light Caesar salad dressing
2 tablespoons pesto
½ cup nonfat sour cream
¼ teaspoon freshly ground pepper

Combine tomato and hot water in a small bowl. Let stand 10 minutes. Drain and coarsely chop tomato; set aside.

Cook potatoes in large saucepan in boiling water to cover 15 to 17 minutes or until tender. Let cool slightly. Cut potatoes into 1-inch pieces; set aside.

Coat a large nonstick skillet with cooking spray; place over medium-high heat until hot. Add tomato, potato, garlic, and green onions to skillet. Sauté 5 minutes. Add salad dressing, deglazing pan by scraping particles that cling to bottom. Cook 1 minute; set aside, and keep warm.

Combine pesto, sour cream and pepper in a large bowl, stirring well. Add potato mixture, and toss gently to combine. Yield: 6 (1-cup) servings.

Per Serving:

Calories 201	Carbohydrate 32.0g	Fiber 3.8g
Fat 5.7g	Cholesterol 2.9mg	Calcium 68mg
Protein 6.1g	Sodium 446mg	Iron 2.7mg

Exchanges: 2 Starch, 1 Fat

Squash and Jicama Salad

Prep time: 15 minutes   Chill time: 2 hours

3 cups cubed yellow squash (about 3 medium)
3 cups julienne-sliced jicama
1 medium-size green pepper, seeded and sliced
    into thin strips
1 cup thinly sliced purple onion
½ cup unsweetened orange juice
2 tablespoons Dijon mustard
2 tablespoons white wine vinegar
2 teaspoons vegetable oil
¼ teaspoon sugar
¼ teaspoon pepper

Arrange squash in a steamer basket over boiling water. Cover and steam 2 minutes. Combine squash, jicama, green pepper, and onion in a heavy-duty, zip-top plastic bag; set aside.

Combine orange juice and remaining 5 ingredients in a small bowl, stirring well. Pour juice mixture over squash mixture; seal bag, and turn until vegetables are coated. Marinate in refrigerator at least 2 hours, turning bag occasionally. Yield: 8 (¾-cup) servings.

Per Serving:

Calories 59	Carbohydrate 10.3g	Fiber 1.6g
Fat 1.6g	Cholesterol 0mg	Calcium 21mg
Protein 1.3g	Sodium 116mg	Iron 0.7mg

Exchange: 2 Vegetable

Gazpacho Mold

Prep time: 15 minutes   Chill time: 8 hours

2 envelopes unflavored gelatin
½ cup cold water
2½ cups no-salt-added vegetable juice
3 tablespoons lemon juice
¼ teaspoon hot sauce
½ cup chopped celery
½ cup chopped green pepper
½ cup peeled, seeded, and chopped cucumber
    Vegetable cooking spray
¼ cup plain nonfat yogurt
¼ cup chopped fresh parsley
¼ cup reduced-calorie mayonnaise

Sprinkle gelatin over water in a small saucepan; let stand 1 minute. Cook over low heat, stirring until gelatin dissolves, about 2 minutes. Add vegetable juice, lemon juice, and hot sauce; stir well. Remove from heat, and chill until the consistency of unbeaten egg white.

Add celery, green pepper, and cucumber to gelatin mixture, stirring gently to combine. Spoon gelatin mixture into a 4-cup mold coated with cooking spray. Cover and chill until firm.

Combine yogurt, parsley, and mayonnaise in a small bowl; stir well. Cover and chill. Unmold gazpacho, and serve with parsley sauce. Yield: 8 servings.

Per Serving:

Calories 56	Carbohydrate 5.8g	Fiber 0.9g
Fat 2.1g	Cholesterol 3mg	Calcium 30mg
Protein 2.7g	Sodium 116mg	Iron 0.5mg

Exchanges: 1 Vegetable, ½ Fat

Can't Take the Heat

To serve this congealed salad, run a knife or thin spatula around edge of the mold. Invert the mold onto a serving dish, and then wrap the mold with a hot towel. The salad will slip out easily.

Tabbouleh

Prep time: 10 minutes   Stand time: 15 minutes
Chill time: 1 hour

1   cup boiling water
1   cup bulgur (cracked wheat), uncooked
1½   cups seeded, chopped tomato
1   cup chopped fresh mint
¾   cup minced fresh parsley
½   cup seeded, chopped cucumber
⅓   cup sliced green onions
½   cup lemon juice
2   tablespoons olive oil
½   teaspoon salt
½   teaspoon garlic powder
⅛   teaspoon ground red pepper
⅛   teaspoon black pepper

Pour water over bulgur in a large bowl; cover and let stand 15 to 20 minutes or until bulgur is tender and water is absorbed. Add tomato and next 4 ingredients; toss well.

Combine lemon juice and remaining 5 ingredients in a small bowl; stir well with a wire whisk. Drizzle lemon juice mixture over bulgur mixture; toss well. Cover and chill at least 1 hour.
Yield: 10 (½-cup) servings.

Per Serving:

Calories 85	Carbohydrate 13.8g	Fiber 3.3g
Fat 3.0g	Cholesterol 0mg	Calcium 18mg
Protein 2.3g	Sodium 125mg	Iron 0.9mg

Exchanges: 1 Starch, ½ Fat

Big on Bulgur

Bulgur, this recipe's main ingredient, is pre-cooked cracked wheat. The grain is steamed, dried, and then cracked to various sizes. Bulgur is available in supermarkets in the rice section and in health food stores.

Southwestern Pasta Salad

Prep time: 10 minutes   Cook time: 10 minutes
Chill time: 2 hours

4   ounces ditalini macaroni, uncooked
½   cup diced sweet red pepper
½   cup diced sweet yellow pepper
1   cup peeled, seeded, and chopped tomato
¼   cup diced purple onion
1   tablespoon plus 1½ teaspoons minced fresh
     cilantro
1   clove garlic, minced
1   small jalapeño pepper, seeded and minced
1½   teaspoons olive oil
1½   teaspoons red wine vinegar
¼   cup crumbled feta cheese
2   tablespoons pine nuts, toasted

Cook macaroni according to package directions, omitting salt and fat. Drain and set aside. Combine sweet red pepper and next 8 ingredients in a large bowl. Stir in macaroni. Cover and chill at least 2 hours. Top with cheese and pine nuts.
Yield: 4 (1-cup) servings.

Per Serving:

Calories 232	Carbohydrate 30.5g	Fiber 3.0g
Fat 10.0g	Cholesterol 13mg	Calcium 88mg
Protein 7.7g	Sodium 175mg	Iron 2.5mg

Exchanges: 2 Starch, 1½ Fat

Tuna-Pasta Salad

Prep time: 5 minutes   Cook time: 10 minutes
Chill time: 30 minutes

8 ounces small shell macaroni, uncooked (about 2 cups)
1 cup shredded carrot
¾ cup diced green pepper
⅔ cup sliced celery
½ cup minced green onions
1 (6½-ounce) can tuna in water, drained and flaked
¼ cup plus 2 tablespoons plain low-fat yogurt
¼ cup reduced-calorie mayonnaise
¼ teaspoon celery seeds
¼ teaspoon salt
¼ teaspoon pepper
   Curly leaf lettuce leaves (optional)

Cook macaroni according to package directions, omitting salt and fat; drain. Rinse with cold water, and drain well.

Combine macaroni, carrot, and next 4 ingredients; toss gently. Combine yogurt and next 4 ingredients; stir well. Add to pasta mixture, tossing gently to combine. Cover and chill thoroughly. To serve, spoon pasta mixture onto individual lettuce-lined salad plates, if desired.
Yield: *7 (1-cup) servings.*

Per Serving:

Calories 191	Carbohydrate 29.1g	Fiber 1.9g
Fat 3.6g	Cholesterol 11mg	Calcium 45mg
Protein 10.3g	Sodium 247mg	Iron 1.9mg

Exchanges: 2 Starch, ½ Fat

Posole Pasta Salad

SuperQuick
Prep time: 5 minutes   Cook time: 12 minutes

8 ounces wagon wheel pasta, uncooked
1 (15½-ounce) can golden hominy, drained
1 (15-ounce) can no-salt-added black beans, drained
⅓ cup chopped purple onion
2 tablespoons chopped fresh cilantro
1 cup low-fat sour cream
1 tablespoon chili powder
¼ teaspoon salt
⅛ teaspoon pepper

Cook pasta according to package directions, omitting salt and fat. Drain; rinse with cold water, and drain well. Place pasta in a large bowl. Add hominy and next 3 ingredients; toss well.

Combine sour cream and remaining 3 ingredients, stirring well. Pour sour cream mixture over pasta mixture; toss well. Serve immediately.
Yield: *7 (1-cup) servings.*

Per Serving:

Calories 250	Carbohydrate 41.5g	Fiber 3.9g
Fat 5.2g	Cholesterol 13mg	Calcium 58mg
Protein 9.5g	Sodium 184mg	Iron 2.6mg

Exchanges: 2½ Starch, 1 Fat

Pondering Posole

Posole, a thick, hearty soup originating in Mexico, traditionally includes flavorful ingredients like pork or chicken, hominy, onion, chiles, and cilantro. You'll think you're south of the border eating this pasta salad variation of posole.

Garden Tortellini

Prep time: 5 minutes   Cook time: 14 minutes
Chill time: 30 minutes

2 (9-ounce) packages fresh cheese-filled
    tortellini
1 cup sliced carrot
1 cup cherry tomatoes, halved
1 (9-ounce) package frozen asparagus spears,
    thawed and cut into 1-inch pieces
1 (6-ounce) package frozen snow pea pods,
    thawed
⅔ cup sliced radishes
1 small purple onion, thinly sliced and
    separated into rings
3 tablespoons water
2 tablespoons lemon juice
2 tablespoons cider vinegar
1½ tablespoons olive oil
1 teaspoon dried basil
½ teaspoon pepper
½ teaspoon salt

Cook tortellini according to package directions, omitting salt and fat; drain. Rinse with cold
water; drain well, and set aside.

Arrange carrot in a steamer basket over boiling water. Cover and steam 3 to 5 minutes or until
crisp-tender. Combine tortellini, carrot, and next 5
ingredients in a large bowl.

Combine water and remaining 6 ingredients;
stir well. Pour over tortellini mixture, and toss gently. Cover and chill. Yield: 11 (1-cup) servings.

Per Serving:

Calories 191	Carbohydrate 27.1g	Fiber 1.7g
Fat 5.3g	Cholesterol 21mg	Calcium 22mg
Protein 8.4g	Sodium 230mg	Iron 0.8mg

Exchanges: 2 Starch, 1 Fat

Touting Tortellini

Tortellini is pasta stuffed with a variety of fill-
ings and shaped into a ring or hat. You can find
fresh tortellini in the refrigerated section of the
supermarket. If you don't use fresh tortellini within a week of purchase, freeze it to retain maximum
freshness.

Beef and Succotash Salad

Prep time: 15 minutes   Cook time: 15 minutes

½ pound lean flank steak
    Vegetable cooking spray
1 tablespoon plus 1 teaspoon minced roasted
    garlic, divided
1 cup frozen baby lima beans
3 tablespoons water
½ cup frozen corn
2 teaspoons olive oil
½ teaspoon Italian seasoning
½ cup coarsely chopped roasted red pepper
¼ cup white wine vinegar
½ head curly leaf lettuce

Partially freeze steak; trim fat from steak.
Slice steak diagonally across grain into thin strips,
and set aside.

Coat a large nonstick skillet with cooking
spray, and place over medium heat until hot. Add 2
teaspoons garlic and lima beans; cook, stirring constantly, 3 minutes. Add water and corn; cover and
cook 3 minutes or until vegetables are crisp-tender,
stirring occasionally. Drain vegetables; place in a
medium bowl, and set aside.

Add olive oil to skillet, and place over medium
heat until hot. Add steak, Italian seasoning, and 1
teaspoon garlic. Cook steak about 3 minutes or to
desired degree of doneness. Drain steak; add steak
and chopped pepper to vegetable mixture, tossing
gently.

Add vinegar and remaining 1 teaspoon garlic
to skillet; cook over medium heat 5 minutes, stirring occasionally. Pour over beef mixture; toss gently to coat. Serve on a lettuce-lined platter.
Yield: 4 (1-cup) servings.

Per Serving:

Calories 194	Carbohydrate 14.7g	Fiber 3.0g
Fat 8.4g	Cholesterol 28mg	Calcium 33mg
Protein 15.2g	Sodium 50mg	Iron 3.1mg

Exchanges: 1½ Medium-Fat Meat, 1 Starch

Grilled Chicken Salad

*Prep time: 23 minutes   Marinate time: 1 hour
Cook time: 10 minutes*

6   (4-ounce) skinned, boned chicken breast
    halves
½   cup unsweetened orange juice
¼   cup honey
1   tablespoon low-sodium soy sauce
    Vegetable cooking spray
6   cups torn red leaf lettuce
2   medium oranges, peeled and sectioned
1½   cups halved red grapes

Place chicken in a large heavy-duty, zip-top plastic bag. Combine orange juice, honey, and soy sauce, stirring well. Divide orange juice mixture in half; set aside half in refrigerator. Pour remaining orange juice mixture over chicken; seal bag, and shake until chicken is coated. Marinate in refrigerator 1 hour, turning bag occasionally.

Remove chicken from marinade, discarding marinade. Coat grill rack with cooking spray; place on grill over medium-hot coals (350° to 400°). Place chicken on rack; grill, covered, 5 minutes on each side or until chicken is done. Slice chicken into thin slices.

Combine lettuce, orange sections, and grapes, tossing gently. Arrange chicken in a spoke fashion evenly on each individual salad plate. Spoon lettuce mixture evenly over chicken. Drizzle reserved orange juice mixture evenly over each serving. Serve immediately. Yield: 6 (1¾-cup) servings.

Per Serving:

Calories 219	Carbohydrate 20.1g	Fiber 2.2g
Fat 3.4g	Cholesterol 72mg	Calcium 51mg
Protein 27.4g	Sodium 110mg	Iron 1.5mg

Exchanges: 3 Very Lean Meat, 1 Vegetable, 1 Fruit

Bag the Marinade

Marinate the chicken in a zip-top plastic bag. There's no messy container to clean up, and it's easy to keep the chicken coated with marinade by shaking or turning the bag occasionally.

Southwestern Chicken Salad

Prep time: 20 minutes   Chill time: 2 hours

2   cups chopped cooked chicken breast
    (skinned before cooking and cooked
    without salt)
1   cup nonfat sour cream
1   (4.5-ounce) can chopped green chiles,
    drained
1   tablespoon taco seasoning mix
1   (7-ounce) package no-oil baked tortilla
    chips
2   cups torn iceberg lettuce
1   cup (4 ounces) shredded reduced-fat sharp
    Cheddar cheese
    Chopped fresh cilantro (optional)

Combine first 4 ingredients in a small bowl.
Cover and chill at least 2 hours.

To serve, place tortilla chips on individual
salad plates; top evenly with chicken mixture.
Sprinkle lettuce and cheese over chicken mixture.
Garnish with cilantro, if desired. Yield: 4 servings.

Per Serving:

Calories 468	Carbohydrate 47.8g	Fiber 4.1g
Fat 10.1g	Cholesterol 87mg	Calcium 271mg
Protein 41.1g	Sodium 655mg	Iron 1.2mg

Exchanges: 4 Very Lean Meat, 3 Starch

Turkey Waldorf Salad with Yogurt Dressing

SuperQuick
Prep time: 15 minutes

1   cup chopped cooked turkey
1   cup unpeeled diced Red Delicious apple
½   cup chopped celery
2   tablespoons chopped walnuts
2   tablespoons raisins
½   cup plain low-fat yogurt
1   tablespoon honey
1   teaspoon grated orange rind
4   green leaf lettuce leaves

Combine first 5 ingredients in a medium
bowl. Combine yogurt, honey, and orange rind;
pour over turkey mixture, and toss gently.

Place 2 lettuce leaves on 2 individual serving
plates; top evenly with turkey mixture. Serve
immediately. Yield: 2 servings.

Per Serving:

Calories 278	Carbohydrate 31.5g	Fiber 3.4g
Fat 6.6g	Cholesterol 47mg	Calcium 173mg
Protein 25.7g	Sodium 120mg	Iron 2.0mg

Exchanges: 2½ Very Lean Meat, ½ Starch, 1½ Fruit, ½ Fat

Rind or Reason

It's easier to grate the colored part of citrus
rind when the fruit is whole. The bitter white part
(pith) beneath the rind or outer skin doesn't contain any of the aromatic oils or flavoring of the
rind.

Smoked Turkey, Potato, and Green Bean Salad

Prep time: 15 minutes   Cook time: 15 minutes

1   pound small round red potatoes
½   cup canned low-sodium chicken broth
½   cup water
2   tablespoons lemon juice
2   tablespoons white wine vinegar
1   tablespoon Dijon mustard
1   tablespoon olive oil
½   teaspoon salt
¼   teaspoon freshly ground pepper
3   cups sliced fresh mushrooms
½   pound green beans, sliced into ¾-inch pieces
¾   pound julienne-sliced smoked turkey
1   cup julienne-sliced sweet red pepper
¾   cup diagonally sliced celery
½   cup diced purple onion
¼   cup minced fresh parsley

Cook potatoes in boiling water to cover until almost tender; drain, reserving water, and set aside. Combine chicken broth and next 7 ingredients in a small bowl; stir well. Place mushrooms in a large bowl; add chicken broth mixture, and toss gently to combine.

Bring reserved water to boil; add green beans, and cook 3 minutes or until crisp-tender. Drain and set aside.

Cut potatoes into quarters, and add to mushroom mixture. Stir in beans, turkey, sweet red pepper, celery, and onion. Transfer to individual serving plates. Sprinkle with parsley.
Yield: 5 (2-cup) servings.

Per Serving:

Calories 250	Carbohydrate 27.0g	Fiber 3.7g
Fat 7.5g	Cholesterol 38mg	Calcium 44mg
Protein 20.6g	Sodium 896mg	Iron 3.7mg

Exchanges: 2½ Lean Meat, 1 Starch, 1 Vegetable

Shrimp and Vegetable Salad

Prep time: 20 minutes   Cook time: 20 minutes

1½   pounds unpeeled medium-size fresh shrimp
⅔   cup water
½   cup chopped onion
⅓   cup dry white wine
¼   teaspoon dried crushed red pepper
1   small sweet red pepper
1   small sweet yellow pepper
1   small green pepper
    Olive oil-flavored vegetable cooking spray
3   carrots, scraped and cut into very thin strips
1   clove garlic, minced
1   small zucchini, cut into very thin strips
1   small yellow squash, cut into very thin strips
½   pound snow pea pods, trimmed
¾   cup plain nonfat yogurt
¼   cup reduced-calorie mayonnaise
2   tablespoons chopped fresh dillweed
1   tablespoon lemon juice
¼   teaspoon salt
¼   teaspoon freshly ground black pepper
    Dash of ground red pepper
7½   cups shredded romaine lettuce

Peel and devein shrimp. Combine water and next 3 ingredients in a nonstick skillet; bring to a boil. Boil 5 minutes. Add shrimp; cook 3 minutes. Remove shrimp, reserving liquid in skillet. Rinse shrimp with cold water; drain. Boil reserved liquid 3 minutes or until reduced by half. Set aside 2 tablespoons liquid; discard remaining liquid.

Seed and cut peppers into very thin strips; set aside. Coat a nonstick skillet with cooking spray; place over medium-high heat until hot. Add carrot and garlic; sauté 2 minutes. Add pepper strips, zucchini, squash, and snow peas; sauté 4 minutes or until crisp-tender. Remove from skillet.

Combine 2 tablespoons reserved liquid, yogurt, and next 6 ingredients; stir well. Arrange lettuce on a serving plate; top with vegetable mixture and shrimp. Serve with yogurt mixture.
Yield: 6 servings.

Per Serving:

Calories 166	Carbohydrate 16.2g	Fiber 4.6g
Fat 4.0g	Cholesterol 114mg	Calcium 150mg
Protein 17.1g	Sodium 345mg	Iron 4.4mg

Exchanges: 1½ Very Lean Meat, ½ Starch, 2 Vegetable

Creamy Buttermilk Dressing

Prep time: 5 minutes   Chill time: 30 minutes

⅓ cup nonfat buttermilk
⅔ cup nonfat mayonnaise
1 tablespoon grated onion
¼ teaspoon pepper
¼ teaspoon salt
¼ teaspoon garlic powder
¼ teaspoon dried thyme
   Dash of curry powder

Combine all ingredients in a small bowl, stirring well with a wire whisk. Cover and chill thoroughly. Serve with salad greens or fresh raw vegetables. Yield: 1 cup.

Per Tablespoon:

Calories 11	Carbohydrate 2.5g	Fiber 0.1g
Fat 0.0g	Cholesterol 0mg	Calcium 7mg
Protein 0.2g	Sodium 172mg	Iron 0.0mg

Exchange: Free

Cheese-Herb Dressing

SuperQuick
Prep time: 5 minutes

3 tablespoons light process cream cheese, softened
2 tablespoons cider vinegar
½ cup plain nonfat yogurt
1 tablespoon chopped fresh parsley
1 teaspoon chopped fresh chives
¼ teaspoon celery seeds
¼ teaspoon salt
1 (2-ounce) jar diced pimiento, drained

Combine cream cheese and vinegar in a small bowl, stirring until smooth. Add yogurt and next 4 ingredients; stir well. Stir in pimiento. Serve with salad greens. Yield: 1 cup.

Per Tablespoon:

Calories 11	Carbohydrate 1.0g	Fiber 0.0g
Fat 0.5g	Cholesterol 2mg	Calcium 19mg
Protein 0.7g	Sodium 57mg	Iron 0.1mg

Exchange: Free

Are You In a Salad Rut?

When you think of salad greens, does iceberg lettuce immediately come to mind? If so, maybe you're in a salad rut. Use your imagination and give your taste buds a flavor trip by experimenting with an array of leafy greens. You can change the flavor, texture, and color of any salad simply by changing greens. And the darker in color your leafy green is, the more nutrient-packed it is.

Try dandelion, turnip, or collard greens, spinach, romaine, or escarole lettuce for a sharp, bitter flavor. For a sweet and succulent flavor, try Boston or butterhead lettuce. Radicchio is a crisp, colorful complement to any salad. Or toss in a little watercress or arugula for a peppery taste. For a taste of them all, select a bag of mixed baby lettuce greens.

Honey French Dressing

Prep time: 5 minutes   Chill time: 30 minutes

½ cup reduced-calorie ketchup
¼ cup cider vinegar
2 tablespoons honey
2 tablespoons water
1 teaspoon low-sodium Worcestershire sauce

Combine all ingredients in a jar. Cover tightly, and shake vigorously. Chill thoroughly. Shake dressing again before serving. Serve with salad greens. Yield: 1 cup.

Per Tablespoon:

Calories 12	Carbohydrate 3.1g	Fiber 0.0g
Fat 0.0g	Cholesterol 0mg	Calcium 0mg
Protein 0.0g	Sodium 3mg	Iron 0.0mg

Exchange: Free

Pesto Dressing

Prep time: 5 minutes   Chill time: 30 minutes

¼ cup part-skim ricotta cheese
¼ cup minced fresh basil
¼ cup minced fresh parsley
¼ cup skim milk
2 tablespoons grated Parmesan cheese
1 medium shallot, quartered
   Dash of ground white pepper

Combine all ingredients in container of an electric blender; cover and process until smooth, stopping once to scrape down sides. Transfer mixture to a small bowl. Cover and chill thoroughly. Serve with salad greens or fresh raw vegetables. Yield: 1⅓ cups.

Per Tablespoon:

Calories 8	Carbohydrate 0.4g	Fiber 0.0g
Fat 0.4g	Cholesterol 1mg	Calcium 20mg
Protein 0.7g	Sodium 15mg	Iron 0.1mg

Exchange: Free

Craving Italian?

For an Italian topping, try Pesto Dressing. It combines ricotta cheese and skim milk for body, and Parmesan cheese and basil for seasoning.

Honey-Anise Dressing

Prep time: 5 minutes   Chill time: 30 minutes

1 vanilla bean, split
½ cup nonfat buttermilk
½ cup 1% low-fat cottage cheese
2 tablespoons honey
⅛ teaspoon anise flavoring

Scrape seeds from inside of vanilla bean. Combine seeds, buttermilk, and remaining ingredients in container of an electric blender; cover and process until smooth, stopping once to scrape down sides. Transfer mixture to a bowl. Cover and chill thoroughly. Serve with mixed fruit salad or salad greens. Yield: 1 cup plus 2 tablespoons.

Per Tablespoon:

Calories 14	Carbohydrate 2.5g	Fiber 0.0g
Fat 0.1g	Cholesterol 0mg	Calcium 12mg
Protein 1.0g	Sodium 33mg	Iron 0.0mg

Exchange: Free

Low in Fat, not Flavor

Nonfat buttermilk and low-fat cottage cheese add a tart flavor and thick, creamy texture without a lot of fat.

Honey-Anise Dressing

Apricot-Mint Dressing

Prep time: 5 minutes   Chill time: 30 minutes

1   (16-ounce) can apricot halves in light syrup,
      drained
¼   cup vanilla low-fat yogurt
1   teaspoon minced fresh mint
⅛   teaspoon ground mace

Combine all ingredients in container of an
electric blender; cover and process until smooth,
stopping once to scrape down sides. Transfer mixture to a small bowl. Cover and chill thoroughly.
Serve with mixed fruit salad or salad greens. Yield:
1 cup plus 2 tablespoons.

Per Tablespoon:

Calories 14	Carbohydrate 3.2g	Fiber 0.1g
Fat 0.1g	Cholesterol 0mg	Calcium 7mg
Protein 0.3g	Sodium 2mg	Iron 0.1mg

Exchange: Free

Fruit Topper

Vanilla low-fat yogurt, pureed apricots, and
fresh mint form a low-fat base in Apricot-Mint
Dressing. Its tangy flavor and smooth consistency
are perfect for fresh fruit or salad greens.

Salad Dressings   141

Chutney Vinaigrette

Prep time: 5 minutes   Chill time: 30 minutes

¼ cup white wine vinegar
3 tablespoons mango chutney
2 tablespoons coarse-grained Dijon mustard
2 teaspoons sugar
1 clove garlic, minced
1½ tablespoons vegetable oil
1½ tablespoons water
⅛ teaspoon freshly ground pepper

Combine first 5 ingredients in container of an electric blender; cover and process at high speed 30 seconds. Combine oil and water. With blender running, gradually add oil mixture in a slow, steady stream. Process 15 seconds. Stir in pepper. Cover and chill thoroughly. Stir well before serving. Serve with salad greens. Yield: ¾ cup.

Per Tablespoon:

Calories 32	Carbohydrate 3.6g	Fiber 0.0g
Fat 1.9g	Cholesterol 0mg	Calcium 2mg
Protein 0.1g	Sodium 83mg	Iron 0.1mg

Exchange: Free

Oriental Vinaigrette

SuperQuick
Prep time: 2 minutes   Cook time: 5 minutes

½ teaspoon unflavored gelatin
⅔ cup plus 1 tablespoon cold water, divided
⅓ cup rice vinegar
1 teaspoon chicken bouillon granules
1 teaspoon sesame seeds
1 teaspoon peeled, minced gingerroot
1 tablespoon low-sodium soy sauce
1 teaspoon honey

Dissolve gelatin in 1 tablespoon water; stir well, and set aside.

Combine remaining ⅔ cup water, vinegar, and remaining 5 ingredients in a saucepan; bring to a boil over medium-high heat. Remove from heat; add gelatin mixture, stirring well. Serve warm or chilled over chicken salad or salad greens. Yield: 1 cup.

Per Tablespoon:

Calories 4	Carbohydrate 0.5g	Fiber 0.0g
Fat 0.2g	Cholesterol 0mg	Calcium 2mg
Protein 0.1g	Sodium 76mg	Iron 0.0mg

Exchange: Free

Soups
and
Sandwiches

Sloppy Joes (page 158)

Chilled Apple Soup

Prep time: 15 minutes   Cook time: 23 minutes
Chill time: 2 hours

- 3 cups peeled, coarsely chopped Rome apple
- 2½ cups unsweetened apple cider
- 3 tablespoons brown sugar, divided
- ½ teaspoon ground cinnamon, divided
- ½ teaspoon vanilla extract
- 2 (1-ounce) slices French bread, trimmed and cut into ¾-inch cubes
  Butter-flavored vegetable cooking spray
- 1 (8-ounce) carton apple cinnamon-flavored low-fat yogurt

Combine apple, cider, and 2 tablespoons sugar in a large saucepan. Bring to a boil; cover, reduce heat, and simmer 15 to 20 minutes or until apple is tender. Let cool slightly. Transfer apple mixture to container of an electric blender or food processor; cover and process until smooth, stopping once to scrape down sides.

Combine apple mixture, ¼ teaspoon cinnamon, and vanilla in a medium bowl, stirring well. Cover and chill at least 2 hours.

Combine remaining 1 tablespoon sugar and ¼ teaspoon cinnamon in a heavy-duty, zip-top plastic bag. Coat bread cubes with cooking spray; add cubes to sugar mixture in bag. Seal bag; shake until cubes are coated. Place cubes on a baking sheet. Bake at 350° for 8 to 10 minutes or until toasted, stirring once. Let cool completely.

To serve, combine apple mixture and yogurt, stirring well. Ladle soup into individual bowls. Top evenly with toasted bread cubes.
Yield: 4 (1-cup) servings.

Per Serving:

Calories 241	Carbohydrate 55.3g	Fiber 3.3g
Fat 1.6g	Cholesterol 4mg	Calcium 28mg
Protein 3.2g	Sodium 90mg	Iron 1.1mg

Exchanges: 1½ Starch, 2 Fruit

Crunchy Croutons

The croutons add a sweet crunch to the soup, but if you don't want to make them, just sprinkle the sugar mixture over the soup before serving.

Cantaloupe Soup

Prep time: 15 minutes   Chill time: 30 minutes

- 5 cups cantaloupe chunks (about 1 medium)
- ⅓ cup unsweetened orange juice
- 1 (8-ounce) carton plain low-fat yogurt
- 2 teaspoons powdered sugar
- 1 teaspoon minced fresh mint
  Fresh mint sprigs (optional)

Place cantaloupe and orange juice in container of an electric blender or food processor; cover and process until smooth, stopping once to scrape down sides. Transfer mixture to a medium bowl.

Combine yogurt, powdered sugar, and 1 teaspoon mint; add to cantaloupe mixture, and stir well. Cover and chill thoroughly.

To serve, ladle soup into individual bowls, and garnish with fresh mint sprigs, if desired.
Yield: 6 (¾-cup) servings.

Per Serving:

Calories 80	Carbohydrate 16.1g	Fiber 1.6g
Fat 1.0g	Cholesterol 2mg	Calcium 85mg
Protein 3.2g	Sodium 39mg	Iron 0.3mg

Exchange: 1 Fruit

Soup's On

You can serve this versatile soup as a satisfying first course or as a refreshing light dessert.

Gazpacho

Prep time: 18 minutes   Chill time: 8 hours

1   (10½-ounce) can low-sodium tomato soup,
     undiluted
1¾ cups no-salt-added tomato juice
⅔   cup peeled, seeded, and finely chopped
     cucumber
½   cup finely chopped green pepper
½   cup finely chopped tomato
⅓   cup finely chopped onion
2   tablespoons red wine vinegar
1   tablespoon oil-free Italian dressing
1   tablespoon lemon juice
1   clove garlic, minced
½   teaspoon pepper
¼   teaspoon salt
¼   teaspoon hot sauce
     Thinly sliced cucumber (optional)

Combine first 13 ingredients in a large bowl; stir well. Cover and chill at least 8 hours.

To serve, ladle soup into individual bowls, and garnish with cucumber slices, if desired.
Yield: 5 (1-cup) servings.

Per Serving:

Calories 75	Carbohydrate 15.2g	Fiber 1.6g
Fat 1.4g	Cholesterol 0mg	Calcium 21mg
Protein 2.1g	Sodium 174mg	Iron 0.8mg

Exchange: 2 Vegetable

Apple-Butternut Soup

Prep time: 15 minutes   Cook time: 30 minutes

2   (14¼-ounce) cans no-salt-added chicken broth
1   small butternut squash, peeled, seeded, and cubed
1   small Granny Smith apple, cored, peeled, and quartered
1   small onion, chopped (about 1 cup)
1   teaspoon sugar
½   teaspoon salt
½   teaspoon curry powder
⅛   teaspoon pepper
1   (5-ounce) can evaporated skimmed milk
    Toasted squash seeds (optional)

Combine first 8 ingredients in a saucepan; bring to a boil. Cover, reduce heat, and simmer 25 minutes or until squash and apple are tender. Transfer mixture, in batches, to container of an electric blender or food processor; cover and process until smooth, stopping once to scrape down sides. Return soup to saucepan; stir in milk. Cook over low heat until thoroughly heated.

To serve, ladle soup into individual bowls, and garnish with toasted squash seeds, if desired. Yield: 7 (1-cup) servings.

Per Serving:

Calories 80	Carbohydrate 16.9g	Fiber 2.0g
Fat 0.2g	Cholesterol 1mg	Calcium 99mg
Protein 2.8g	Sodium 196mg	Iron 0.6mg

Exchange: 1 Starch

Toast 'em

To toast squash seeds, spread seeds in a single layer in a shallow pan, and bake at 350° for 10 to 12 minutes, stirring occasionally.

Cheddar Cheese Soup

Prep time: 10 minutes   Cook time: 22 minutes

    Vegetable cooking spray
1   teaspoon margarine
1   cup finely chopped celery
1   cup finely chopped onion
½   cup nonfat sour cream
¼   cup plain low-fat yogurt
⅓   cup all-purpose flour
2   (10½-ounce) cans low-sodium chicken broth
¾   cup skim milk
1   teaspoon white wine Worcestershire sauce
¼   teaspoon garlic powder
⅛   teaspoon salt
⅛   teaspoon ground white pepper
⅛   teaspoon ground red pepper
6   (⅔-ounce) slices nonfat process Cheddar cheese

Coat a medium nonstick skillet with cooking spray. Add margarine, and place over medium heat until margarine melts. Add celery; sauté 3 minutes. Add onion; sauté 7 minutes or until vegetables are tender. Set aside.

Combine sour cream, yogurt, and flour in a large heavy saucepan; stir well with a wire whisk. Gradually add broth and next 6 ingredients, stirring constantly. Stir in onion mixture; cook over medium heat 15 minutes or until thickened and bubbly, stirring often. Add cheese slices, and stir until cheese melts.

To serve, ladle soup into individual bowls. Yield: 5 (1-cup) servings.

Per Serving:

Calories 135	Carbohydrate 16.0g	Fiber 0.7g
Fat 2.1g	Cholesterol 1mg	Calcium 76mg
Protein 11.8g	Sodium 509mg	Iron 1.1mg

Exchanges: 1 Very Lean Meat, 1 Starch, ½ Fat

Asparagus-Blue Cheese Soup

SuperQuick

Prep time: 15 minutes   Cook time: 10 minutes

2   (10-ounce) packages frozen asparagus spears
1   teaspoon reduced-calorie margarine
¼   cup chopped onion
1   (14¼-ounce) can no-salt-added chicken broth, divided
1½ cups 1% low-fat milk
3   tablespoons crumbled blue cheese
½   teaspoon salt
¼   teaspoon cracked black pepper

Cook asparagus according to package directions. Drain and set aside. Melt margarine in a small nonstick skillet over medium-high heat. Add onion; sauté until tender.

Combine asparagus, onion, and 1 cup broth in container of an electric blender; cover and process until smooth, stopping once to scrape down sides. Pour asparagus mixture into a saucepan. Add remaining broth, milk, cheese, and salt to asparagus mixture. Cook, stirring constantly, until cheese melts.

To serve, ladle soup into individual bowls; sprinkle soup evenly with pepper.
Yield: 6 (1-cup) servings.

Per Serving:

Calories 85	Carbohydrate 8.2g	Fiber 1.1g
Fat 3.4g	Cholesterol 8mg	Calcium 133mg
Protein 6.2g	Sodium 343mg	Iron 0.8mg

Exchanges: ½ Starch, 1 Fat

Plan Ahead

You can make this soup a day or two ahead and keep it in the refrigerator. When you reheat it, warm over low heat, but don't bring to a boil or the soup may curdle.

Black Bean Soup

Prep time: 15 minutes   Cook time: 30 minutes

1   tablespoon olive oil
1   cup chopped onion
½   cup chopped carrot
½   cup chopped green pepper
¼   cup chopped celery
2   (15-ounce) cans black beans, rinsed and drained
1   (14½-ounce) can no-salt-added tomatoes, undrained and chopped
1   (10-ounce) can tomatoes with chiles, undrained and chopped
1   cup water
½   cup no-salt-added beef broth
½   teaspoon ground cumin
½   teaspoon pepper
¼   teaspoon garlic powder

Heat oil in a large saucepan over medium-high heat until hot. Add onion, carrot, green pepper, and celery; sauté until tender. Add beans and remaining ingredients. Bring mixture to a boil. Cover, reduce heat, and simmer 30 minutes, stirring occasionally.

To serve, ladle soup into individual bowls.
Yield: 8 (1-cup) servings.

Per Serving:

Calories 145	Carbohydrate 24.3g	Fiber 4.4g
Fat 2.3g	Cholesterol 0mg	Calcium 48mg
Protein 7.4g	Sodium 363mg	Iron 2.1mg

Exchanges: 1½ Starch, ½ Fat

How to Keep Soup

Store this soup in an airtight container in the freezer up to 3 months, if desired. Thaw in the refrigerator, and then reheat.

White Bean Soup

Prep time: 18 minutes   Cook time: 18 minutes

Vegetable cooking spray
1   tablespoon olive oil
2   (4-ounce) skinned, boned chicken breast
       halves, coarsely chopped
3   ounces Canadian bacon, coarsely chopped
¼   cup chopped onion
3   cloves garlic, minced
1   (14¼-ounce) can no-salt-added chicken
       broth
1   (4½-ounce) can chopped green chiles,
       undrained
¾   cup water
½   teaspoon ground coriander
¼   teaspoon ground cumin
⅛   teaspoon ground white pepper
1   (15-ounce) can cannellini beans, drained
¼   cup (1 ounce) shredded reduced-fat
       Monterey Jack cheese

Coat a large saucepan with cooking spray;
add oil. Place over medium-high heat until hot.
Add chicken and next 3 ingredients; sauté 3 minutes or until chicken is done. Remove chicken mixture from pan, and set aside.

Add broth, chiles, water, coriander, cumin,
and pepper to pan. Bring to a boil; reduce heat,
and simmer 10 minutes. Add chicken mixture and
beans; cook 5 minutes or until thoroughly heated.

To serve, ladle soup into individual bowls;
sprinkle each serving with 2 teaspoons cheese.
Yield: 6 (1-cup) servings.

Per Serving:

Calories 161	Carbohydrate 11.1g	Fiber 3.9g
Fat 5.0g	Cholesterol 32mg	Calcium 60mg
Protein 16.2g	Sodium 351mg	Iron 1.5mg

Exchanges: 2 Lean Meat, 1 Starch

French Onion Soup

SuperQuick

Prep time: 5 minutes   Cook time: 20 minutes

Vegetable cooking spray
2   medium onions, sliced and separated into
       rings
3   cups canned no-salt-added beef broth
1   tablespoon low-sodium Worcestershire
       sauce
¼   teaspoon salt
¼   teaspoon pepper
2   (½-inch) slices French bread
2   tablespoons (½ ounce) shredded
       Gruyère cheese
Freshly ground pepper (optional)

Coat a large saucepan with cooking spray;
place over medium-high heat until hot. Add onion,
and sauté 2 minutes or until tender. Add broth,
Worcestershire sauce, salt, and ¼ teaspoon pepper;
bring to a boil. Reduce heat, and simmer, uncovered, 15 minutes.

Place bread slices on a baking sheet, and broil
5½ inches from heat (with electric oven door partially opened) 1 minute or until lightly browned.
Turn bread over; sprinkle evenly with cheese. Broil
1 minute or until cheese melts.

To serve, ladle soup into individual bowls; top
each serving with a toasted bread slice, and sprinkle with freshly ground pepper, if desired. Serve
immediately. Yield: 2 (1½-cup) servings.

Per Serving:

Calories 169	Carbohydrate 24.5g	Fiber 1.9g
Fat 3.1g	Cholesterol 9mg	Calcium 98mg
Protein 5.9g	Sodium 503mg	Iron 0.8mg

Exchanges: 1 Starch, 1 Vegetable, 1 Fat

A Swiss Stand-in

Gruyère cheese is similar to Swiss cheese.
Gruyère is a pale yellow, firm cheese with small
holes throughout. Substitute an equal amount of
Swiss for Gruyère to get a similar rich, nutty
flavor in this soup. Swiss cheese has about 10
fewer calories per ounce.

French Onion Soup

Citrus Sweet Potato Soup

Prep time: 15 minutes   Cook time: 40 minutes

2¼ cups canned no-salt-added chicken broth
1½ cups unsweetened orange juice
1   cup sliced carrot
2   medium-size sweet potatoes (about 1
       pound), peeled and cubed
1   large clove garlic, minced
1   bay leaf
¼   teaspoon salt
⅛   teaspoon ground white pepper
¼   cup plus 1 tablespoon vanilla nonfat yogurt
       Freshly grated nutmeg (optional)

Combine first 6 ingredients in a medium saucepan. Bring to a boil; cover, reduce heat, and simmer 30 minutes or until vegetables are tender. Remove from heat, and let cool 10 minutes. Remove and discard bay leaf.

Transfer mixture, in batches, to container of an electric blender or food processor; cover and process until smooth, stopping once to scrape down sides. Return pureed mixture to saucepan. Add salt and pepper. Cook over medium heat until thoroughly heated, stirring occasionally.

To serve, ladle soup into individual bowls. Top each serving with 1 tablespoon yogurt. Sprinkle with freshly grated nutmeg, if desired. Yield: 5 (1-cup) servings.

Per Serving:

Calories 145	Carbohydrate 31.7g	Fiber 3.2g
Fat 0.3g	Cholesterol 0mg	Calcium 60mg
Protein 3.1g	Sodium 149mg	Iron 0.7mg

Exchanges: 1½ Starch, ½ Fruit

A Spicy Substitute

White pepper adds spiciness without affecting the appearance of this light-colored, sweet soup. If you don't have white pepper, use black; the flavor will be similar.

Pasta Vegetable Soup

Prep time: 5 minutes   Cook time: 25 minutes

4   cups canned no-salt-added chicken broth
3   cups water
1   cup dried tomatoes (packed without oil)
6   ounces bow tie pasta, uncooked
4   green onions, sliced
1   tablespoon balsamic vinegar
1   clove garlic, minced
1   (10-ounce) package frozen leaf spinach,
       thawed and drained

Combine first 3 ingredients in a Dutch oven. Bring to a boil; cover, reduce heat, and simmer 10 minutes or until tomato is soft. Remove tomato from mixture. Let cool slightly; cut into thin strips. Return tomato to pan. Stir in pasta, green onions, vinegar, and garlic. Bring to a boil; cover, reduce heat, and simmer 15 minutes or until pasta is tender. Remove from heat; stir in spinach.

To serve, ladle soup into individual bowls. Yield: 9 (1-cup) servings.

Per Serving:

Calories 102	Carbohydrate 17.8g	Fiber 1.6g
Fat 1.4g	Cholesterol 0mg	Calcium 47mg
Protein 4.8g	Sodium 151mg	Iron 1.5mg

Exchanges: 1 Starch, 1 Vegetable

Lemon Tortellini Soup

SuperQuick
Prep time: 10 minutes   Cook time: 15 minutes

Vegetable cooking spray
1 cup sliced fresh mushrooms
½ cup sliced green onions
1 clove garlic, minced
2 (14¼-ounce) cans no-salt-added chicken broth
¼ teaspoon salt
1 (10-ounce) package frozen broccoli flowerets, thawed
1 (9-ounce) package fresh cheese-filled tortellini, uncooked
2 tablespoons fresh lemon juice
Grated lemon rind (optional)

Coat a large Dutch oven with cooking spray; place over medium-high heat until hot. Add mushrooms, green onions, and garlic; sauté until tender.

Add broth and salt; bring to a boil. Add broccoli; cover, reduce heat, and simmer 5 minutes. Add tortellini; cook 5 minutes or until tender. Stir in lemon juice.

To serve, ladle soup into individual bowls. Garnish with lemon rind, if desired. Yield: 6 (1-cup) servings.

Per Serving:

Calories 160	Carbohydrate 25.2g	Fiber 2.8g
Fat 2.3g	Cholesterol 20mg	Calcium 133mg
Protein 9.2g	Sodium 267mg	Iron 1.8mg

Exchanges: 1½ Starch, 1 Vegetable, ½ Fat

Split Pea Soup

Prep time: 15 minutes   Cook time: 1 hour, 30 minutes

1 (16-ounce) package dried green split peas
4 cups water
4 cups canned no-salt-added chicken broth
1 teaspoon salt
1 teaspoon dried thyme
¼ teaspoon liquid smoke
3 cloves garlic, minced
2 bay leaves
2 cups sliced carrot
1½ cups peeled, diced potato
1 cup chopped celery
¾ cup chopped onion
¼ cup dry white wine
2 tablespoons dried parsley flakes
2 tablespoons lemon juice

Sort and wash peas; place in a Dutch oven. Add water and next 6 ingredients. Bring to a boil; reduce heat, and simmer, uncovered, 1 hour.

Add carrot and remaining ingredients. Bring to a boil; reduce heat, and simmer, uncovered, 30 minutes or until vegetables are tender. Remove and discard bay leaves.

Transfer mixture, in batches, into container of an electric blender or food processor; cover and process until smooth, stopping once to scrape down sides. Return pureed mixture to Dutch oven; stir well.

To serve, ladle soup into individual bowls. Serve immediately. Yield: 10 (1-cup) servings.

Per Serving:

Calories 210	Carbohydrate 38.1g	Fiber 4.4g
Fat 0.7g	Cholesterol 0mg	Calcium 48mg
Protein 12.5g	Sodium 269mg	Iron 2.8mg

Exchanges: 1 Very Lean Meat, 2 Starch

Chunky Chicken and Mushroom Soup

SuperQuick

Prep time: 10 minutes   Cook time: 15 minutes

Vegetable cooking spray
3 tablespoons reduced-calorie margarine
1 (8-ounce) package sliced fresh mushrooms
1½ cups sliced green onions
¼ cup all-purpose flour
3½ cups skim milk
1 tablespoon chicken-flavored bouillon granules
2½ cups chopped cooked chicken breast

Coat a large saucepan with cooking spray; add margarine. Place over medium-high heat until margarine melts. Add mushrooms and green onions; sauté until tender.

Add flour; cook, stirring constantly, 1 minute. Gradually add milk and bouillon granules; cook over medium heat, stirring constantly, until mixture is thickened. Stir in chicken; cook until thoroughly heated.

To serve, ladle soup into individual bowls. Yield: 4 (1½-cup) servings.

Per Serving:

Calories 360	Carbohydrate 20.9g	Fiber 1.5g
Fat 11.1g	Cholesterol 98mg	Calcium 299mg
Protein 44.1g	Sodium 895mg	Iron 2.6mg

Exchanges: 4 Very Lean Meat, 1 Starch, 1 Vegetable, 1 Fat

Vegetable Beef Soup

Prep time: 20 minutes   Cook time: 25 minutes

Vegetable cooking spray
½ pound ground round
2⅓ cups chopped cabbage
2 cups chopped celery
1⅓ cups frozen sliced carrot, thawed
1 cup frozen chopped onion, thawed
½ cup frozen chopped green pepper, thawed
2 (14¼-ounce) cans no-salt-added beef broth
2 (14½-ounce) cans no-salt-added whole tomatoes, undrained and chopped
1 (11-ounce) can no-salt-added whole-kernel corn, drained
1 teaspoon dried oregano
¾ teaspoon salt
½ teaspoon dried thyme
½ teaspoon pepper

Coat a Dutch oven with cooking spray; place over medium-high heat until hot. Add ground round; cook until meat is browned, stirring until it crumbles. Remove from pan; drain and pat dry with paper towels. Wipe drippings from pan with a paper towel.

Coat pan with cooking spray; place over medium-high heat until hot. Add cabbage, celery, carrot, onion, and green pepper; sauté 5 minutes or until tender. Return meat to pan. Add broth and remaining ingredients. Bring to a boil; cover, reduce heat, and simmer 25 to 30 minutes or until vegetables are tender.

To serve, ladle soup into individual bowls.
Yield: 6 (2-cup) servings.

Per Serving:

Calories 170	Carbohydrate 23.2g	Fiber 4.3g
Fat 3.1g	Cholesterol 23mg	Calcium 106mg
Protein 11.9g	Sodium 404mg	Iron 2.5mg

Exchanges: 1 Lean Meat, ½ Starch, 3 Vegetable

Chicken Vegetable Soup

Prep time: 12 minutes   Cook time: 30 minutes

3½ cups water
1 tablespoon chicken-flavored bouillon granules
1 (14½-ounce) can no-salt-added whole tomatoes, undrained and chopped
¼ cup dried minced onion
1 teaspoon dried basil
1 teaspoon paprika
¾ teaspoon minced garlic
1 cup sliced carrot
1 (8-ounce) can mushroom stems and pieces, drained
1 cup diced zucchini
1 cup diced cooked chicken breast (skinned before cooking and cooked without salt or fat)
2 tablespoons dry red wine

Combine first 7 ingredients in a Dutch oven. Bring to a boil; cover, reduce heat, and simmer 10 minutes.

Add carrot; cover and simmer 10 minutes. Add mushrooms and remaining ingredients; simmer, uncovered, 8 minutes.

To serve, ladle soup into individual bowls.
Yield: 7 (1-cup) servings.

Per Serving:

Calories 83	Carbohydrate 10.5g	Fiber 1.2g
Fat 1.6g	Cholesterol 16mg	Calcium 43mg
Protein 7.5g	Sodium 492mg	Iron 1.2mg

Exchanges: 1 Very Lean Meat, 2 Vegetable

Chicken in a Flash

To prepare cooked chicken quickly to use as an ingredient in a recipe, use your microwave oven. Count on ½ cup of chopped or diced chicken per chicken breast half. To microwave chicken for this recipe, arrange 2 boned and skinned chicken breast halves in a baking dish. Microwave, covered, at HIGH 3 to 5 minutes or until done, turning dish once.

Spicy Vegetarian Chili

Prep time: 18 minutes   Cook time: 25 minutes

7   ounces wagon wheel pasta, uncooked
    Vegetable cooking spray
1½ cups finely chopped onion
1⅓ cups finely chopped green pepper
2   cloves garlic, minced
1   tablespoon chili powder
1   teaspoon ground cumin
½   teaspoon garlic powder
½   teaspoon dried crushed red pepper
1   (28-ounce) can crushed tomatoes with
    puree, undrained
½   pound firm tofu, drained and crumbled
2   (15-ounce) cans kidney beans, drained
½   cup (2 ounces) shredded reduced-fat
    Cheddar cheese

Cook pasta according to package directions, omitting salt and fat; drain. Set aside.

Coat a Dutch oven with cooking spray, and place over medium-high heat until hot. Add onion, green pepper, and garlic; sauté until tender. Add chili powder, cumin, garlic powder, and crushed red pepper; cook, stirring constantly, 1 minute. Stir in tomato and tofu. Bring mixture to a boil; reduce heat, and simmer, uncovered, 15 minutes. Add beans, and cook 10 additional minutes or until bean mixture is thoroughly heated.

To serve, place ½ cup pasta into each of 7 individual bowls, and spoon 1 cup chili over each serving. Top servings evenly with cheese.
Yield: 7 (1½-cup) servings.

Per Serving:

Calories 298	Carbohydrate 49.0g	Fiber 5.5g
Fat 4.5g	Cholesterol 5mg	Calcium 175mg
Protein 17.2g	Sodium 372mg	Iron 6.3mg

Exchanges: 1 Very Lean Meat, 2 Starch, 2 Vegetable, 1 Fat

Southwestern Turkey Chili

Prep time: 15 minutes   Cook time: 30 minutes

    Vegetable cooking spray
1½ pounds raw skinless turkey breast, cut into
    1-inch cubes
1½ cups chopped onion
1½ cups chopped green pepper
4   cloves garlic, crushed
4   (14½-ounce) cans no-salt-added stewed
    tomatoes, undrained
2   (15-ounce) cans pinto beans, drained and
    rinsed
2   (4½-ounce) cans chopped green chiles,
    undrained
1   (6-ounce) can no-salt-added tomato paste
1   (1¼-ounce) envelope chili seasoning mix
⅔   cup water
½   cup chopped fresh parsley or cilantro
1   jalapeño pepper, seeded and minced
1   tablespoon lemon juice
1   teaspoon ground cumin
⅛   teaspoon ground cloves

Coat a Dutch oven with cooking spray; place over medium-high heat until hot. Add turkey and next 3 ingredients. Cook, stirring constantly, until turkey is done. Stir in tomato and remaining ingredients; bring to a boil. Cover, reduce heat; and simmer 30 minutes, stirring occasionally.

To serve, ladle chili into individual bowls.
Yield: 10 (1½-cup) servings.

Per Serving:

Calories 245	Carbohydrate 34.3g	Fiber 4.1g
Fat 1.6g	Cholesterol 41mg	Calcium 99mg
Protein 24.0g	Sodium 424mg	Iron 4.0mg

Exchanges: 2 Very Lean Meat, 1 Starch, 3 Vegetable

Beef Burgundy Stew

Prep time: 10 minutes   Cook time: 45 minutes

¼ cup all-purpose flour
¼ teaspoon pepper
1¼ pounds lean boneless top sirloin steak, trimmed and cut into ¾-inch cubes
    Vegetable cooking spray
2 cups sliced fresh mushrooms
1 cup diagonally sliced carrot
1 cup water
1 cup dry red wine
1 (10½-ounce) can French onion soup
8 ounces medium egg noodles, uncooked

Combine flour and pepper in a large heavy-duty, zip-top plastic bag; add meat. Shake bag until meat is well coated.

Coat a Dutch oven with cooking spray; place over medium-high heat until hot. Add meat, and cook until meat is browned on all sides. Add mushrooms and next 4 ingredients; bring to a boil. Cover, reduce heat, and simmer 30 minutes, stirring occasionally. Uncover and cook 10 minutes.

Cook pasta according to package directions, omitting salt and fat; drain.

To serve, spoon noodles evenly into individual bowls; ladle ¾ cup stew over each serving.
Yield: 7 (1½-cup) servings.

Per Serving:

Calories 328	Carbohydrate 40.3g	Fiber 4.1g
Fat 7.0g	Cholesterol 89mg	Calcium 30mg
Protein 24.8g	Sodium 416mg	Iron 4.8mg

Exchanges: 3 Lean Meat, 2 Starch, ½ Vegetable

Red, Red Wine

The red wine gives this stew its hearty, rich flavor. If you prefer not to use alcohol, use a nonalcoholic red wine or 1 cup no-salt-added beef broth.

Pork Succotash Stew

Prep time: 15 minutes   Cook time: 20 minutes

1 (1-pound) lean boneless pork loin roast
    Vegetable cooking spray
1 cup chopped onion
3 cups water
1 (10-ounce) package frozen baby lima beans
1 (10-ounce) package frozen whole-kernel corn
1 (4½-ounce) can chopped green chiles, undrained
1 medium-size sweet red pepper, seeded and chopped
2 teaspoons vegetable-flavored bouillon granules
⅛ teaspoon pepper
⅛ teaspoon paprika

Trim fat from pork; cut pork into ½-inch cubes. Coat a Dutch oven with cooking spray; place over medium-high heat until hot. Add pork cubes and onion; cook until pork is browned and onion is tender, stirring often.

Add water and remaining ingredients. Bring to a boil; cover, reduce heat, and simmer 20 to 30 minutes or until pork and vegetables are tender.

To serve, ladle stew into individual bowls.
Yield: 4 (1¾-cup) servings.

Per Serving:

Calories 193	Carbohydrate 22.1g	Fiber 2.7g
Fat 3.2g	Cholesterol 49mg	Calcium 28mg
Protein 20.2g	Sodium 362mg	Iron 2.5mg

Exchanges: 2 Very Lean Meat, 1½ Starch

Sweet on Succotash

Lima beans, corn, and sweet red pepper make this stew reminiscent of a true succotash. For a quick complete meal, add cornbread and a tossed salad.

Spicy Seafood Stew

Prep time: 15 minutes   Cook time: 30 minutes

Vegetable cooking spray
1 teaspoon olive oil
1½ cups chopped onion
3 tablespoons chopped fresh parsley
2 cloves garlic, minced
1 (16-ounce) can Cajun-style stewed tomatoes, undrained
2 (8-ounce) cans no-salt-added tomato sauce
2 cups canned no-salt-added chicken broth
¼ cup dry sherry
2 bay leaves
½ teaspoon dried thyme
½ teaspoon pepper
¼ teaspoon hot sauce
½ pound large fresh shrimp, peeled and deveined
½ pound red snapper fillets, cut into 2-inch pieces
½ pound fresh sea scallops

Coat a Dutch oven with cooking spray; add oil, and place over medium-high heat until hot. Add onion, parsley, and garlic; sauté until tender. Stir in stewed tomatoes and next 7 ingredients. Bring to a boil; cover, reduce heat, and simmer 20 minutes.

Add shrimp, snapper, and scallops to tomato mixture. Simmer 10 minutes or until fish flakes easily when tested with a fork. Remove and discard bay leaves.

To serve, ladle stew into individual bowls. Yield: 6 (1½-cup) servings.

Per Serving:

Calories 193	Carbohydrate 16.2g	Fiber 1.9g
Fat 2.8g	Cholesterol 70mg	Calcium 49mg
Protein 22.4g	Sodium 461mg	Iron 1.2mg

Exchanges: 3 Very Lean Meat, 1 Starch

Creamy Clam Chowder

Prep time: 15 minutes   Cook time: 25 minutes

1¼ cups peeled, diced potato
½ cup water
⅓ cup chopped celery
⅓ cup chopped onion
1 tablespoon reduced-calorie margarine
1 (12-ounce) can evaporated skimmed milk
1 cup skim milk
1 tablespoon cornstarch
1 (10-ounce) can whole shelled clams, drained
¼ teaspoon salt
⅛ teaspoon ground white pepper

Combine first 5 ingredients in a Dutch oven; place over medium-high heat, and bring to a boil. Cover, reduce heat, and simmer 15 minutes or until potato is tender.

Combine evaporated milk, skim milk, and cornstarch in a small bowl; add to potato mixture. Add clams, salt, and pepper. Cook over medium heat, stirring constantly, 10 minutes or until thickened and bubbly.

To serve, ladle chowder into individual bowls. Yield: 5 (1-cup) servings.

Per Serving:

Calories 177	Carbohydrate 22.0g	Fiber 1.0g
Fat 2.4g	Cholesterol 26mg	Calcium 297mg
Protein 16.5g	Sodium 291mg	Iron 10.1mg

Exchanges: 1½ Lean Meat, 1 Starch, ½ Skim Milk

A Low-Fat Secret

Reduce calories, fat, and cholesterol in cream-based soups by using skim or low-fat milk in place of whipping cream or half-and-half.

Focaccia Garden Sandwich

Prep time: 15 minutes   Chill time: 30 minutes

12 dried tomatoes (packed without oil)
½ cup hot water
1½ (8-ounce) containers fat-free garden vegetable cream cheese, softened
3 tablespoons sweet pickle relish
2 (10-ounce) thin crust Italian flat breads
1 large cucumber, thinly sliced
1 cup coarsely shredded carrot
1 cup alfalfa sprouts

Combine tomatoes and water in a small bowl; let stand 10 minutes. Drain and chop tomato. Combine tomato, cream cheese, and pickle relish, stirring well.

Spread half of cream cheese mixture over top of each flat bread. Arrange half of cucumber slices over 1 flat bread. Top with carrot, sprouts, remaining cucumber slices, and remaining flat bread, cream cheese side down. Wrap in plastic wrap, and chill thoroughly.

To serve, remove plastic wrap, and cut into wedges. Yield: 6 servings.

Per Serving:

Calories 341	Carbohydrate 50.5g	Fiber 2.2g
Fat 6.1g	Cholesterol 9mg	Calcium 15mg
Protein 21.5g	Sodium 969mg	Iron 0.3mg

Exchanges: 2 Very Lean Meat, 2½ Starch, 1 Vegetable, 1 Fat

An Inside Tip

We used Boboli for the Italian bread shell, but you can use any brand of Italian flat bread.

Beef Roll-Ups

Prep time: 25 minutes

10 dried tomatoes (packed without oil)
1 cup hot water
½ cup nonfat cream cheese, softened
6 (8-inch) flour tortillas
2 cups shredded fresh spinach
¾ cup alfalfa sprouts
¼ cup light Italian wine and cheese salad dressing
9 ounces thinly sliced lean roast beef

Combine tomatoes and hot water in a small bowl; let stand 10 minutes. Drain and coarsely chop tomato. Combine tomato and cream cheese. Spread cheese mixture evenly over 1 side of tortillas.

Combine spinach and sprouts; add dressing, and toss. Spoon spinach mixture evenly over cream cheese mixture. Arrange roast beef over spinach mixture. Roll up tortillas, jellyroll fashion. Serve immediately. Yield: 6 servings.

Per Serving:

Calories 258	Carbohydrate 29.3g	Fiber 2.6g
Fat 8.5g	Cholesterol 39mg	Calcium 128mg
Protein 15.9g	Sodium 763mg	Iron 2.9mg

Exchanges: 1½ Lean Meat, 1 Starch

Serve 'em Up

These sandwich roll-ups are best eaten right away. They get soggy if they stand.

Sloppy Joes

SuperQuick
Prep time: 5 minutes   Cook time: 20 minutes

	Vegetable cooking spray
1	cup chopped onion
½	cup chopped green pepper
1½	pounds ground round
1	cup ketchup
1	(8-ounce) can no-salt-added tomato sauce
1	tablespoon dark brown sugar
1½	tablespoons low-sodium Worcestershire sauce
1½	tablespoons lemon juice
1½	tablespoons prepared mustard
¼	teaspoon garlic powder
¼	teaspoon freshly ground pepper
8	reduced-calorie whole wheat hamburger buns

Coat a large nonstick skillet with cooking spray; place over medium-high heat until hot. Add onion and green pepper, and sauté 4 minutes or until tender. Add ground round, and cook until beef is browned, stirring until it crumbles. Drain and pat dry with paper towels. Wipe drippings from skillet with a paper towel.

Return beef mixture to skillet. Add ketchup and next 7 ingredients. Bring to a boil; reduce heat, and simmer 10 minutes, stirring occasionally.

To serve, spoon meat mixture evenly onto bottom halves of buns. Top with remaining bun halves. Yield: 8 servings.

Per Serving:

Calories 231	Carbohydrate 22.7g	Fiber 3.5g
Fat 5.5g	Cholesterol 52mg	Calcium 19mg
Protein 21.6g	Sodium 572mg	Iron 3.0mg

Exchanges: 2 Lean Meat, 1½ Starch

Tangy Beef Pockets

*Prep time: 15 minutes   Marinate time: 15 minutes
Cook time: 16 minutes*

1½	pounds lean flank steak
¼	cup lemon juice
2	tablespoons water
1¼	teaspoons ground cumin
1	teaspoon garlic powder
¼	teaspoon pepper
⅛	teaspoon ground ginger
½	cup plus 2 tablespoons plain nonfat yogurt
1	tablespoon chopped fresh parsley
2	teaspoons skim milk
	Vegetable cooking spray
3	(6-inch) whole wheat pita bread rounds, cut in half crosswise
2	cups finely shredded romaine lettuce
1	cup seeded, chopped tomato (about 2 medium)

Trim fat from steak; slice diagonally across grain into ¼-inch-thick strips. Place steak in a large shallow dish. Combine lemon juice and next 5 ingredients; pour mixture over steak. Cover and marinate in refrigerator at least 15 minutes.

Combine yogurt, parsley, and milk in a small bowl; stir well, and set aside.

Remove steak from marinade, discarding marinade. Place steak on rack of a broiler pan coated with cooking spray. Broil 3 inches from heat (with electric oven door partially opened) 3 minutes on each side or to desired degree of doneness.

Wrap pita bread halves in aluminum foil, and bake at 350° for 10 minutes or until thoroughly heated. Line pita halves with shredded lettuce, and divide steak evenly among halves. Top each pita bread half with chopped tomato and 2 tablespoons yogurt mixture. Yield: 6 servings.

Per Serving:

Calories 298	Carbohydrate 16.8g	Fiber 3.1g
Fat 13.5g	Cholesterol 60mg	Calcium 87mg
Protein 25.0g	Sodium 202mg	Iron 3.5mg

Exchanges: 3 Lean Meat, 1 Starch, 1 Vegetable, ½ Fat

Vegetable-Turkey Hero

Prep time: 15 minutes   Stand time: 15 minutes

1   (16-ounce) round loaf sourdough bread
¼   cup white balsamic vinegar
1   tablespoon olive oil
1   teaspoon dried oregano
1   teaspoon dried parsley flakes
½   teaspoon pepper
2   cloves garlic, minced
1   cup sliced fresh mushrooms
6   (¼-inch-thick) tomato slices
2   (¼-inch-thick) purple onion slices,
       separated into rings
2   cups shredded zucchini
8   (1-ounce) slices lean turkey
6   (1-ounce) slices part-skim mozzarella cheese

Slice bread in half horizontally, using an electric or serrated knife. Carefully remove soft bread from inside of each half, leaving ½-inch-thick shells. Set aside; reserve soft bread for another use.

Combine vinegar and next 5 ingredients in a shallow baking dish; add mushrooms, tomato slices, and onion. Let stand 15 to 20 minutes.

Drain with a slotted spoon, reserving marinade. Brush marinade evenly inside bread cavities. Spoon 1 cup zucchini into bottom half; arrange half of mushroom mixture over zucchini. Layer with 4 turkey slices and 3 cheese slices. Repeat layers with remaining zucchini, mushroom mixture, turkey, and cheese. Top with remaining half of loaf. To serve, slice loaf into wedges.
Yield: 8 servings.

Per Serving:

Calories 239	Carbohydrate 25.4g	Fiber 1.3g
Fat 7.1g	Cholesterol 32mg	Calcium 200mg
Protein 18.5g	Sodium 374mg	Iron 2.1mg

Exchanges: 2 Lean Meat, 1½ Starch

Holiday Hoagie

SuperQuick
Prep time: 15 minutes

½   cup canned jellied whole-berry cranberry
       sauce
1   tablespoon prepared horseradish
¼   cup plus 2 tablespoons nonfat mayonnaise
½   teaspoon rubbed sage
4   (2½-ounce) submarine rolls, split
4   green leaf lettuce leaves
8   ounces thinly sliced cooked turkey breast

Combine cranberry sauce and horseradish,
stirring well. Combine mayonnaise and sage, stirring well. Spread mayonnaise mixture evenly over
bottom halves of rolls. Arrange lettuce and turkey
evenly over mayonnaise mixture. Spoon cranberry
mixture evenly over turkey. Top with remaining
roll halves. Yield: 4 servings.

Per Serving:

Calories 363	Carbohydrate 51.4g	Fiber 0.6g
Fat 6.1g	Cholesterol 44mg	Calcium 35mg
Protein 24.3g	Sodium 750mg	Iron 4.0mg

Exchanges: 2 Very Lean Meat, 2 Starch, 1 Fruit, 1 Fat

A Second Time Around

Turn your leftover holiday turkey and cranberry sauce into hearty sandwiches.

Fruited Ham Sandwich

SuperQuick
Prep time: 15 minutes

1   tablespoon reduced-calorie margarine
1   ripe red pear, thinly sliced
1   tablespoon finely chopped walnuts
1   teaspoon sugar
⅓   cup nonfat cream cheese
4   (1¼-ounce) slices honey wheatberry bread,
       toasted
6   ounces thinly sliced reduced-fat, low-salt
       ham

Melt margarine in a medium nonstick skillet.
Add pear, walnuts, and sugar. Cook over low heat
8 minutes or until pear is tender, stirring occasionally; set aside.

Spread about 1½ tablespoons cream cheese
over 1 side of each bread slice; top evenly with
ham. Spoon pear mixture evenly over ham; serve
immediately. Yield: 4 servings.

Per Serving:

Calories 228	Carbohydrate 30.7g	Fiber 4.6g
Fat 6.6g	Cholesterol 26mg	Calcium 82mg
Protein 15.1g	Sodium 665mg	Iron 0.5mg

Exchanges: 1½ Very Lean Meat, 2 Starch, 1 Fat

A "Pearfect" Arrangement

To make these open-face sandwiches more
colorful, use half of a red pear and half of a green
pear, and arrange slices in alternating colors on the
bread.

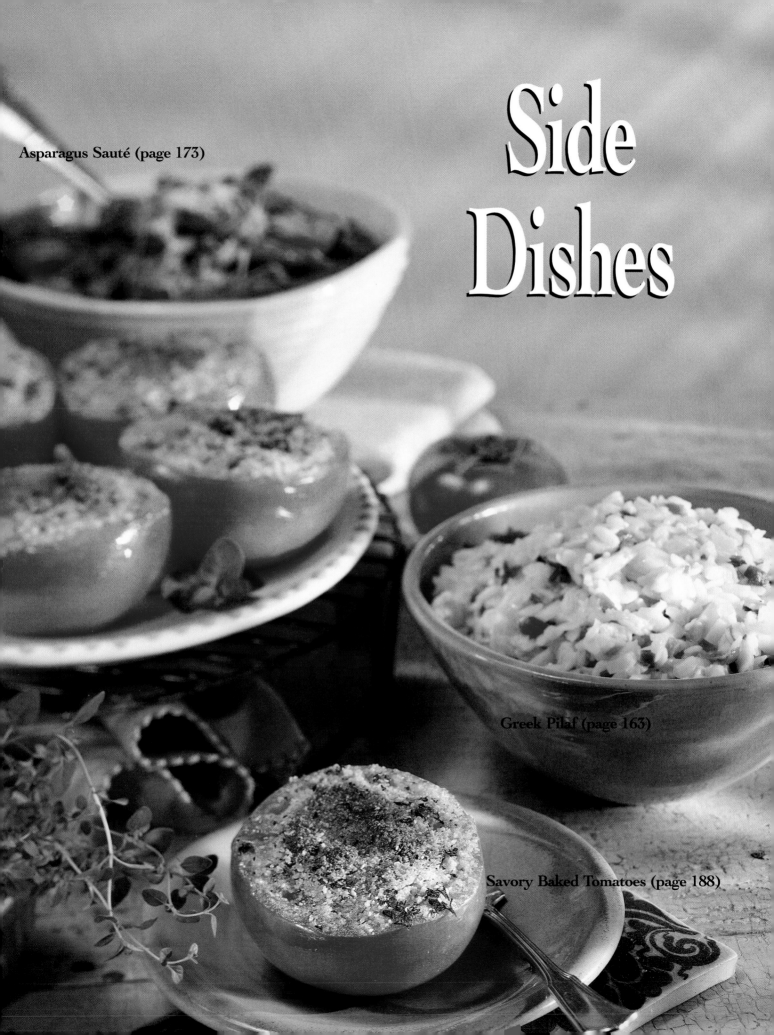

Asparagus Sauté (page 173)

Side Dishes

Greek Pilaf (page 163)

Savory Baked Tomatoes (page 188)

Broccoli-Rice Casserole

Prep time: 15 minutes   Cook time: 25 minutes

3   cups chopped fresh broccoli
1   tablespoon plus 2 teaspoons margarine,
      divided
¼   cup chopped onion
3   tablespoons all-purpose flour
½   teaspoon dry mustard
1¼ cups skim milk
⅛   teaspoon pepper
1¾ cups cooked long-grain rice (cooked without
      salt or fat)
1   cup (4 ounces) shredded reduced-fat sharp
      Cheddar cheese
¼   cup nonfat mayonnaise
      Vegetable cooking spray
⅓   cup crushed unsalted Melba toast (about 5
      slices)

Cook broccoli in boiling water 3 minutes or until crisp-tender. Drain and plunge into cold water; drain again. Set aside.

Melt 1 tablespoon plus 1 teaspoon margarine in a medium saucepan over medium heat; add onion, and sauté 3 minutes or until tender. Add flour and mustard; cook, stirring constantly with a wire whisk, 1 minute. Gradually add milk, stirring constantly. Cook, stirring constantly, 2 additional minutes or until thickened and bubbly. Remove from heat; stir in pepper.

Combine broccoli, milk mixture, rice, cheese, and mayonnaise in a bowl; stir well. Spoon into a shallow 2-quart baking dish coated with cooking spray.

Melt remaining 1 teaspoon margarine, and combine with Melba toast crumbs; sprinkle over broccoli mixture. Bake at 350° for 25 minutes or until thoroughly heated. Yield: 8 (½-cup) servings.

Per Serving:

Calories 161	Carbohydrate 20.2g	Fiber 1.4g
Fat 5.6g	Cholesterol 10mg	Calcium 196mg
Protein 8.0g	Sodium 271mg	Iron 1.0mg

Exchanges: 1 Starch, 1 Vegetable, 1 Fat

Vegetable Pilaf

Prep time: 10 minutes   Cook time: 25 minutes

1⅓ cups water
1   teaspoon chicken-flavored bouillon granules
½   cup long-grain rice, uncooked
½   cup water
1½ cups sliced fresh mushrooms
1¼ cups shredded carrot
½   cup chopped fresh parsley
⅓   cup thinly sliced green onions
¼   teaspoon pepper
¼   cup chopped pecans, toasted

Combine 1⅓ cups water and bouillon granules in a medium saucepan; bring to a boil, and add rice. Cover, reduce heat, and simmer 20 minutes or until liquid is absorbed and rice is tender.

Add ½ cup water, mushrooms, carrot, parsley, green onions, and pepper to rice; stir well. Cover and cook over low heat 5 minutes. Sprinkle with toasted pecans. Yield: 4 (1-cup) servings.

Per Serving:

Calories 164	Carbohydrate 25.8g	Fiber 2.7g
Fat 5.7g	Cholesterol 0mg	Calcium 37mg
Protein 3.6g	Sodium 225mg	Iron 2.3mg

Exchanges: 1 Starch, 1 Vegetable, 1 Fat

Streamline Prep Time

While rice simmers, toast chopped pecans in a baking pan at 350° for about 10 minutes.

Greek Pilaf

Prep time: 5 minutes   Cook time: 30 minutes

   Vegetable cooking spray
1 tablespoon olive oil
6 green onions, finely chopped
¾ cup orzo, uncooked
¾ cup instant rice, uncooked
1 (14¼-ounce) can no-salt-added chicken
      broth
1¼ cups water
¼ teaspoon salt
⅛ teaspoon pepper
1¼ cups peeled, diced cucumber
⅓ cup crumbled feta cheese
2 tablespoons diced pimiento, drained

   Coat a large nonstick skillet with cooking
spray; add oil. Place over medium-high heat until
hot. Add green onions, and sauté until tender. Add
orzo; sauté, stirring constantly, 2 minutes. Add
rice; sauté 2 minutes. Stir in chicken broth, water,
salt, and pepper. Bring to a boil; cover, reduce heat,
and simmer 20 to 25 minutes or until liquid is
absorbed and rice is tender.
   Remove from heat, and stir in cucumber, feta
cheese, and pimiento. Yield: 6 (1-cup) servings.

Per Serving:

Calories 197	Carbohydrate 30.5g	Fiber 1.2g
Fat 5.3g	Cholesterol 8mg	Calcium 67mg
Protein 6.3g	Sodium 241mg	Iron 1.9mg

Exchanges: 2 Starch, 1 Fat

Brown Rice Primavera
SuperQuick
Prep time: 8 minutes   Cook time: 12 minutes

¾ cup water
½ teaspoon chicken-flavored bouillon granules
2 cloves garlic, minced
¾ cup instant brown rice, uncooked
   Vegetable cooking spray
1 cup frozen green beans, thawed and drained
1 cup sliced fresh mushrooms
½ cup diced sweet red pepper
2 tablespoons grated Parmesan cheese

   Combine first 3 ingredients in a medium
saucepan; bring to a boil. Stir in rice; cover, reduce
heat, and simmer 5 minutes. Remove from heat,
and let stand 5 minutes or until liquid is absorbed.
Set aside, and keep warm.
   Coat a large nonstick skillet with cooking
spray; place over medium heat until hot. Add green
beans; sauté 2 minutes, stirring often. Add mushrooms and red pepper; sauté, stirring constantly, 3
minutes or until crisp-tender. Add green bean mixture and Parmesan cheese to rice mixture; toss
well. Yield: 3 (1-cup) servings.

Per Serving:

Calories 229	Carbohydrate 44.2g	Fiber 2.4g
Fat 3.1g	Cholesterol 3mg	Calcium 93mg
Protein 7.3g	Sodium 214mg	Iron 2.4mg

Exchanges: 2 Starch, ½ Vegetable, ½ Fat

Microwave It Right

   Combine first 4 ingredients in a 1½-quart
baking dish.
   Cover with heavy-duty plastic wrap, and
microwave at HIGH 6 minutes. Let stand, covered, 5 minutes.
   Place green beans in a 1-quart casserole.
Cover with heavy-duty plastic wrap, and
microwave at HIGH 3 minutes. Stir in mushrooms and pepper. Cover and microwave at
HIGH 3 to 4 minutes or until vegetables are crisp-
tender. Add green bean mixture and Parmesan
cheese to rice mixture; toss well.

Lemon Risotto

Prep time: 5 minutes   Cook time: 30 minutes

2	(14¼-ounce) cans no-salt-added chicken broth
2	teaspoons olive oil
½	cup chopped onion
1	clove garlic, crushed
1	cup Arborio rice, uncooked
¼	teaspoon salt
½	teaspoon grated lemon rind
3	tablespoons fresh lemon juice

Pour chicken broth into a medium saucepan; place over medium heat. Bring just to a boil; cover, reduce heat, and simmer.

Heat oil in a large skillet over medium-high heat. Add onion and garlic; cook, stirring constantly, until tender. Add rice, stirring well. Add half of broth to rice mixture; stir constantly 3 minutes. Cover, reduce heat, and simmer 10 minutes. Repeat procedure with remaining broth. Stir in salt, lemon rind, and lemon juice. Serve immediately. Yield: 6 (½-cup) servings.

Per Serving:

Calories 158	Carbohydrate 28.3g	Fiber 0.7g
Fat 2.8g	Cholesterol 0mg	Calcium 5mg
Protein 3.5g	Sodium 175mg	Iron 1.5mg

Exchanges: 1½ Starch, ½ Fat

Wild Rice Bulgur

Prep time: 10 minutes   Cook time: 30 minutes

	Olive oil-flavored vegetable cooking spray
¾	cup chopped onion
¾	cup chopped celery
2	cloves garlic, minced
2¾	cups canned no-salt-added chicken broth
1	cup bulgur (cracked wheat), uncooked
⅓	cup instant wild rice, uncooked
½	teaspoon salt

Coat a Dutch oven with cooking spray; place over medium-high heat until hot. Add onion, celery, and garlic, and sauté until crisp-tender. Add broth, and bring to a boil. Stir in bulgur, rice, and salt. Cover, reduce heat, and simmer 30 minutes or until liquid is absorbed and bulgur is tender. Yield: 8 (½-cup) servings.

Per Serving:

Calories 101	Carbohydrate 21.0g	Fiber 4.0g
Fat 0.4g	Cholesterol 0mg	Calcium 18mg
Protein 3.6g	Sodium 164mg	Iron 0.7mg

Exchange: 1 Starch

Fresh Corn Polenta with Jalapeños

Prep time: 10 minutes   Chill time: 8 hours
Cook time: 30 minutes

3½ cups canned no-salt-added chicken broth
1   cup fresh corn cut from cob (about 3 ears)
½   cup skim milk
½   teaspoon salt
1   cup quick-cooking polenta, uncooked
1   small jalapeño pepper, seeded and minced
     Vegetable cooking spray
2   ounces reduced-fat sharp Cheddar cheese,
     cut into ½-inch-wide strips

Combine first 4 ingredients in a large saucepan; bring to a boil. Add polenta in a slow, steady stream, stirring constantly. Reduce heat; cook over medium-low heat, stirring constantly, 10 minutes or until mixture pulls away from sides of pan. Add jalapeño pepper.

Line an 8½- x 4½- x 3-inch loafpan with heavy-duty plastic wrap. Spoon polenta mixture into prepared pan; cover and chill 8 hours.

Remove polenta from pan; remove plastic wrap. Cut polenta into 8 equal slices, about 1 inch thick. Cut each slice diagonally into 2 triangles. Place polenta triangles on a baking sheet coated with cooking spray. Bake at 425° for 11 to 12 minutes or until golden. Remove from oven; arrange cheese strips on top of polenta triangles. Bake 4 to 5 additional minutes or until cheese melts. Serve immediately. Yield: 8 servings.

Per Serving:

Calories 124	Carbohydrate 21.1g	Fiber 1.6g
Fat 1.9g	Cholesterol 5mg	Calcium 83mg
Protein 5.1g	Sodium 209mg	Iron 0.9mg

Exchange: 1½ Starch

Summer Goodness

Summer's sweet, fresh corn tastes best in the polenta, but you can use thawed frozen whole-kernel corn. And, if you've never tried polenta, this is the time to do so. Polenta has the same grainy texture and flavor as grits and cornbread—they all come from ground corn. Polenta can be served as a spoonable side dish like grits or cooled and cut into slices or wedges as in this recipe.

Seasoned Couscous

SuperQuick
Prep time: 10 minutes   Cook time: 5 minutes

     Vegetable cooking spray
½   teaspoon peanut oil
½   cup sliced green onions
1½   cups water
2   teaspoons chicken-flavored bouillon
     granules
1   cup couscous, uncooked
2   teaspoons low-sodium soy sauce
⅔   cup peeled, seeded, and chopped tomato
2   tablespoons chopped fresh parsley
¼   teaspoon freshly ground pepper

Coat a medium saucepan with cooking spray; add oil. Place over medium-high heat until hot. Add green onions; sauté until tender. Add water and bouillon granules; bring to a boil. Stir in couscous and soy sauce. Remove from heat; cover and let stand 5 minutes or until liquid is absorbed and couscous is tender. Stir in tomato, parsley, and pepper. Yield: 4 (1-cup) servings.

Per Serving:

Calories 176	Carbohydrate 34.8g	Fiber 2.4g
Fat 1.8g	Cholesterol 0mg	Calcium 14mg
Protein 6.4g	Sodium 485mg	Iron 1.3mg

Exchange: 2 Starch

Couscous for a Quick Fix

Couscous (koos-koos), an ideal side dish with any entrée, is a tiny, round pasta from the Middle East. It's ready in about 5 minutes and absorbs flavor easily. Serve couscous instead of mashed potatoes or rice one night; you'll enjoy the change in texture and flavor.

Orange-Ginger Couscous

SuperQuick

Prep time: 5 minutes   Cook time: 5 minutes

1   cup canned no-salt-added chicken broth
¾   cup unsweetened orange juice
1   teaspoon minced crystallized ginger
¼   teaspoon ground cinnamon
¼   teaspoon salt
⅛   teaspoon ground red pepper
1   cup plus 2 tablespoons couscous, uncooked
½   cup raisins
     Orange rind strips (optional)

Combine first 6 ingredients in a medium saucepan; bring to a boil. Remove from heat, and stir in couscous and raisins. Cover and let stand 5 minutes or until liquid is absorbed and couscous is tender. Fluff couscous with a fork before serving. Garnish with orange rind, if desired. Serve immediately. Yield: 5 (¾-cup) servings.

Per Serving:

Calories 203	Carbohydrate 45.2g	Fiber 2.3g
Fat 0.5g	Cholesterol 0mg	Calcium 14mg
Protein 5.8g	Sodium 124mg	Iron 1.3mg

Exchanges: 2 Starch, 1 Fruit

Lemon-Garlic Bow Ties

SuperQuick

Prep time: 5 minutes   Cook time: 11 minutes

6 ounces farfalle (bow tie pasta), uncooked
1 tablespoon reduced-calorie margarine
2 cloves garlic, minced
3 tablespoons grated Parmesan cheese
1 teaspoon grated lemon rind
3 tablespoons lemon juice
1 (2-ounce) jar diced pimiento, drained

Cook pasta according to package directions, omitting salt and fat; drain well. Place pasta in a serving bowl. Set aside, and keep warm.

Melt margarine in a small saucepan over medium heat; add garlic. Cook, stirring constantly, until garlic is golden. Remove from heat. Add cheese, lemon rind, and lemon juice. Add lemon mixture and pimiento to pasta; toss well. Serve immediately. Yield: 4 (¾-cup) servings.

Per Serving:

Calories 198	Carbohydrate 34.0g	Fiber 1.0g
Fat 3.7g	Cholesterol 3mg	Calcium 64mg
Protein 7.3g	Sodium 102mg	Iron 1.9mg

Exchanges: 2 Starch, ½ Fat

In a Pinch

For convenience use 1 teaspoon minced garlic from a jar in place of fresh garlic. And if you don't have farfalle on hand, any pasta that is similar in size and thickness, such as penne, fusilli, rigatoni, or rotini will do.

Orecchiette with Asparagus, Blue Cheese, and Walnuts

SuperQuick

Prep time: 10 minutes   Cook time: 15 minutes

2½ quarts water
1 teaspoon chicken-flavored bouillon granules
8 ounces orecchiette (small disk-shaped pasta), uncooked
1 pound fresh asparagus spears
3 tablespoons crumbled blue cheese
2 tablespoons raspberry-flavored vinegar
1 teaspoon sugar
¼ teaspoon salt
¼ teaspoon freshly ground pepper
2 tablespoons finely chopped walnuts, toasted

Combine water and bouillon granules in a Dutch oven; bring to a boil. Add pasta, and cook 11 to 13 minutes or until tender; drain well. Place in a serving bowl. Set aside, and keep warm.

Snap off tough ends of asparagus. Remove scales from stalks with a vegetable peeler, if desired. Cut asparagus into 1-inch pieces. Arrange asparagus in a steamer basket over boiling water. Cover and steam 7 minutes or until crisp-tender; drain.

Add asparagus, blue cheese, and next 4 ingredients to pasta; toss well. Sprinkle with chopped walnuts. Serve pasta immediately.
Yield: 5 (1-cup) servings.

Per Serving:

Calories 232	Carbohydrate 37.9g	Fiber 2.5g
Fat 5.0g	Cholesterol 4mg	Calcium 52mg
Protein 9.3g	Sodium 284mg	Iron 2.4mg

Exchanges: 2 Starch, ½ Vegetable, 1 Fat

Vegetable-Pasta Toss

Prep time: 10 minutes   Cook time: 20 minutes

Vegetable cooking spray
½ cup chopped onion
2 cloves garlic, minced
1 cup low-sodium chicken broth
1 large carrot, scraped and cut into very thin strips
2 tablespoons chopped fresh basil
¼ teaspoon salt
⅛ teaspoon pepper
1 cup rotini, uncooked
1 medium zucchini, cut into very thin strips
½ cup (2 ounces) shredded reduced-fat sharp Cheddar cheese

Coat a large saucepan with cooking spray; place over medium heat until hot. Add onion and garlic; sauté until tender. Add broth and next 4 ingredients; bring to a boil. Stir in pasta. Reduce heat, and simmer 20 minutes or until pasta is tender, stirring occasionally.

Remove from heat; stir in zucchini and cheese. Cover and let stand 2 minutes or until cheese melts. Transfer to a serving dish.
Yield: 4 (¾-cup) servings.

Per Serving:

Calories 184	Carbohydrate 27.6g	Fiber 1.3g
Fat 3.9g	Cholesterol 10mg	Calcium 148mg
Protein 9.4g	Sodium 278mg	Iron 0.7mg

Exchanges: ½ Lean Meat, 1½ Starch, 1 Vegetable

Spinach Noodle Bake

Prep time: 5 minutes   Cook time: 40 minutes

1 (10-ounce) package frozen chopped spinach
1 (8-ounce) package fettuccine, broken in half
1¼ cups (5 ounces) shredded 50% less-fat Swiss cheese
1 cup 1% low-fat cottage cheese
1 (8-ounce) carton low-fat sour cream
2 teaspoons dried Italian seasoning
1 teaspoon ground white pepper
Vegetable cooking spray

Cook spinach according to package directions, omitting salt; drain well.

Cook pasta according to package directions, omitting salt and fat; drain well.

Combine spinach, pasta, Swiss cheese, and next 4 ingredients in a large bowl; toss well. Spoon spinach mixture into a 2-quart baking dish coated with cooking spray. Bake at 325° for 30 minutes or until bubbly. Yield: 10 servings.

Per Serving:

Calories 181	Carbohydrate 20.6g	Fiber 1.5g
Fat 5.5g	Cholesterol 17mg	Calcium 257mg
Protein 11.8g	Sodium 159mg	Iron 1.9mg

Exchanges: 1 Medium-Fat Meat, 1 Starch, 1 Vegetable

Fettuccine Primavera

SuperQuick

Prep time: 15 minutes   Cook time: 5 minutes

¼ cup reduced-calorie margarine
2 cups thinly sliced broccoli flowerets
1 cup thinly sliced carrot
½ cup sliced green onions
3 tablespoons sliced fresh basil
2 cloves garlic, minced
2 cups sliced fresh mushrooms
½ cup dry white wine
¼ teaspoon salt
¼ teaspoon pepper
3½ cups hot cooked fettuccine (cooked without salt or fat)
3 tablespoons freshly grated Parmesan cheese

Melt margarine in a large saucepan over medium-high heat; add broccoli and next 4

ingredients; cook, stirring constantly, 5 minutes or until vegetables are crisp-tender.

Add mushrooms, wine, salt, and pepper to vegetable mixture; cook, stirring constantly, 2 minutes or until mushrooms are tender. Combine vegetable mixture, pasta, and cheese in a large bowl; toss gently. Yield: *7 (1-cup) servings.*

Per Serving:

Calories 185	Carbohydrate 25.2g	Fiber 2.9g
Fat 5.9g	Cholesterol 3mg	Calcium 78mg
Protein 6.5g	Sodium 227mg	Iron 1.9mg

Exchanges: 1 Starch, 1½ Vegetable, 1 Fat

Very Cherry Cranberries

SuperQuick
Prep time: 5 minutes   Cook time: 20 minutes

1   (12-ounce) package fresh or frozen
      cranberries
1   cup frozen pitted sweet cherries
⅓   cup sugar
½   cup cranberry-cherry drink
1   vanilla bean, split
¼   cup chopped pecans or almonds, toasted

Combine first 5 ingredients in a medium
saucepan, stirring well. Bring to a boil; reduce
heat, and simmer, uncovered, 20 minutes or until
cranberry mixture thickens. Remove and discard
vanilla bean. Spoon cranberry mixture into a serving bowl; sprinkle with nuts. Serve immediately.
Yield: 6 (⅓-cup) servings.

Per Serving:

Calories 134	Carbohydrate 27.0g	Fiber 1.1g
Fat 3.3g	Cholesterol 0mg	Calcium 10mg
Protein 1.1g	Sodium 1mg	Iron 0.3mg

Exchanges: 2 Fruit, ½ Fat

'Tis the Season

Serve this sweet-tart side dish with the holiday turkey or ham instead of traditional cranberry
sauce.

Prune-Topped Oranges

SuperQuick
Prep time: 15 minutes   Cook time: 2 minutes

2   large seedless oranges, cut in half crosswise
2   teaspoons Triple Sec or other orange-
      flavored liqueur
4   orange-flavored prunes, chopped
2   tablespoons nutlike cereal nuggets
2   tablespoons dark brown sugar
      Grated orange rind (optional)

Loosen sections of orange halves. Sprinkle
orange liqueur over orange halves.

Combine prunes, cereal, and brown sugar.
Top orange halves evenly with prune mixture.
Place orange halves in an 8-inch square baking
dish, and broil 5½ inches from heat (with electric
oven door partially opened) 2 to 3 minutes or until
browned and bubbly. Garnish with grated orange
rind, if desired. Serve immediately.
Yield: 4 servings.

Per Serving:

Calories 95	Carbohydrate 22.4g	Fiber 3.8g
Fat 0.8g	Cholesterol 0mg	Calcium 40mg
Protein 1.4g	Sodium 33mg	Iron 0.5mg

Exchange: 1½ Fruit

Orange Variation

If you can't find orange-flavored prunes at
your local supermarket, you can use regular
prunes in this recipe.

Amaretto Pears

SuperQuick
Prep time: 10 minutes   Cook time: 15 minutes

4	firm ripe Bosc pears
½	cup plus 1 tablespoon water, divided
⅓	cup sugar
¼	cup golden raisins
3	tablespoons amaretto
¼	teaspoon ground nutmeg
⅛	teaspoon salt
1	tablespoon cornstarch

Peel and core pears; cut each pear into 8 wedges. Combine pear wedges, ½ cup water, sugar, and next 4 ingredients in a skillet. Bring to a boil. Cover, reduce heat, and simmer 10 minutes or until pear wedges are tender.

Combine remaining 1 tablespoon water and cornstarch, stirring well. Add cornstarch mixture to pear mixture; cook, stirring constantly, 1 minute or until thickened and bubbly. Yield: 6 servings.

Per Serving:

Calories 141	Carbohydrate 33.2g	Fiber 2.9g
Fat 1.7g	Cholesterol 0mg	Calcium 15mg
Protein 0.8g	Sodium 55mg	Iron 0.4mg

Exchanges: 1 Starch, 1 Fruit

The Core of the Matter

Use an apple corer to core and slice a peeled pear in one step. Center the corer over the stem of the pear and press down firmly.

Maple Baked Fruits

Prep time: 10 minutes   Cook time: 30 minutes

2	(15-ounce) cans sliced peaches in light syrup
1	(16-ounce) can pear halves in juice
1	(15¼-ounce) can pineapple chunks in juice
1½	tablespoons lemon juice
1	teaspoon maple flavoring
¼	cup firmly packed brown sugar
2	tablespoons reduced-calorie margarine

Drain peaches, discarding liquid; set peaches aside. Drain pears and pineapple, reserving ¼ cup juice from each can. Discard remaining juice. Set fruit aside. Combine reserved juice, lemon juice, and maple flavoring.

Place fruit in an 8-inch square baking dish. Pour juice mixture over fruit. Sprinkle with sugar; dot with margarine. Cover and bake at 350° for 30 minutes or until thoroughly heated.
Yield: 8 (½-cup) servings.

Per Serving:

Calories 111	Carbohydrate 29.5g	Fiber 1.5g
Fat 2.1g	Cholesterol 0mg	Calcium 17mg
Protein 0.7g	Sodium 33mg	Iron 0.5mg

Exchange: 2 Fruit

How Sweet It Is!

Serve this saucy side dish in small compote dishes or custard cups. The sweet fruit is excellent paired with ham or pork. You can even drizzle some of the cooked fruit liquid over the meat.

Baked Acorn Squash

Prep time: 5 minutes   Cook time: 1 hour

2   medium acorn squash (about 1 pound)
2   tablespoons brown sugar
2   tablespoons unsweetened orange juice
2   teaspoons reduced-calorie margarine, melted
¼   teaspoon ground cinnamon
¼   teaspoon ground nutmeg
1   tablespoon finely chopped pecans, toasted

Cut squash in half crosswise; remove and discard seeds. Place squash halves, cut side down, in a 13- x 9- x 2-inch baking dish. Add water to depth of ½ inch. Bake, uncovered, at 350° for 40 minutes. Remove from oven, and invert squash halves.

Combine brown sugar and next 4 ingredients in a small bowl, stirring well. Spoon brown sugar mixture evenly into squash halves. Bake, uncovered, 20 additional minutes, basting occasionally. Sprinkle with pecans. Yield: 4 servings.

Per Serving:

Calories 89	Carbohydrate 17.6g	Fiber 1.5g
Fat 2.6g	Cholesterol 0mg	Calcium 45mg
Protein 1.1g	Sodium 24mg	Iron 0.9mg

Exchange: 1 Starch

Asparagus Dijon

SuperQuick
Prep time: 12 minutes   Cook time: 7 minutes

1½   pounds fresh asparagus spears
1   cup nonfat buttermilk
1   tablespoon cornstarch
2   teaspoons Dijon mustard
¾   teaspoon lemon juice
½   teaspoon dried tarragon
¼   teaspoon ground white pepper

Snap off tough ends of asparagus. Remove scales from spears with a vegetable peeler, if desired. Arrange asparagus in a steamer basket over boiling water. Cover and steam 7 minutes or until crisp-tender. Set aside, and keep warm.

Combine buttermilk and cornstarch in a small saucepan; stir well. Cook over medium heat, stirring constantly, until thickened and bubbly. Remove from heat; stir in mustard, lemon juice, tarragon, and pepper.

Arrange asparagus on a serving platter. Spoon sauce over asparagus. Serve immediately. Yield: 6 servings.

Per Serving:

Calories 43	Carbohydrate 7.1g	Fiber 0.9g
Fat 0.5g	Cholesterol 1mg	Calcium 69mg
Protein 3.7g	Sodium 103mg	Iron 0.7mg

Exchange: 1½ Vegetable

Asparagus Sauté

SuperQuick
Prep time: 5 minutes   Cook time: 10 minutes

1   pound fresh asparagus spears
     Vegetable cooking spray
1   clove garlic, minced
10   cherry tomatoes, halved
½   teaspoon dried oregano
⅛   teaspoon dried thyme
     Dash of pepper
2   tablespoons freshly grated Parmesan cheese

Snap off tough ends of asparagus. Remove scales from spears with a vegetable peeler, if desired. Cut asparagus spears diagonally into 1-inch pieces. Arrange asparagus pieces in a steamer basket over boiling water. Cover and steam 4 to 5 minutes or until crisp-tender.

Coat a large nonstick skillet with cooking spray; place over medium-high heat until hot. Add asparagus and garlic; cook, stirring constantly, 4 to 5 minutes or until tender. Stir in tomato halves, oregano, thyme, and pepper. Cook, stirring constantly, 1 minute or until thoroughly heated. Transfer mixture to a serving dish, and sprinkle with Parmesan cheese. Yield: 4 servings.

Per Serving:

Calories 47	Carbohydrate 6.3g	Fiber 1.5g
Fat 1.5g	Cholesterol 2mg	Calcium 66mg
Protein 3.9g	Sodium 71mg	Iron 1.0mg

Exchange: 1½ Vegetable

Spicy Beets

SuperQuick
Prep time: 8 minutes   Cook time: 10 minutes

¼   cup plus 2 tablespoons sugar
1   tablespoon cornstarch
2   teaspoons grated orange rind
½   teaspoon salt
¼   teaspoon ground cinnamon
¼   teaspoon pepper
½   cup water
¼   cup plus 2 tablespoons red wine vinegar
2   (16-ounce) cans whole beets, drained
     Grated orange rind (optional)

Combine first 6 ingredients in a medium non-aluminum saucepan. Stir in water and vinegar. Bring mixture to a boil over medium heat. Cook, stirring constantly, 1 minute or until thickened. Add beets, and cook over medium-low heat 10 minutes or until thoroughly heated, stirring often. Garnish with orange rind, if desired.
Yield: 6 (½-cup) servings.

Per Serving:

Calories 92	Carbohydrate 23.2g	Fiber 0.8g
Fat 0.1g	Cholesterol 0mg	Calcium 22mg
Protein 1.0g	Sodium 447mg	Iron 0.7mg

Exchanges: 1 Starch, 1 Vegetable

To Pepper or Not to Pepper

Pepper adds a slightly spicy flavor to the beets in this recipe. For a milder version of glazed beets, omit the pepper.

Szechuan Broccoli

SuperQuick

Prep time: 8 minutes   Cook time: 8 minutes

1   tablespoon low-sodium soy sauce
1   tablespoon cider vinegar
½   teaspoon sugar
2   teaspoons sesame seeds
     Vegetable cooking spray
1   teaspoon vegetable oil
¼   teaspoon dried crushed red pepper
½   teaspoon peeled, minced gingerroot
2   cloves garlic, minced
5   cups coarsely chopped broccoli

Combine first 3 ingredients in a small bowl; set aside.

Place a large nonstick skillet or wok over medium heat until hot. Add sesame seeds; cook 1 minute or until browned. Remove seeds, and set aside.

Coat skillet with cooking spray; add oil, and place over medium-high heat until hot. Add red pepper, gingerroot, and garlic; sauté 30 seconds. Add broccoli; sauté 1 minute. Add soy sauce mixture; stir well. Cover and cook 2 minutes or until broccoli is crisp-tender. Sprinkle with sesame seeds. Yield: 4 (1-cup) servings.

Per Serving:

Calories 63	Carbohydrate 8.4g	Fiber 3.9g
Fat 2.6g	Cholesterol 0mg	Calcium 79mg
Protein 4.2g	Sodium 154mg	Iron 1.4mg

Exchange: 2 Vegetable

Brussels Sprouts with Shallots

Prep time: 10 minutes   Cook time: 19 minutes

2   (8-ounce) packages frozen brussels sprouts
2   teaspoons reduced-calorie margarine
4   shallots, cut in half lengthwise and thinly sliced crosswise
½   cup unsweetened orange juice
¼   cup water
2   tablespoons sugar
½   teaspoon chicken-flavored bouillon granules
⅛   teaspoon pepper

Cook brussels sprouts according to package directions, omitting salt. Drain and set aside.

Melt margarine in a large nonstick skillet over medium-high heat. Add shallot; sauté 2 minutes or until tender.

Combine orange juice and remaining 4 ingredients in a small bowl; stir well. Add orange juice mixture to shallot. Bring to a boil; reduce heat, and simmer, uncovered, 3 minutes. Stir in brussels sprouts; cook 2 minutes or until thoroughly heated, stirring occasionally. Transfer to a serving dish. Serve with a slotted spoon.
Yield: 7 (½-cup) servings.

Per Serving:

Calories 64	Carbohydrate 13.2g	Fiber 2.9g
Fat 1.0g	Cholesterol 0mg	Calcium 33mg
Protein 2.6g	Sodium 87mg	Iron 1.1mg

Exchanges: ½ Starch, 1 Vegetable

Italian Broccoli and Tomatoes

SuperQuick

Prep time: 12 minutes   Cook time: 10 minutes

1   **pound fresh broccoli**
2   **medium tomatoes, each cut into 8 wedges**
2   **tablespoons water**
½   **teaspoon garlic powder**
½   **teaspoon dried oregano**
½   **cup (2 ounces) shredded nonfat mozzarella cheese**
2   **tablespoons sliced ripe olives**

Remove broccoli leaves, and cut broccoli into small spears. Arrange broccoli in a steamer basket over boiling water. Cover and steam 5 to 8 minutes or until crisp-tender. Drain and place in a large saucepan.

Add tomato wedges, water, garlic powder, and oregano to pan; stir gently. Cook over medium-low heat, uncovered, 10 to 15 minutes or until thoroughly heated, stirring occasionally. Sprinkle with cheese and olives. Remove from heat. Cover and let stand 2 to 3 minutes or until cheese melts. Yield: 4 (1-cup) servings.

Per Serving:

Calories 61	Carbohydrate 9.3g	Fiber 3.7g
Fat 1.0g	Cholesterol 0mg	Calcium 52mg
Protein 5.2g	Sodium 211mg	Iron 1.3mg

Exchange: 2 Vegetable

Sweet-and-Sour Cabbage

SuperQuick

Prep time: 7 minutes   Cook time: 10 minutes

 1 medium Granny Smith apple, cored and
      sliced
 2 tablespoons lemon juice
      Vegetable cooking spray
 1 small onion, sliced and separated into rings
 5 cups shredded red cabbage
¼ cup unsweetened white grape juice
 2 tablespoons dry white wine
 2 tablespoons balsamic vinegar
¼ teaspoon salt
⅛ teaspoon pepper

Combine sliced apple and lemon juice in a
small bowl; toss gently, and set aside.

Coat a large nonstick skillet with cooking
spray; place over medium-high heat until hot. Add
onion; sauté until tender. Add cabbage; sauté 3 to 4
minutes or until crisp-tender. Add apple mixture,
grape juice, and remaining ingredients; stir gently.
Cook 1 to 2 minutes or until thoroughly heated.
Yield: 5 (1-cup) servings.

Per Serving:

Calories 51	Carbohydrate 11.1g	Fiber 2.7g
Fat 0.3g	Cholesterol 0mg	Calcium 42mg
Protein 1.3g	Sodium 132mg	Iron 0.6mg

Exchanges: ½ Starch, 1 Vegetable

Don't Be Blue

To avoid a blue color that sometimes occurs
when cooking red cabbage, cut the cabbage with a
long-bladed stainless steel knife or use the slicing
disc of a food processor. And make sure the recipe
calls for some type of acidic ingredient like vinegar, wine, or lemon juice. The acid will help maintain the rich magenta color of red cabbage.

Creamy Cabbage and Fennel

Prep time: 15 minutes   Cook time: 25 minutes

      Vegetable cooking spray
3½ cups thinly sliced red cabbage
  1 large Granny Smith apple, peeled, cored
        and thinly sliced
1¾ cups chopped fennel bulb
  ¾ cup unsweetened apple juice
  2 tablespoons dark brown sugar
  ¼ teaspoon salt
  ¼ teaspoon freshly ground pepper
  ⅓ cup light process cream cheese, softened
  2 tablespoons coarsely chopped walnuts,
        toasted

Coat a large nonstick skillet with cooking
spray; place over medium heat until hot. Add cabbage and apple; cook 5 minutes, stirring occasionally. Add fennel, and cook 5 minutes or until cabbage and apple are tender.

Stir in apple juice and next 3 ingredients.
Bring to a boil; cover, reduce heat, and simmer 10
minutes or until liquid evaporates. Remove from
heat; add cream cheese, stirring until smooth.
Sprinkle with walnuts. Yield: 4 (¾-cup) servings.

Per Serving:

Calories 144	Carbohydrate 22.8g	Fiber 2.5g
Fat 5.0g	Cholesterol 11mg	Calcium 108mg
Protein 4.5g	Sodium 265mg	Iron 1.9mg

Exchanges: 1 Vegetable, 1 Fruit, 1 Fat

Lemon-Dill Baby Carrots

SuperQuick
Prep time: 3 minutes   Cook time: 15 minutes

1   (16-ounce) package fresh baby carrots
1   tablespoon lemon juice
1   teaspoon cornstarch
⅓   cup water
1   teaspoon dried dillweed
1   teaspoon reduced-calorie margarine
¼   teaspoon grated lemon rind
⅛   teaspoon salt
    Dash of pepper

Arrange carrots in a steamer basket over boiling water. Cover and steam 10 minutes or until crisp-tender. Transfer carrots to a serving bowl. Set aside, and keep warm.

Combine lemon juice and cornstarch in a medium saucepan; stir until smooth. Gradually add water; cook over medium heat, stirring constantly, 1 minute or until thickened. Remove from heat; stir in dillweed and remaining 4 ingredients. Pour over carrots, and toss gently. Yield: 4 servings.

Per Serving:

Calories 53	Carbohydrate 11.3g	Fiber 1.6g
Fat 0.8g	Cholesterol 0mg	Calcium 42mg
Protein 1.3g	Sodium 147mg	Iron 0.8mg

Exchange: 2 Vegetable

Cauliflower with Cheese Sauce

SuperQuick
Prep time: 10 minutes   Cook time: 15 minutes

1   large cauliflower (about 2½ pounds), broken into flowerets
1   cup water
2   tablespoons margarine
2   tablespoons all-purpose flour
1   cup skim milk
1   cup (4 ounces) cubed loaf light process cheese spread
¼   teaspoon dry mustard
⅛   teaspoon ground white pepper
2   teaspoons chopped fresh parsley

Place cauliflower in a large saucepan; add water. Bring to a boil; cover, reduce heat, and simmer 8 to 10 minutes or until tender. Drain well. Transfer to a serving dish, and keep warm.

Melt margarine in a heavy saucepan over medium heat; add flour. Cook, stirring constantly with a wire whisk, 1 minute. Gradually add milk, stirring constantly. Cook, stirring constantly, until mixture is thickened and bubbly. Add cheese, mustard, and pepper, stirring until cheese melts.

Spoon sauce over cauliflower, and sprinkle with parsley. Serve immediately. Yield: 8 servings.

Per Serving:

Calories 108	Carbohydrate 11.6g	Fiber 3.3g
Fat 4.7g	Cholesterol 1mg	Calcium 69mg
Protein 7.0g	Sodium 300mg	Iron 0.7mg

Exchanges: ½ Medium-Fat Meat, ½ Starch, 1 Vegetable

Mexican Corn

SuperQuick

Prep time: 10 minutes   Cook time: 10 minutes

Vegetable cooking spray
2   teaspoons margarine
2   cups frozen yellow corn, thawed
6   tablespoons water
¼   cup chopped green pepper
¼   cup chopped sweet red pepper
¼   cup chopped purple onion
2   tablespoons chopped fresh cilantro
¼   teaspoon salt

Coat a medium nonstick skillet with cooking spray; add margarine. Place over medium-high heat until hot.

Add corn and remaining ingredients, stirring well to combine. Cook vegetable mixture over medium heat 10 minutes or until vegetables are tender, stirring occasionally.
Yield: 2 (1-cup) servings.

Per Serving:

Calories 199	Carbohydrate 37.8g	Fiber 5.2g
Fat 5.6g	Cholesterol 0mg	Calcium 16mg
Protein 5.6g	Sodium 346mg	Iron 1.4mg

Exchanges: 2 Starch, 1 Fat

Shear Cooking

Use kitchen shears to chop fresh cilantro or parsley. Place herb sprigs in a glass measuring cup, and snip until chopped. It's easy to measure — and less messy.

South-of-the-Border Corn

SuperQuick

Prep time: 2 minutes   Cook time: 20 minutes

12   half-ears frozen corn
 1   tablespoon reduced-calorie margarine, melted
 1   tablespoon hot water
 ½   teaspoon ground cumin
 ½   teaspoon paprika
 ¼   teaspoon salt
 ¼   teaspoon garlic powder
 ¼   teaspoon dried cilantro
     Dash of ground red pepper

Cook corn according to package directions; transfer corn to a serving platter. Combine margarine and remaining 7 ingredients in a small bowl; stir well. Brush mixture over corn.
Yield: 12 servings.

Per Serving:

Calories 93	Carbohydrate 19.1g	Fiber 2.8g
Fat 2.2g	Cholesterol 0mg	Calcium 4mg
Protein 2.5g	Sodium 129mg	Iron 0.6mg

Exchange: 1 Starch

Green Beans Provençal

SuperQuick

Prep time: 5 minutes   Cook time: 8 minutes

  1 (9-ounce) package frozen cut green beans,
        thawed
 12 small cherry tomatoes, halved
  3 tablespoons chopped purple onion
  2 tablespoons white wine vinegar
  2 tablespoons water
  1 tablespoon grated Parmesan cheese
 ¼ teaspoon dried thyme
 ¼ teaspoon pepper
  1 clove garlic, minced
  2 teaspoons olive oil

Arrange beans in a steamer basket over boiling water. Cover and steam 8 minutes or until crisp-tender. Drain beans, and plunge into cold water; drain.

Combine beans, tomato, and onion; toss gently. Combine vinegar and remaining 6 ingredients; stir well. Pour over bean mixture; toss well to coat. Yield: 4 (¾-cup) servings.

Per Serving:

Calories 58	Carbohydrate 7.0g	Fiber 1.9g
Fat 2.9g	Cholesterol 1mg	Calcium 48mg
Protein 2.1g	Sodium 36mg	Iron 1.2mg

Exchanges: 1 Vegetable, ½ Fat

Green Beans, Peasant Style

Prep time: 10 minutes   Cook time: 22 minutes

  1 pound fresh green beans
  1 tablespoon olive oil
  1 cup chopped onion
  2 cloves garlic, crushed
  1 (14½ ounce) can no-salt-added whole
        tomatoes, drained and chopped
 ⅓ cup dry red wine
 ½ teaspoon dried oregano
 ½ teaspoon pepper

Wash beans; trim ends, and remove strings. Arrange beans in a steamer basket over boiling water. Cover and steam 5 minutes or until crisp-tender; drain. Set aside, and keep warm.

Heat olive oil in a large nonstick skillet over medium-high heat until hot. Add onion and garlic; sauté until tender. Add tomato and remaining 3 ingredients. Cook over low heat 15 minutes, stirring occasionally. Remove from heat; add beans, tossing well to combine. Yield: 7 (½-cup) servings.

Per Serving:

Calories 61	Carbohydrate 8.4g	Fiber 1.7g
Fat 2.0g	Cholesterol 0mg	Calcium 44mg
Protein 1.8g	Sodium 10mg	Iron 1.0mg

Exchanges: 1½ Vegetable, ½ Fat

A Range of Flavor

When selecting olive oil, keep in mind how much olive flavor appeals to you. Olive oils labeled extra virgin and virgin have the most olive flavor. Pure, refined, and extra light olive oils are milder. All olive oils contain the same amount of beneficial monounsaturated fat and the same number of calories, approximately 119 per tablespoon.

Rancher's Beans

Prep time: 8 minutes   Cook time: 20 minutes

Vegetable cooking spray
1/4 cup chopped onion
1 (16-ounce) can light red kidney beans, undrained
1 (15.8-ounce) can Great Northern beans, undrained
1 (8-ounce) can no-salt-added tomato sauce
3 tablespoons no-salt-added tomato juice
1 tablespoon prepared mustard
2 tablespoons brown sugar
1/4 teaspoon garlic powder
1/8 teaspoon pepper

Coat a medium saucepan with cooking spray; place over medium-high heat until hot. Add onion; sauté until tender.

Add kidney beans and remaining ingredients. Cook over medium heat, uncovered, 20 minutes or until slightly thickened. Yield: 9 (1/2-cup) servings.

Per Serving:

Calories 139	Carbohydrate 26.1g	Fiber 4.1g
Fat 0.4g	Cholesterol 0mg	Calcium 51mg
Protein 9.1g	Sodium 242mg	Iron 2.6mg

Exchanges: 1 Very Lean Meat, 1 1/2 Starch

Creole Lima Beans

Prep time: 20 minutes   Cook time: 12 minutes

Vegetable cooking spray
½ cup chopped celery
½ cup chopped green pepper
½ cup chopped onion
1 (16-ounce) package frozen baby lima beans, thawed
1 cup diced tomato
1 cup spicy hot vegetable juice
¼ teaspoon dried crushed red pepper

Coat a large nonstick skillet with cooking spray; place over medium-high heat until hot. Add celery, green pepper, and onion; sauté until tender.

Stir in lima beans and remaining ingredients; bring to a boil over medium heat. Cover, reduce heat, and simmer 12 to 15 minutes or until beans are tender. Yield: 16 (¾-cup) servings.

Per Serving:

Calories 45	Carbohydrate 8.6g	Fiber 1.0g
Fat 0.2g	Cholesterol 0mg	Calcium 16mg
Protein 2.5g	Sodium 96mg	Iron 1.0mg

Exchange: ½ Starch

Tangy White Beans

SuperQuick
Prep time: 7 minutes

1 (15.8-ounce) can Great Northern beans, drained
1 cup seeded, chopped tomato
½ cup chopped fresh parsley
½ cup chopped celery
¼ cup white wine vinegar
1½ tablespoons Dijon mustard
⅛ teaspoon ground white pepper

Combine first 4 ingredients in a medium bowl; toss gently.

Combine vinegar, mustard, and pepper; stir well. Add to bean mixture, tossing gently. Yield: 4 (¾-cup) servings.

Per Serving:

Calories 78	Carbohydrate 13.3g	Fiber 7.5g
Fat 0.8g	Cholesterol 0mg	Calcium 22mg
Protein 3.8g	Sodium 182mg	Iron 1.5mg

Exchange: 1 Starch

Mushroom Newburg

Prep time: 12 minutes   Cook time: 22 minutes

Vegetable cooking spray
2 (8-ounce) packages sliced fresh mushrooms
½ teaspoon salt, divided
¼ teaspoon pepper
3 tablespoons dry sherry
3 tablespoons all-purpose flour
2 cups skim milk
¼ cup instant nonfat dry milk powder
2 tablespoons reduced-calorie margarine
6 (1-ounce) slices white bread

Coat a large nonstick skillet with cooking spray; place over medium-high heat until hot. Add mushrooms; sauté 6 minutes or until mushrooms are tender and liquid evaporates. Add ¼ teaspoon salt, pepper, and sherry; sauté 1 minute.

Place flour in a medium saucepan; gradually add milk, stirring until smooth. Stir in remaining ¼ teaspoon salt, milk powder, and margarine. Cook over medium heat, stirring constantly with a wire whisk, until thickened and bubbly. Add mushroom mixture to milk mixture, stirring well. Set aside, and keep warm.

Remove and discard crust from bread; cut each piece in half diagonally. Place bread on a large baking sheet. Bake at 400° for 6 minutes or until toasted. To serve, spoon mushroom mixture over toasted bread. Yield: 6 servings.

Per Serving:

Calories 153	Carbohydrate 22.9g	Fiber 1.5g
Fat 3.7g	Cholesterol 3mg	Calcium 182mg
Protein 8.2g	Sodium 401mg	Iron 1.7mg

Exchanges: 1 Starch, 1 Vegetable, ½ Fat

A Boost of Calcium

Calcium-rich instant nonfat dry milk powder is great to add to a recipe to get thick, creamy results. It also has a longer shelf life and is less expensive than fresh milk.

Crumb-Topped Onions

SuperQuick
Prep time: 10 minutes   Cook time: 12 minutes

4 small Vidalia or other sweet onions
¼ cup canned no-salt-added beef broth
¼ cup plus 2 tablespoons crushed reduced-fat round buttery crackers (7 crackers)
1½ tablespoons reduced-calorie margarine, melted
¼ teaspoon freshly ground black pepper
⅛ teaspoon ground red pepper
¼ cup plus 2 tablespoons (1½ ounces) shredded reduced-fat Swiss cheese

Peel onions, and cut in half crosswise. Arrange onion halves, cut side up, in an 11- x 7- x 1½-inch baking dish (if necessary, cut a thin slice off bottom of onions so they will sit flat). Pour broth over onion. Cover with heavy-duty plastic wrap, and vent. Microwave at HIGH 10 minutes, rotating dish a half-turn after 5 minutes.

Combine cracker crumbs and next 3 ingredients; sprinkle crumb mixture evenly over onion halves. Sprinkle evenly with cheese. Broil 5½ inches from heat (with electric oven door partially opened) 2 minutes or until cheese melts. Serve immediately. Yield: 4 servings.

Per Serving:

Calories 118	Carbohydrate 12.8g	Fiber 2.0g
Fat 5.5g	Cholesterol 7mg	Calcium 147mg
Protein 5.2g	Sodium 102mg	Iron 0.3mg

Exchanges: ½ Starch, 1 Vegetable, 1 Fat

Don't Cry

If Vidalia onions aren't available, look for other sweet onions like Walla Walla or Maui.

Sautéed Peppers and Onions

SuperQuick

Prep time: 10 minutes   Cook time: 6 minutes

- 1 large onion
- 1 large green pepper
- 1 large sweet red pepper
- 1 large sweet yellow pepper
  Vegetable cooking spray
- 2 teaspoons olive oil
- ¼ teaspoon dried thyme
- ⅛ teaspoon salt
- ⅛ teaspoon pepper

Cut onion into ¼-inch slices, and separate into rings. Slice peppers into ¼-inch rings; remove and discard membranes and seeds.

Coat a large nonstick skillet with cooking spray; add oil. Place over medium-high heat until hot. Add onion and pepper slices; sauté 6 to 8 minutes or until crisp-tender. Sprinkle with thyme, salt, and ⅛ teaspoon pepper. Yield: 4 servings.

Per Serving:

Calories 75	Carbohydrate 12.5g	Fiber 0.8g
Fat 2.9g	Cholesterol 0mg	Calcium 39mg
Protein 1.9g	Sodium 75mg	Iron 1.2mg

Exchanges: 2 Vegetable, ½ Fat

Mexican Potato Cakes

SuperQuick

Prep time: 12 minutes   Cook time: 8 minutes

- 4 cups frozen shredded hash browns, thawed
- ½ cup frozen chopped onion, thawed
- ⅓ cup (1.3 ounces) shredded Monterey Jack cheese with peppers
- 3 tablespoons all-purpose flour
- 2 tablespoons seeded and chopped jalapeño pepper
- 2 teaspoons chili powder
- ½ teaspoon salt
- ½ teaspoon freshly ground pepper
- 1 egg, beaten
  Olive oil-flavored vegetable cooking spray

Combine first 9 ingredients in a medium bowl. Shape potato mixture into 8 patties.

Coat a large nonstick skillet with cooking spray; place over medium-high heat until hot. Add potato patties, and cook 4 minutes on each side or until browned. Yield: 8 servings.

Per Serving:

Calories 84	Carbohydrate 12.9g	Fiber 0.7g
Fat 2.3g	Cholesterol 31mg	Calcium 48mg
Protein 3.1g	Sodium 191mg	Iron 0.8mg

Exchanges: 1 Starch, ½ Fat

The Skinny on Hash Browns

For these potato cakes make sure you buy frozen shredded hash browns without added salt or fat.

O'Brien Potato Casserole

Prep time: 7 minutes   Cook time: 45 minutes

1   (24-ounce) package frozen hash browns
      with onions and peppers, thawed
1   (10¾-ounce) can reduced-fat, reduced-
      sodium cream of mushroom soup,
      undiluted
1   (2-ounce) jar diced pimiento, drained
⅔   cup 1% low-fat milk
½   cup low-fat sour cream
½   teaspoon salt
2   cloves garlic, minced
      Vegetable cooking spray
½   cup soft reduced-calorie whole wheat
      breadcrumbs, toasted

Combine first 7 ingredients, stirring well. Spoon potato mixture into an 8-inch square baking dish coated with cooking spray. Sprinkle breadcrumbs over top of potato mixture; bake at 350° for 45 to 50 minutes or until bubbly.
Yield: 8 (¾-cup) servings.

Per Serving:

Calories 118	Carbohydrate 20.8g	Fiber 2.6g
Fat 3.2g	Cholesterol 10mg	Calcium 45mg
Protein 3.1g	Sodium 346mg	Iron 0.2mg

Exchange: 1½ Starch

Breadcrumb Basics

Make soft breadcrumbs by tearing fresh or slightly stale bread into small pieces. If you need a large amount of soft breadcrumbs, use a food processor to crumble several slices of bread at one time.

Roasted Red Potatoes

Prep time: 5 minutes   Cook time: 28 minutes

16   small round red potatoes, quartered
1   tablespoon vegetable oil
½   teaspoon garlic powder
½   teaspoon onion powder
¼   teaspoon salt
⅛   teaspoon ground red pepper
⅛   teaspoon paprika

Place potato in a 13- x 9- x 2-inch pan. Add oil and remaining ingredients; toss well. Bake at 450° for 28 minutes or until tender and browned. Yield: 6 servings.

Per Serving:

Calories 178	Carbohydrate 35.5g	Fiber 3.8g
Fat 2.5g	Cholesterol 0mg	Calcium 29mg
Protein 4.7g	Sodium 210mg	Iron 2.8mg

Exchanges: 2 Starch, ½ Fat

Roasted Red Potatoes

Scalloped Potato and Leeks

Prep time: 18 minutes   Cook time: 25 minutes

Vegetable cooking spray
2 cups thinly sliced leek
2 cloves garlic, minced
1½ tablespoons margarine
2½ tablespoons all-purpose flour
2 cups skim milk
½ teaspoon salt
½ teaspoon ground red pepper
¼ teaspoon ground white pepper
6 cups frozen diced potato, thawed
1 cup (4 ounces) shredded Gruyère cheese
2 tablespoons freshly grated Parmesan cheese

Coat a Dutch oven with cooking spray; place over medium heat until hot. Add leek and garlic; sauté until tender. Remove leek mixture from Dutch oven, and set aside.

Melt margarine in Dutch oven over low heat; add flour, stirring until smooth. Gradually add milk, stirring constantly with a wire whisk. Cook over medium heat, stirring constantly, until mixture is slightly thickened and bubbly. Stir in salt, red pepper, and white pepper. Return leek mixture to Dutch oven. Add potato, stirring to combine.

Spoon half of potato mixture into an 11- x 7- x 1½-inch baking dish coated with cooking spray. Top with half of Gruyère cheese. Repeat layers with remaining half of potato mixture and Gruyère cheese. Sprinkle with Parmesan cheese. Bake at 400° for 25 to 30 minutes or until bubbly and golden. Yield: 14 servings.

Per Serving:

Calories 123	Carbohydrate 16.1g	Fiber 0.5g
Fat 4.3g	Cholesterol 10mg	Calcium 152mg
Protein 5.1g	Sodium 167mg	Iron 0.8mg

Exchanges: 1 Starch, 1 Fat

Sweet Potato Wedges

SuperQuick

Prep time: 12 minutes   Cook time: 6 minutes

1 tablespoon margarine
1 tablespoon unsweetened orange juice
¼ teaspoon ground cinnamon
2 medium sweet potatoes (about 1 pound), peeled and each cut lengthwise into 8 wedges

Place margarine in an 8-inch square baking dish; microwave at HIGH 30 seconds or until melted. Stir in orange juice and cinnamon; add potato, tossing to coat. Cover with wax paper. Microwave at HIGH 6 to 8 minutes or until tender, stirring after 3 minutes. Yield: 4 servings.

Per Serving:

Calories 147	Carbohydrate 28.1g	Fiber 3.4g
Fat 3.2g	Cholesterol 0mg	Calcium 28mg
Protein 1.9g	Sodium 48mg	Iron 0.7mg

Exchanges: 1½ Starch, ½ Fat

Sweet Potato and Apple Casserole

Prep time: 20 minutes   Cook time: 1 hour

3   tablespoons sugar
½   teaspoon ground cinnamon
    Dash of ground white pepper
4   small sweet potatoes (about 1½ pounds), peeled and sliced
2   large red cooking apples (about 1 pound), cored and sliced lengthwise
    Vegetable cooking spray
2   tablespoons reduced-calorie margarine, melted

Combine first 3 ingredients; set aside.

Layer half each of sweet potato and apple in an 8-inch square baking dish coated with cooking spray; sprinkle with half of sugar mixture. Drizzle with half of margarine. Repeat layering procedure with remaining ingredients.

Cover and bake at 350° for 1 hour or until potato and apple are tender. Yield: 8 servings.

Per Serving:

Calories 153	Carbohydrate 33.3g	Fiber 4.2g
Fat 2.3g	Cholesterol 0mg	Calcium 24mg
Protein 1.4g	Sodium 38mg	Iron 0.6mg

Exchanges: 1 Starch, 1 Fruit, ½ Fat

Spinach with Dilled Feta

SuperQuick
Prep time: 10 minutes   Cook time: 5 minutes

1   tablespoon water
2   (10-ounce) packages fresh spinach
¼   cup crumbled feta cheese
2   tablespoons chopped fresh dillweed
1   tablespoon fresh lemon juice
⅛   teaspoon freshly ground pepper
    Lemon wedges (optional)

Place water and spinach in a Dutch oven. Bring to a boil; cover and cook over medium heat just until spinach wilts. Add cheese and next 3 ingredients; toss well. Serve with lemon wedges, if desired. Yield: 4 (1-cup) servings.

Per Serving:

Calories 52	Carbohydrate 5.9g	Fiber 5.7g
Fat 2.0g	Cholesterol 6mg	Calcium 185mg
Protein 5.2g	Sodium 192mg	Iron 4.2mg

Exchanges: ½ Medium-Fat Meat, 1 Vegetable

It's a Wash

Particles of dirt cling tightly to spinach, so it may be gritty if you don't wash it carefully. After washing, pinch the spiny stems from each leaf. Or, buy already-washed and trimmed spinach. Many markets wash, trim, and bag fresh produce to help save you time. Ready-to-use washed and trimmed spinach usually comes in 10-ounce packages, which are roughly equivalent to 1 pound of fresh untrimmed spinach or 2½ cups of torn spinach.

Tangy Greens and Onion

Prep time: 10 minutes   Cook time: 20 minutes

1   pound fresh turnip greens
     Vegetable cooking spray
1   teaspoon vegetable oil
½   cup diced onion
2   tablespoons balsamic vinegar
2   teaspoons sugar
½   teaspoon dried crushed red pepper
¼   teaspoon salt

Remove tough stems from greens, and wash thoroughly. Drain (do not pat dry). Place greens in a large Dutch oven (do not add water). Cover and cook over medium heat 8 to 10 minutes or until tender. Drain well; pat dry with paper towels. Coarsely chop greens, and set aside.

Coat a large nonstick skillet with cooking spray; add oil. Place over medium-high heat until hot. Add onion, and sauté 3 minutes or until tender. Add greens, vinegar, and remaining ingredients; stir well. Cook, uncovered, 5 minutes or until thoroughly heated. Yield: 4 (½-cup) servings.

Per Serving:

Calories 47	Carbohydrate 8.1g	Fiber 2.3g
Fat 1.6g	Cholesterol 0mg	Calcium 168mg
Protein 1.4g	Sodium 183mg	Iron 1.1mg

Exchange: 1 Vegetable

Savory Baked Tomatoes

SuperQuick

Prep time: 10 minutes   Cook time: 15 minutes

6   medium tomatoes
¼   teaspoon salt
3   tablespoons Italian-seasoned breadcrumbs
1   tablespoon grated Parmesan cheese
1   tablespoon chopped fresh parsley
⅛   teaspoon pepper
     Vegetable cooking spray

Cut off top of each tomato; discard tops. Sprinkle cut side of tomatoes with salt. Combine breadcrumbs, Parmesan cheese, chopped parsley, and pepper; sprinkle evenly over tomatoes. Place tomatoes in an 11- x 7- x 1½-inch baking dish coated with cooking spray. Bake at 350° for 15 to 20 minutes or until thoroughly heated.
Yield: 6 servings.

Per Serving:

Calories 44	Carbohydrate 8.4g	Fiber 1.7g
Fat 0.9g	Cholesterol 1mg	Calcium 22mg
Protein 1.9g	Sodium 224mg	Iron 0.7mg

Exchange: 1 Vegetable

Fresh from the Vine

You get more than just great flavor and juiciness when tomatoes are at their peak of ripeness. You also get a hefty helping of vitamins A and C, which may reduce the risk of some types of cancer. Research shows that tomatoes also contain lycopene, a substance that studies suggest may have cancer-fighting properties.

Grilled Zucchini Slices

SuperQuick

Prep time: 10 minutes   Cook time: 5 minutes

3   large zucchini
⅓   cup canned no-salt-added chicken broth
2   tablespoons low-sodium soy sauce
2   tablespoons balsamic vinegar
½   teaspoon garlic powder
     Vegetable cooking spray

Slice zucchini lengthwise into ¼-inch-thick slices.

Combine broth and next 3 ingredients; brush over zucchini slices. Coat grill rack with cooking spray; place on grill over medium-hot coals (350° to 400°). Place zucchini slices on rack, and grill, uncovered, 2 minutes on each side or until tender, brushing often with broth mixture.
Yield: 4 servings.

Per Serving:

Calories 30	Carbohydrate 4.9g	Fiber 0.8g
Fat 0.5g	Cholesterol 0mg	Calcium 24mg
Protein 2.0g	Sodium 211mg	Iron 0.7mg

Exchange: 1 Vegetable

Zucchini Italienne

SuperQuick

Prep time: 10 minutes   Cook time: 3 minutes

     Vegetable cooking spray
5   cups sliced zucchini (about 4 medium)
2   cups diced tomato
1   tablespoon minced fresh basil or 1 teaspoon dried basil
1½   teaspoons minced fresh oregano or ½ teaspoon dried oregano
½   cup (2 ounces) shredded part-skim mozzarella cheese
     Fresh basil sprig (optional)

Coat a large nonstick skillet with cooking spray; place over medium-high heat until hot. Add zucchini, and sauté 3 to 4 minutes or until crisp-tender. Add tomato, minced basil, and oregano; cook until thoroughly heated. Transfer to a serving dish, and sprinkle with cheese. Garnish with basil sprig, if desired. Yield: 4 servings.

Per Serving:

Calories 86	Carbohydrate 10.6g	Fiber 2.2g
Fat 3.0g	Cholesterol 8mg	Calcium 130mg
Protein 6.5g	Sodium 81mg	Iron 1.3mg

Exchanges: 2 Vegetable, ½ Fat

Grilled Summer Vegetables

Grilled Summer Vegetables

SuperQuick

Prep time: 6 minutes   Cook time: 10 minutes

1   medium-size sweet red pepper, cut into 6 strips
1   small eggplant (about ½ pound), cut crosswise into slices (½ inch thick)
1   small zucchini, quartered lengthwise
1   small yellow squash, quartered lengthwise
3   tablespoons red wine vinegar
1   tablespoon olive oil
½   teaspoon dried oregano
⅛   teaspoon pepper
    Vegetable cooking spray
¼   teaspoon salt

Combine first 4 ingredients.

Combine vinegar and next 3 ingredients in a small bowl; stir well with a wire whisk. Brush vegetables with vinegar mixture.

Coat grill rack with cooking spray; place on grill over medium-hot coals (350° to 400°). Place vegetables on rack, and grill, uncovered, 5 minutes on each side or until crisp-tender, turning once. Transfer to a serving platter; sprinkle with salt. Yield: 4 servings.

Per Serving:

Calories 66	Carbohydrate 7.9g	Fiber 2.0g
Fat 3.8g	Cholesterol 0mg	Calcium 38mg
Protein 1.7g	Sodium 151mg	Iron 1.0mg

Exchanges: 1½ Vegetable, ½ Fat

Zucchini with Baby Carrots

SuperQuick

Prep time: 8 minutes   Cook time: 10 minutes

2   medium zucchini
¾   cup fresh baby carrots
⅓   cup water
¼   teaspoon chicken-flavored bouillon granules
¼   teaspoon dried Italian seasoning
¼   teaspoon coarsely ground pepper
⅛   teaspoon garlic powder

Cut zucchini crosswise into ½-inch-thick diagonal slices. Set aside.

Combine carrots and remaining 5 ingredients in a large nonstick skillet; bring to a boil. Cover, reduce heat, and simmer 5 minutes, stirring occasionally. Add zucchini; cover and cook 3 to 4 minutes or until vegetables are crisp-tender, stirring occasionally. Yield: 5 (1-cup) servings.

Per Serving:

Calories 37	Carbohydrate 8.4g	Fiber 2.3g
Fat 0.3g	Cholesterol 0mg	Calcium 31mg
Protein 1.6g	Sodium 61mg	Iron 0.7mg

Exchange: 1½ Vegetable

Pasta in Creamy Wine Sauce (page 195)

Spicy Grilled Lamb Chops (page 194)

Quick Menus

Strawberry Spritzer (page 194)

Grilled Vegetable Kabobs (page 195)

Dinner on the Patio
(photo on page 193)

Strawberry Spritzer (1 cup)
Spicy Grilled Lamb Chops
Pasta in Creamy Wine Sauce
Grilled Vegetable Kabobs (2 skewers)

Serves 4
Total calories per serving: 691
30% calories from fat
Dinner on the table in: 50 minutes

Strawberry Spritzer

2   (16-ounce) packages frozen unsweetened
    strawberries, thawed
1   (48-ounce) bottle white grape juice, chilled
1   (25-ounce) bottle sparkling water, chilled

Place strawberries in container of an electric
blender; cover and process until smooth. Combine
strawberry puree, grape juice, and sparkling water
in a large pitcher; stir well. Serve immediately.
Yield: 13 (1-cup) servings.

Per Serving:

Calories 99	Carbohydrate 24.7g	Fiber 0.6g
Fat 0.1g	Cholesterol 0mg	Calcium 30mg
Protein 0.7g	Sodium 6mg	Iron 0.8mg

Exchange: 1½ Fruit

Spicy Grilled Lamb Chops

8   (4-ounce) lean lamb loin chops (1 inch
    thick)
1   teaspoon ground ginger
½   teaspoon ground coriander
½   teaspoon ground cumin
¼   teaspoon ground cloves
¼   teaspoon ground red pepper
¼   teaspoon black pepper
    Vegetable cooking spray

Trim fat from chops. Combine ginger and
next 5 ingredients; stir well. Rub chops with ginger
mixture. Cover and marinate in refrigerator at least
15 minutes.

Coat grill rack with cooking spray; place on
grill over medium-hot coals (350° to 400°). Place
chops on rack, and grill, covered, 8 to 10 minutes
on each side or to desired degree of doneness.
Yield: 4 servings.

Per Serving:

Calories 250	Carbohydrate 0.7g	Fiber 0.1g
Fat 11.3g	Cholesterol 108mg	Calcium 27mg
Protein 34.1g	Sodium 96mg	Iron 2.6mg

Exchange: 4 Lean Meat

Pasta in Creamy Wine Sauce

6 ounces angel hair pasta, uncooked
Vegetable cooking spray
1 clove garlic, minced
¼ cup chopped green onions
¼ cup dry white wine
¼ cup light process cream cheese
½ cup low-fat sour cream
¼ teaspoon salt
¼ teaspoon freshly ground pepper
2 tablespoons freshly grated Parmesan cheese

Cook pasta according to package directions, omitting salt and fat; drain. Set aside; keep warm.

Coat a small nonstick skillet with cooking spray; place over medium heat until hot. Add garlic and green onions; sauté until tender. Add wine; bring to a boil. Reduce heat, and simmer, uncovered, 3 minutes or until liquid is reduced by half. Set aside, and keep warm.

Place cream cheese in a small saucepan; cook over low heat, stirring constantly, 2 minutes or until melted. Add sour cream, salt, and pepper, stirring until thoroughly heated. Stir in wine mixture.

Place pasta in a serving bowl. Add cheese mixture; toss well. Sprinkle with grated cheese. Serve immediately. Yield: 4 (¾-cup) servings.

Per Serving:

Calories 255	Carbohydrate 34.9g	Fiber 1.2g
Fat 7.6g	Cholesterol 22mg	Calcium 100mg
Protein 9.0g	Sodium 289mg	Iron 1.9mg

Exchanges: ½ Lean Meat, 2 Starch, 1 Fat

Grilled Vegetable Kabobs

½ cup balsamic vinegar
1 tablespoon olive oil
½ teaspoon dried basil
½ teaspoon garlic powder
¼ teaspoon pepper
2 medium onions, quartered
1 medium zucchini, cut into 8 pieces
1 medium-size sweet yellow pepper, cut into 1½-inch pieces
1 medium-size sweet red pepper, cut into 1½-inch pieces
Vegetable cooking spray

Soak 8 (6-inch) wooden skewers in water at least 30 minutes. Set aside.

Combine first 5 ingredients in a large bowl. Add onion, zucchini, and sweet peppers; toss gently to coat. Cover and marinate in refrigerator at least 15 minutes, stirring occasionally. Remove vegetables from marinade, using a slotted spoon; reserve marinade.

Thread onion, zucchini, and sweet peppers alternately onto skewers. Coat grill rack with cooking spray; place on grill over medium-hot coals (350° to 400°). Place kabobs on rack; grill, covered, 12 to 16 minutes or until tender, turning and basting occasionally with marinade. Serve warm. Yield: 4 servings.

Per Serving:

Calories 87	Carbohydrate 12.6g	Fiber 2.9g
Fat 4.0g	Cholesterol 0mg	Calcium 31mg
Protein 2.2g	Sodium 7mg	Iron 1.7mg

Exchanges: 2 Vegetables, ½ Fat

Meal Plan for Dinner on the Patio

- First, soak the skewers for Grilled Vegetable Kabobs. Meanwhile, cut up and marinate the vegetables.

- Prepare Spicy Grilled Lamb Chops, and marinate in refrigerator.

- Thread vegetables onto skewers, and cook the pasta for Pasta in Creamy Wine Sauce.

- Place the vegetables and meat on the grill at the same time.

- While these are grilling, finish the pasta recipe.

- Prepare Strawberry Spritzer just before serving.

Marinated Pasta Salad (page 198)

Broccoli with Creamy Chive Sauce (page 198)

Chicken Piccata (opposite page)

Fast, Fresh Family Supper

Chicken Piccata
Broccoli with Creamy Chive Sauce
Marinated Pasta Salad

Serves 4
Total calories per serving: 309
26% calories from fat
Supper on the table in: 1 hour

Chicken Piccata

4 (4-ounce) skinned, boned chicken breast
    halves
2 tablespoons all-purpose flour
1 teaspoon paprika
⅛ teaspoon ground red pepper
    Vegetable cooking spray
2 tablespoons dry white wine
2 tablespoons lemon juice
2 teaspoons reduced-calorie margarine
½ teaspoon chicken-flavored bouillon granules
1 tablespoon chopped fresh parsley
    Lemon wedges (optional)

Place chicken between 2 sheets of heavy-duty plastic wrap, and flatten to ¼-inch thickness, using a meat mallet or rolling pin. Combine flour, paprika, and pepper in a shallow bowl; dredge chicken in flour mixture.

Coat a large nonstick skillet with cooking spray; place over medium-high heat until hot. Add chicken, and cook 3 minutes on each side or until done. Remove to a serving platter, and keep warm.

Add wine, lemon juice, margarine, and bouillon granules to skillet. Cook, stirring constantly, 1 minute or until margarine melts. To serve, drizzle wine mixture over chicken, and sprinkle with chopped parsley. Garnish with lemon wedges, if desired. Yield: 4 servings.

Per Serving:

Calories 160	Carbohydrate 4.2g	Fiber 0.3g
Fat 3.0g	Cholesterol 66mg	Calcium 17mg
Protein 26.8g	Sodium 196mg	Iron 1.2mg

Exchange: 4 Very Lean Meat

Meal Plan for Fast, Fresh Family Supper

- Prepare Marinated Pasta Salad, and let it chill at least 1 hour.

- Microwave the broccoli for Broccoli with Creamy Chive Sauce. Set aside; keep warm.

- Prepare Chicken Piccata; keep warm.

- Prepare sauce for broccoli; drizzle over broccoli, and serve supper.

Broccoli with Creamy Chive Sauce

2 (10-ounce) packages frozen broccoli spears, thawed
⅓ cup water
½ teaspoon chicken-flavored bouillon granules
1 tablespoon reduced-calorie margarine
1 tablespoon all-purpose flour
 Dash of ground white pepper
2½ tablespoons skim milk
1½ teaspoons freeze-dried chives
¾ teaspoon lemon juice
½ teaspoon prepared mustard

Arrange broccoli spears crosswise in an 11- x 7- x 1½-inch baking dish. Cover with heavy-duty plastic wrap, and vent. Microwave at HIGH 6 to 8 minutes.

Place water in a 1-cup glass measure, and microwave, uncovered, at HIGH 40 seconds. Add bouillon granules, stirring until dissolved. Set aside.

Place margarine in a 1-cup glass measure; microwave, uncovered, at HIGH 10 seconds or until margarine melts. Add flour and pepper; stir well. Add reserved bouillon and milk; stir until smooth. Microwave at HIGH 1 to 2 minutes or until thickened and bubbly, stirring after 1 minute. Stir in chives, lemon juice, and mustard.

Drain broccoli, and transfer to serving plates. Drizzle sauce over broccoli. Yield: 4 servings.

Per Serving:

Calories 69	Carbohydrate 9.7g	Fiber 3.0g
Fat 2.4g	Cholesterol 0mg	Calcium 71mg
Protein 5.0g	Sodium 167mg	Iron 1.1mg

Exchanges: 2 Vegetable, ½ Fat

Marinated Pasta Salad

3 ounces bow tie pasta, uncooked
1 cup chopped tomato
1 small onion, cut in half vertically and thinly sliced
3 tablespoons small ripe olives, halved
1 tablespoon chopped fresh parsley
1 tablespoon white wine vinegar
2 teaspoons olive oil
½ teaspoon dried basil
½ teaspoon dried oregano
½ teaspoon pepper
¼ teaspoon salt

Cook pasta according to package directions, omitting salt and fat. Rinse with cold water, and drain well.

Combine pasta and remaining ingredients in a medium bowl; toss gently. Cover and chill at least 1 hour. Yield: 4 servings.

Per Serving:

Calories 80	Carbohydrate 11.3g	Fiber 1.8g
Fat 3.4g	Cholesterol 0mg	Calcium 24mg
Protein 1.9g	Sodium 215mg	Iron 1.1mg

Exchanges: ½ Starch, 1 Vegetable, ½ Fat

Casual Weekend Dinner

Individual Chicken Pot Pies (page 200)

Casual Weekend Dinner

Individual Chicken Pot Pies
Tomatoes Vinaigrette
Chocolate-Cinnamon Cake (1 wedge)
Serves 4
Total calories per serving: 538
23% calories from fat
Dinner on the table in: 1 hour

Individual Chicken Pot Pies

1   (10¾-ounce) can low-sodium cream of
      chicken soup, undiluted
1   cup water
¾   teaspoon poultry seasoning
2   cups diced cooked chicken breast
1   (10-ounce) package frozen mixed vegetables,
      thawed
¾   cup sliced fresh mushrooms
      Vegetable cooking spray
¾   cup self-rising flour
1   tablespoon margarine
¼   cup plus 2 tablespoons skim milk

Combine soup, water, and poultry seasoning
in a medium bowl; stir well. Add chicken, mixed
vegetables, and mushrooms, and stir well.

Spoon chicken mixture evenly into 4 individual baking dishes coated with cooking spray.
Place flour in a bowl; cut in margarine with
pastry blender until mixture resembles coarse
meal. Stir in skim milk. Divide dough into 4 equal
portions; drop 1 portion over each serving. Bake at
450° for 12 minutes or until golden. Yield: 4 servings.

Per Serving:

Calories 317	Carbohydrate 27.0g	Fiber 0.3g
Fat 7.3g	Cholesterol 75mg	Calcium 123mg
Protein 30.4g	Sodium 701mg	Iron 2.2mg

Exchanges: 3 Very Lean Meat, 2 Starch, 1 Fat

Meal Plan for Casual Weekend Dinner

• Prepare Tomatoes Vinaigrette, and chill at least 30 minutes.

• Next prepare Chocolate-Cinnamon Cake and, while it bakes, assemble
  Individual Chicken Pot Pies.

• While the cake cools, bake the pot pies.

Tomatoes Vinaigrette

⅓ cup water
3 tablespoons cider vinegar
1 tablespoon chopped purple onion
¼ teaspoon ground coriander
⅛ teaspoon sugar
⅛ teaspoon dry mustard
⅛ teaspoon paprika
   Dash of chili powder
   Dash of garlic powder
2 medium tomatoes, cut into ¼-inch slices
   Green leaf lettuce (optional)

Combine first 9 ingredients. Place tomato in an 11- x 7- x 1½-inch baking dish. Pour vinegar mixture over tomato. Cover and marinate in refrigerator at least 30 minutes. Serve with a slotted spoon. Serve on individual lettuce-lined salad plates, if desired. Yield: 4 servings.

Per Serving:

Calories 17	Carbohydrate 4.0g	Fiber 0.9g
Fat 0.2g	Cholesterol 0mg	Calcium 5mg
Protein 0.6g	Sodium 6mg	Iron 0.4mg

Exchange: ½ Vegetable

Chocolate-Cinnamon Cake

½ cup nonfat buttermilk
3 tablespoons vegetable oil
1 egg
¾ cup all-purpose flour
½ teaspoon baking soda
⅔ cup firmly packed brown sugar
3 tablespoons unsweetened cocoa
½ teaspoon ground cinnamon
½ teaspoon vanilla extract
   Vegetable cooking spray
⅓ cup regular oats, uncooked
2 tablespoons brown sugar
   Dash of ground cinnamon

Combine buttermilk, oil, and egg in a medium bowl; beat at low speed of an electric mixer 1 minute. Combine flour and next 4 ingredients; add to buttermilk mixture. Beat at low speed just until blended. Beat at high speed 2 additional minutes. Stir in vanilla. Pour batter into an 8-inch round cakepan coated with cooking spray.

Combine oats, 2 tablespoons brown sugar, and dash of cinnamon; sprinkle over batter. Bake at 350° for 25 minutes or until a wooden pick inserted in center comes out clean. Cool in pan 10 minutes. Cut into 8 wedges. Yield: 8 servings.

Per Wedge:

Calories 204	Carbohydrate 33.2g	Fiber 0.7g
Fat 6.5g	Cholesterol 28mg	Calcium 47mg
Protein 3.7g	Sodium 112mg	Iron 1.6mg

Exchanges: 2 Starch, 1 Fat

Garlic Mashed Potatoes (opposite page)

Lemon green beans (page 204)

Salsa Meat Loaf (opposite page)

Down-Home Supper

Salsa Meat Loaf (1 serving)
Garlic Mashed Potatoes
Lemon green beans (1 cup)
Chocolate Silk Pudding
Serves 4
Total calories per serving: 507
18% calories from fat
Supper on the table in: 1 hour, 5 minutes

Salsa Meat Loaf

1   pound ground round
1   cup salsa, divided
⅔   cup soft whole wheat breadcrumbs
1   egg white, lightly beaten
¼   teaspoon salt
¼   teaspoon rubbed sage
¼   teaspoon pepper
    Vegetable cooking spray

Combine meat, ½ cup salsa, breadcrumbs, and next 4 ingredients in a large bowl. Shape mixture into a 6- x 4-inch loaf, and place on a rack coated with cooking spray. Place rack in a roasting pan. Bake at 400° for 55 minutes. Brush remaining ½ cup salsa over loaf, and bake 5 additional minutes. Let stand 5 minutes before slicing. Yield: 6 servings.

Per Serving:

Calories 126	Carbohydrate 4.5g	Fiber 1.0g
Fat 3.4g	Cholesterol 43mg	Calcium 28mg
Protein 18.8g	Sodium 282mg	Iron 2.0mg

Exchanges: 3 Very Lean Meat, 1 Vegetable

Garlic Mashed Potatoes

4   medium baking potatoes, peeled and cubed (about 2 pounds)
3   large cloves garlic, peeled and halved
¼   cup nonfat sour cream
2   tablespoons skim milk
1   tablespoon reduced-calorie margarine
½   teaspoon salt
    Dash of ground white pepper

Place potato and garlic in a large saucepan; add water to cover. Bring to a boil; cover, reduce heat, and simmer 20 minutes or until tender. Drain potato and garlic; transfer to a large bowl. Beat potato and garlic at medium speed of an electric mixer 1 minute or until smooth. Add sour cream and remaining ingredients, beating well. Yield: 4 servings.

Per Serving:

Calories 163	Carbohydrate 30.3g	Fiber 4.1g
Fat 2.1g	Cholesterol 0mg	Calcium 82mg
Protein 7.2g	Sodium 357mg	Iron 7.4mg

Exchange: 2 Starch

Meal Plan for Down-Home Supper

- Prepare the Chocolate Silk Pudding and chill at least 1 hour.

- Prepare Salsa Meat Loaf and, while it bakes, make Garlic Mashed Potatoes, and steam the green beans. You'll even have a couple of slices of meat loaf left over for a sandwich tomorrow.

Lemon Green Beans in a Flash

Preserve flavor, texture, and nutrients by cooking fresh vegetables in a steamer basket. Steaming allows vegetables to cook without the addition of fat and, because the food is not cooked in water, vitamin loss is minimal. Add herbs or spices to the water to infuse the vegetables with additional flavor.

To steam fresh green beans for this menu, trim 1 pound beans. Wash and arrange in a steamer basket over boiling water. Cover and steam 5 to 8 minutes or until crisp-tender. Drain beans, and sprinkle with 2 teaspoons grated lemon rind.

Chocolate Silk Pudding

- 2 cups skim milk
- ⅓ cup sugar
- 3 tablespoons unsweetened cocoa
- 3 tablespoons cornstarch
- 1½ tablespoons reduced-calorie margarine
- ½ teaspoon vanilla extract
- ¼ teaspoon almond extract
- 1 tablespoon plus 1 teaspoon sliced almonds, toasted

Place milk in a 1½-quart glass measure. Microwave, uncovered, at HIGH 3 to 3½ minutes or just until milk is hot, but not boiling. Combine sugar, cocoa, and cornstarch; stir into hot milk. Microwave, uncovered, at HIGH 3 minutes or until thickened, stirring after 1½ minutes. Add margarine and flavorings, stirring well. Spoon chocolate mixture evenly into 4 individual dessert dishes. Cover and chill at least 1 hour.

Top each serving with 1 teaspoon sliced almonds before serving. Yield: 4 (½-cup) servings.

Per Serving:

Calories 184	Carbohydrate 30.3g	Fiber 0.3g
Fat 4.5g	Cholesterol 3mg	Calcium 163mg
Protein 5.8g	Sodium 108mg	Iron 0.8mg

Exchanges: 2 Starch, 1 Fat

Southern-Style Supper

Calico Cornbread (page 207)

Crunchy Coleslaw (page 206)

Oven-Fried Catfish (page 206)

Southern-Style Supper

Oven-Fried Catfish
Crunchy Coleslaw
Calico Cornbread (1 wedge)
Banana Pudding

Serves 4
Total calories per serving: 577
23% calories from fat
Supper on the table in: 50 minutes

Oven-Fried Catfish

1 tablespoon reduced-calorie mayonnaise
1 tablespoon low-fat sour cream
1 teaspoon lemon juice
½ cup crushed corn flakes cereal
1 tablespoon dried parsley flakes
½ teaspoon paprika
¼ teaspoon pepper
¼ teaspoon garlic powder
4 (4-ounce) farm-raised catfish fillets
Vegetable cooking spray

Combine mayonnaise, sour cream, and lemon juice; stir well. Combine cereal and next 4 ingredients. Brush mayonnaise mixture evenly over fillets; dredge in cereal mixture.

Place fillets on rack of a broiler pan coated with cooking spray. Bake at 450° for 12 to 15 minutes or until fish flakes easily when tested with a fork. Yield: 4 servings.

Per Serving:

Calories 192	Carbohydrate 10.2g	Fiber 0.2g
Fat 6.5g	Cholesterol 68mg	Calcium 51mg
Protein 21.8g	Sodium 234mg	Iron 2.1mg

Exchanges: 3 Very Lean Meat, ½ Starch, ½ Fat

Crunchy Coleslaw

¼ cup plus 2 tablespoons cider vinegar
2 teaspoons vegetable oil
1 tablespoon plus 1 teaspoon sugar
1 teaspoon Dijon mustard
¼ teaspoon salt
¼ teaspoon ground white pepper
4 cups slaw mix
¼ cup chopped onion

Combine first 6 ingredients; stir well with a wire whisk.

Combine slaw mix and onion in a bowl; pour dressing mixture over slaw, and toss gently. Cover and chill. Yield: 4 (1-cup) servings.

Per Serving:

Calories 74	Carbohydrate 13.3g	Fiber 2.1g
Fat 2.4g	Cholesterol 0mg	Calcium 3mg
Protein 1.1g	Sodium 214mg	Iron 0.2mg

Exchanges: 2 Vegetable, ½ Fat

Calico Cornbread

1 cup all-purpose flour
⅔ cup yellow cornmeal
½ teaspoon baking soda
¼ teaspoon salt
1 tablespoon sugar
¼ teaspoon pepper
⅔ cup nonfat buttermilk
1 (7-ounce) can Mexican-style corn, drained
½ cup fresh or frozen chopped onion, thawed
2 tablespoons margarine, melted
1 egg, lightly beaten
   Vegetable cooking spray

Place a 9-inch cast-iron skillet in a 450° oven 5 minutes or until hot.

Combine first 6 ingredients in a large bowl; make a well in center of mixture. Combine buttermilk and next 4 ingredients; add to dry ingredients, stirring just until moistened.

Coat skillet with cooking spray; immediately pour batter into hot skillet. Bake at 450° for 20 minutes or until golden. Cut into 10 wedges. Yield: 10 servings.

Per Wedge:

Calories 136	Carbohydrate 22.2g	Fiber 1.4g
Fat 3.5g	Cholesterol 23mg	Calcium 48mg
Protein 4.3g	Sodium 245mg	Iron 1.1mg

Exchanges: 1½ Starch, ½ Fat

Banana Pudding

1 tablespoon sugar
2 teaspoons cornstarch
1 egg, separated
¾ cup plus 2 tablespoons skim milk
¼ teaspoon vanilla extract
16 reduced-fat vanilla wafers
1 large banana, sliced (1 cup)
1 egg white
   Dash of cream of tartar
1 tablespoon sugar

Combine 1 tablespoon sugar and cornstarch in a small heavy saucepan. Beat egg yolk; combine egg yolk and milk, mixing well. Stir into dry ingredients; cook over medium heat, stirring constantly, until smooth and thickened. Remove from heat; stir in vanilla. Let cool.

Arrange wafers in bottom and around sides of a 1-quart baking dish. Combine pudding mixture and banana; stir gently. Spoon over wafers.

Beat 2 egg whites and cream of tartar at high speed of an electric mixer until foamy. Gradually add 1 tablespoon sugar, beating until stiff peaks form and sugar dissolves (2 to 4 minutes). Spread meringue over pudding mixture, sealing to edge of dish. Bake at 325° for 15 minutes. Yield: 4 servings.

Per Serving:

Calories 175	Carbohydrate 33.2g	Fiber 1.4g
Fat 2.6g	Cholesterol 56mg	Calcium 76mg
Protein 5.3g	Sodium 111mg	Iron 0.4mg

Exchanges: 2 Starch, ½ Fat

Meal Plan for Southern-Style Supper

• Prepare Banana Pudding.

• While pudding bakes, make Crunchy Coleslaw, and place it in the refrigerator to chill.

• Next, prepare Calico Cornbread, and while it bakes, assemble the Oven-Fried Catfish.

• When the cornbread is finished baking, bake the catfish.

Tossed Greens and Grilled Vegetables (page 210)

Honey-Ginger Pork Tenderloins (opposite page)

Grill Out Tonight

Honey-Ginger Pork Tenderloins
Tossed Greens and Grilled Vegetables
French Bread (1 slice)

Serves 4
Total calories per serving: 352
21% calories from fat
Dinner on the table in: 35 minutes

Honey-Ginger Pork Tenderloins

2 (½-pound) pork tenderloins
¼ cup plus 2 tablespoons low-sodium soy sauce
3 tablespoons honey
1 tablespoon peeled, minced gingerroot
1 tablespoon minced garlic
1 tablespoon reduced-calorie ketchup
¼ teaspoon onion powder
¼ teaspoon ground red pepper
¼ teaspoon ground cinnamon
Vegetable cooking spray

Place pork in an 11- x 7- x 1½-inch baking dish. Combine soy sauce and next 7 ingredients, stirring well; pour over pork. Cover and marinate in refrigerator at least 15 minutes, turning once.

Remove pork from marinade, reserving marinade. Coat grill rack with cooking spray; place on grill over medium-hot coals (350° to 400°). Place pork on rack. Cook 20 to 25 minutes, turning often. Let pork stand 10 minutes. Slice diagonally across grain into thin slices, and transfer to a serving platter.

Place reserved marinade in a saucepan; bring to a boil. Remove from heat. Spoon evenly over pork. Yield: 4 servings.

Per Serving:

Calories 212	Carbohydrate 14.1g	Fiber 0.1g
Fat 4.5g	Cholesterol 83mg	Calcium 13mg
Protein 25.9g	Sodium 646mg	Iron 1.5mg

Exchanges: 3 Lean Meat, 1 Starch

Meal Plan for Grill Out Tonight

• Marinate Honey-Ginger Pork Tenderloins in the refrigerator at least 15 minutes.

• Meanwhile, prepare the salad dressing for Tossed Greens and Grilled Vegetables; cut vegetables, and wash greens for salad.

• Put pork and vegetables on the grill, and cook. After 8 to 10 minutes remove the vegetables, and let cool while pork continues to cook.

• Toss salad, and drizzle with dressing. Remove pork from the grill, and slice.

• Slice French bread.

Tossed Greens and Grilled Vegetables

2 tablespoons white wine vinegar
1 tablespoon water
2 teaspoons olive oil
1 teaspoon Dijon mustard
1 teaspoon dried basil
½ teaspoon dried oregano
½ teaspoon chicken-flavored bouillon granules
¼ teaspoon pepper
1 large yellow squash, halved lengthwise
½ small eggplant, halved lengthwise
  Vegetable cooking spray
3 cups torn Bibb lettuce
2 cups torn curly endive
8 cherry tomatoes, halved

Combine first 8 ingredients in a small bowl; stir well. Brush 1 tablespoon vinegar mixture evenly over squash and eggplant halves.

Coat grill rack with cooking spray; place on grill over medium-hot coals (350° to 400°). Place squash and eggplant on rack, and grill, uncovered, 8 to 10 minutes, turning often. Remove from grill, and set aside until cool enough to handle.

Cut squash and eggplant into 1-inch pieces; place in a salad bowl. Add lettuce, endive, and tomato halves; drizzle with remaining vinegar mixture, and toss gently. Yield: 4 (2-cup) servings.

Per Serving:

Calories 67	Carbohydrate 9.3g	Fiber 2.6g
Fat 3.1g	Cholesterol 0mg	Calcium 52mg
Protein 2.5g	Sodium 150mg	Iron 1.3mg

Exchanges: 2 Vegetable, ½ Fat

Garlic's Great

For a flavor-packed spread for French bread, try roasted garlic. Peel outer skin from each garlic head, and discard skin (do not peel or separate cloves). Cut off top one-third of each garlic head. Place garlic, cut side up, on a piece of heavy-duty aluminum foil. Fold foil over garlic, sealing tightly. Place garlic on grill rack, and cook, covered, 30 minutes or until garlic is soft. Let the garlic cool, and squeeze the pulp from the cloves. Spread garlic pulp on French bread slices.

Mexican Meal for Two

Taco Salad (page 212)

Mexican Meal for Two

Frozen Margaritas (1 serving)
Taco Salad

Serves 2
Total calories per serving: 478
19% calories from fat
Dinner on the table in: 35 minutes

Frozen Margaritas

2¾ cups water
1 cup tequila
1 (12-ounce) can frozen lemonade
   concentrate, thawed and undiluted
½ cup unsweetened orange juice
½ cup lime juice
   Lime wedges (optional)

Combine first 5 ingredients in a large container. Stir well. Cover and freeze at least 1 hour, stirring occasionally. To serve, stir mixture, and pour into chilled glasses. Garnish with lime wedges, if desired. Yield: 8 (¾-cup) servings.

Per Serving:

Calories 154	Carbohydrate 23.1g	Fiber 0.2g
Fat 0.1g	Cholesterol 0mg	Calcium 6mg
Protein 0.3g	Sodium 2mg	Iron 0.3mg

Exchange: **1½ Fruit**

Mock Margaritas

1 (6-ounce) can frozen lemonade concentrate,
   thawed and undiluted
1 (6-ounce) can frozen lime concentrate,
   thawed and undiluted
½ cup sifted powdered sugar
3¼ cups crushed ice
1½ cups club soda, chilled
Lime slices (optional)

Combine lemonade and limeade concentrates, powdered sugar, and crushed ice in a large plastic container; stir well. Cover and freeze.

Remove mixture from freezer 30 minutes before serving.

Spoon mixture into container of an electric blender; add club soda. Cover and process until smooth. Pour into glasses; garnish with lime slices, if desired. Yield: 6 (1-cup) servings.

Per Serving:

Calories 143	Carbohydrate 37.3g	Fiber 0.1g
Fat 0.1g	Cholesterol 0mg	Calcium 6mg
Protein 0.1g	Sodium 14mg	Iron 0.4mg

Exchange: **2 Fruit**

Meal Plan for Mexican Meal for Two

- For a head start, prepare Frozen Margaritas the night before, and freeze.

- Take the frozen margarita mixture out of the freezer about 30 minutes before serving to allow mixture to become slushy.

- Prepare meat mixture for Taco Salad. While meat cooks, assemble the rest of the salad ingredients.

- For a nonalcoholic drink, try Mock Margaritas for 467 calories per meal.

Taco Salad

2 (8-inch) flour tortillas
  Vegetable cooking spray
⅓ pound ground round
½ cup water
2 tablespoons chopped green onions
2 teaspoons chili powder
⅛ teaspoon ground cumin
2 cups shredded iceberg lettuce
¾ cup seeded, chopped tomato
2 tablespoons (½ ounce) reduced-fat shredded
  Cheddar cheese
2 tablespoons nonfat sour cream
½ cup no-salt-added salsa

Cut each tortilla into 8 wedges; place on a baking sheet. Bake at 350° for 10 to 12 minutes or until lightly browned. Set aside.

Coat a large nonstick skillet with cooking spray; place over medium-high heat until hot. Add ground round, and cook over medium heat until browned, stirring until meat crumbles. Drain and pat dry with paper towels. Wipe drippings from skillet with a paper towel.

Return meat to skillet; add water and next 3 ingredients, stirring well to combine. Bring to a boil; reduce heat, and simmer 10 minutes.

For each salad, layer half of tortilla wedges, shredded lettuce, meat mixture, and chopped tomato on each of 2 serving plates. Top each with 1 tablespoon cheese, 1 tablespoon sour cream, and ¼ cup salsa. Yield: 2 servings.

Per Serving:

Calories 324	Carbohydrate 35.4g	Fiber 3.8g
Fat 10.0g	Cholesterol 50mg	Calcium 155mg
Protein 23.9g	Sodium 427mg	Iron 4.3mg

Exchanges: 2 Lean Meat, 2 Starch, 2 Vegetable

Menu Helper

Main-dish salads can be easy, complete, one-dish-meal alternatives. With 10 grams of protein, this Taco Salad is a meal in itself.

As a general guide, add julienne-sliced beef, turkey, or ham (2 ounces per serving) to a green salad. Or mix the same amount of chicken or pork into your favorite low-fat potato salad. Create a main-dish pasta salad by adding cheese or cooked meat to a basic recipe. To enhance the flavor of cold leftover meat, heat it briefly in a nonstick skillet before adding it to your salad, even if the salad is chilled.

Hearty Fireside Dinner

Chunky Beef Stew
Savory Rosemary Muffins (1 each)

Serves 4
Total calories per serving: 396
20% calories from fat
Dinner on the table in: 50 minutes

Savory Rosemary Muffins (opposite page)

Chunky Beef Stew (opposite page)

Chunky Beef Stew

1   pound lean, boneless top round steak
2½ tablespoons all-purpose flour
⅛   teaspoon salt
⅛   teaspoon pepper
     Vegetable cooking spray
2   cups water
¾   cup coarsely chopped onion
2   teaspoons beef-flavored bouillon granules
½   teaspoon dried sage
¼   teaspoon dried thyme
2   bay leaves
¾   pound new potatoes, quartered
3   large stalks celery, diagonally cut into 1-inch
     pieces
2   large carrots, scraped and diagonally cut
     into 1-inch pieces

Trim fat from steak. Cut steak into 1-inch cubes. Combine flour, salt, and pepper; dredge steak in flour mixture, and set aside.

Coat a Dutch oven with cooking spray; place over medium-high heat until hot. Add steak, and cook until browned on all sides, stirring occasionally. Add water and remaining ingredients, stirring well. Bring to a boil; cover, reduce heat, and simmer 30 minutes or until vegetables are tender, stirring occasionally. Remove and discard bay leaves. Yield: 4 (1½-cup) servings.

Per Serving:

Calories 266	Carbohydrate 24.2g	Fiber 3.6g
Fat 5.3g	Cholesterol 65mg	Calcium 44mg
Protein 29.1g	Sodium 649mg	Iron 4.2mg

Exchanges: 3 Lean Meat, 1 Starch, 1 Vegetable

Savory Rosemary Muffins

¾   cup all-purpose flour
¼   cup whole wheat flour
1   teaspoon baking powder
⅛   teaspoon salt
¾   teaspoon dried rosemary
½   cup skim milk
1   tablespoon olive oil
1   tablespoon honey
1   egg, lightly beaten
     Vegetable cooking spray
1   tablespoon toasted wheat germ

Combine first 5 ingredients in a medium bowl; make a well in center of mixture. Combine milk, oil, honey, and egg; add to dry ingredients, stirring just until moistened. Spoon batter into muffin pans coated with cooking spray, filling two-thirds full. Sprinkle each muffin with ½ teaspoon wheat germ. Bake at 400° for 14 minutes. Remove from pans immediately. Yield: 6 muffins.

Per Muffin:

Calories 130	Carbohydrate 20.5g	Fiber 1.3g
Fat 3.6g	Cholesterol 37mg	Calcium 81mg
Protein 4.4g	Sodium 71mg	Iron 1.3mg

Exchanges: 1½ Starch, ½ Fat

Meal Plan for Hearty Fireside Dinner

• Make Chunky Beef Stew, and while it simmers, assemble the ingredients for the muffins.

• During the last 15 minutes the stew is simmering, bake Savory Rosemary Muffins to time perfectly for a steaming-hot meal.

Pizza-on-the-Grill (opposite page)

Italian Bistro Lunch

Pizza-on-the-Grill
Green Salad with Wine Vinaigrette
Serves 4
Total calories per serving: 363
29% calories from fat
Lunch on the table in: 35 minutes

Pizza-on-the-Grill

Vegetable cooking spray
¾ cup peeled, seeded, and chopped plum
    tomato (about 3 medium)
3 tablespoons evaporated skimmed milk
⅛ teaspoon garlic powder
1 (10-ounce) can refrigerated pizza dough
¼ cup torn fresh basil leaves
4 (¾-ounce) slices Canadian bacon, cut into
    thin strips
¾ cup (3 ounces) shredded part-skim
    mozzarella cheese

Coat a small nonstick skillet with cooking spray; place over medium-high heat until hot. Add tomato; sauté 2 minutes. Add milk. Bring mixture to a boil; reduce heat, and simmer 1 minute, stirring occasionally. Remove from heat, and stir in garlic powder. Set aside.

Roll dough into a 12- x 10-inch rectangle on a large piece of aluminum foil. Lightly coat pizza dough with cooking spray. Coat grill rack with cooking spray; place on grill over medium-hot coals (350° to 400°). Place dough, sprayed side down, on rack; remove foil. Grill, uncovered, 2 to 3 minutes or until top of crust is slightly set and bottom is lightly browned. (Pierce any air bubbles with a fork.)

Remove crust from grill. Lightly spray top of crust with cooking spray, and turn crust over. Spread tomato mixture over crust. Sprinkle with basil, and top with bacon. Sprinkle with cheese. Grill 3 to 5 additional minutes or until bottom is browned and cheese melts. Yield: 4 servings.

Per Serving:

Calories 292	Carbohydrate 38.4g	Fiber 1.8g
Fat 7.8g	Cholesterol 23mg	Calcium 181mg
Protein 17.0g	Sodium 808mg	Iron 0.5mg

Exchanges: 1 High-Fat Meat, 2 Starch, 1 Vegetable

Meal Plan for Italian Bistro Lunch

- Prepare the vinaigrette dressing for Green Salad with Wine Vinaigrette; chill.

- Make the pizza sauce for Pizza-on-the-Grill.

- Assemble the pizza, and grill. Combine lettuces and vegetables for salad; set aside. Drizzle salads with vinaigrette.

Green Salad with Wine Vinaigrette

2   cups torn Boston lettuce
2   cups torn romaine lettuce
½   cup alfalfa sprouts
1   small purple onion, thinly sliced and
      separated into rings
1   small cucumber, thinly sliced
3   tablespoons water
2   tablespoons white wine vinegar
1   tablespoon olive oil
1   teaspoon sugar
1   teaspoon lemon juice
¼   teaspoon pepper
⅛   teaspoon garlic powder

Place first 5 ingredients in large bowl, tossing gently to combine. Place 1½ cups lettuce mixture on each of 4 individual serving plates. Set aside.

Combine water and remaining 6 ingredients in a small bowl; stir vigorously with a wire whisk until blended. Pour vinegar mixture evenly over salads. Yield: 4 servings.

Per Serving:

Calories 71	Carbohydrate 7.9g	Fiber 2.5g
Fat 3.8g	Cholesterol 0mg	Calcium 33mg
Protein 2.7g	Sodium 11mg	Iron 1.1mg

Exchanges: 1½ Vegetable, ½ Fat

Homemade Vinegars

Making your own flavored vinegar is simple.

Step 1. Insert strips of citrus rind or a few sprigs of your favorite herb into clean, dry decorative bottles.

Step 2. For flavor and color variations, pour red or white wine vinegar, rice, cider, or champagne vinegar into the bottles. Avoid using sharp, flavorless white distilled vinegar.

Step 3. Cover and let vinegar stand at room temperature 2 weeks. Then pour it through a wire-mesh strainer (lined with cheesecloth, if necessary) into bottles, discarding rind or herbs. Seal bottles with corks or airtight lids. Store in refrigerator or a cool, dark place up to 6 months.

Company's Coming

Asparagus and Onion Toss (page 220)

Garlic Potato Wedges (page 221)

Sirloin with Sweet Red Pepper Relish (page 220)

Company's Coming

Sirloin with Sweet Red Pepper Relish
Asparagus and Onion Toss
Garlic Potato Wedges
Strawberry Sorbet (1 serving)

Serves 4
Total calories per serving: 448
24% calories from fat
Dinner on the table in: 50 minutes

Sirloin with Sweet Red Pepper Relish

1   cup finely chopped sweet red pepper
½   cup finely chopped onion
¼   cup white wine vinegar
3   tablespoons sugar
⅛   teaspoon black pepper
1   (1-pound) lean boneless beef sirloin steak
⅛   teaspoon salt
⅛   teaspoon black pepper
     Vegetable cooking spray

Combine first 5 ingredients in a small saucepan. Bring to a boil; cover, reduce heat, and simmer 8 to 10 minutes or until tender. Remove from heat; set aside, and keep warm.

Trim fat from meat. Cut meat into 4 equal pieces; sprinkle with salt and ⅛ teaspoon pepper. Place steaks on rack of a broiler pan coated with cooking spray. Broil 5½ inches from heat (with electric oven door partially opened) 6 to 8 minutes on each side or to desired degree of doneness. Transfer steaks to individual serving plates; top with relish, using a slotted spoon. Yield: 4 servings.

Per Serving:

Calories 221	Carbohydrate 12.7g	Fiber 0.9g
Fat 6.4g	Cholesterol 76mg	Calcium 15mg
Protein 26.3g	Sodium 133mg	Iron 3.4mg

Exchanges: 3 Lean Meat, ½ Starch, 1 Vegetable

Asparagus and Onion Toss

1   pound fresh asparagus spears
1   cup sliced green onions (about 4 green onions)
1   cup sliced radishes
¼   cup white wine vinegar
2   teaspoons olive oil
2   tablespoons water
½   teaspoon dried thyme
½   teaspoon dried basil
¼   teaspoon pepper
⅛   teaspoon salt

Snap off tough ends of asparagus. Remove scales from stalks with a vegetable peeler, if desired. Cut asparagus diagonally into 1½-inch pieces. Cook asparagus in boiling water to cover 3 minutes or until crisp-tender. Drain well; rinse with cold water, and drain again.

Combine asparagus, green onions, and radishes in a large bowl. Combine vinegar and remaining 6 ingredients in a small bowl; stir well with a wire whisk. Pour over vegetable mixture, tossing gently to coat. Cover and chill up to 2 hours. Yield: 4 (1-cup) servings.

Per Serving:

Calories 58	Carbohydrate 7.5g	Fiber 3.0g
Fat 2.7g	Cholesterol 0mg	Calcium 47mg
Protein 3.1g	Sodium 83mg	Iron 1.6mg

Exchanges: 1½ Vegetable, ½ Fat

Garlic Potato Wedges

2   medium baking potatoes (about 1 pound)
2   teaspoons olive oil
⅛   teaspoon salt
⅛   teaspoon garlic powder
⅛   teaspoon ground red pepper
⅛   teaspoon paprika
    Vegetable cooking spray

Scrub potatoes. Cut each into 12 wedges; brush with olive oil. Combine salt and next 3 ingredients in a large heavy-duty, zip-top plastic bag. Add potato wedges; seal bag, and shake to coat well. Place potato wedges, skin side down, in a single layer on a baking sheet coated with cooking spray. Bake at 375° for 25 minutes or until tender and lightly browned, turning once.
Yield: 4 servings.

Per Serving:

Calories 102	Carbohydrate 18.4g	Fiber 1.8g
Fat 2.4g	Cholesterol 0mg	Calcium 15mg
Protein 2.4g	Sodium 81mg	Iron 1.4mg

Exchanges: 1 Starch, ½ Fat

Strawberry Sorbet

½   teaspoon unflavored gelatin
3   tablespoons cold water
4   cups sliced fresh strawberries
½   cup sugar
1   cup sparkling white grape juice, chilled

Sprinkle gelatin over cold water in a small saucepan; let stand 1 minute. Cook over low heat, stirring until gelatin dissolves, about 2 minutes. Set aside.

Position knife blade in food processor bowl; add strawberries and sugar. Process until smooth, stopping occasionally to scrape down sides. Spoon strawberry mixture into a medium bowl; add gelatin mixture and grape juice, stirring well.

Pour mixture into freezer container of a 4-quart hand-turned or electric freezer. Freeze 45 minutes according to manufacturer's instructions. Pack freezer with additional ice and rock salt, and let stand 1 hour before serving, if desired. Store any remaining sorbet in freezer.
Yield: 11 (½-cup) servings.

Per Serving:

Calories 67	Carbohydrate 16.7g	Fiber 1.5g
Fat 0.2g	Cholesterol 0mg	Calcium 8mg
Protein 0.5g	Sodium 54mg	Iron 0.2mg

Exchange: 1 Fruit

Meal Plan for Company's Coming

- Make Strawberry Sorbet for dessert the night before or purchase at store.

- Prepare Asparagus and Onion Toss, and chill up to 2 hours.

- Next, make the pepper relish for Sirloin with Sweet Red Pepper Relish.

- Prepare Garlic Potato Wedges, and after they finish baking, broil the steaks.

Chinese Chicken Salad (page 224)

A Taste of the Orient

Orange-Ginger Tea
Egg Drop Soup
Chinese Chicken Salad
Lemon Tea Cakes (2 each)
Serves 4
Total calories per serving: 374
23% calories from fat
Lunch on the table in: 1 hour

Orange-Ginger Tea

4¼ cups water
1   (2-inch) piece gingerroot, peeled and sliced
4   regular-size tea bags
3   tablespoons sugar
2   teaspoons orange extract
½   teaspoon ground ginger

Combine water and sliced gingerroot in a saucepan; bring to a boil. Pour boiling ginger mixture over tea bags; steep 5 minutes. Strain tea; discard ginger and tea bags. Stir in sugar, orange extract, and ground ginger. Serve warm or chilled. Yield: 4 (1-cup) servings.

Per Serving:

Calories 51	Carbohydrate 10.1g	Fiber 0.0g
Fat 0.0g	Cholesterol 0mg	Calcium 1mg
Protein 0.1g	Sodium 1mg	Iron 0.0mg

Exchange: ½ Starch

Meal Plan for a Taste of the Orient

• Prepare the Lemon Tea Cakes up to 2 days in advance.

• Prepare Chinese Chicken Salad.

• Right before mealtime, prepare Egg Drop Soup and Orange-Ginger Tea. Or, if you want to serve the tea chilled, prepare it early in the day, and chill it.

Egg Drop Soup

2   cups canned low-sodium chicken broth
1½ cups water
1   tablespoon low-sodium soy sauce
¼   cup canned sliced mushrooms, drained
2   tablespoons dry sherry
1   tablespoon plus 1 teaspoon cornstarch
1   egg
1   egg white, lightly beaten
¼   cup thinly sliced green onions

Combine first 3 ingredients in a saucepan; bring to a boil. Add mushrooms. Combine sherry and cornstarch; add to broth mixture. Cook over medium heat, stirring constantly, 1 minute. Combine egg and egg white. Slowly pour egg mixture into boiling broth mixture, stirring constantly. Ladle soup into individual bowls; sprinkle each serving with 1 tablespoon green onions.
Yield: 4 (1-cup) servings.

Per Serving:

Calories 64	Carbohydrate 5.2g	Fiber 0.2g
Fat 2.1g	Cholesterol 55mg	Calcium 13mg
Protein 4.1g	Sodium 191mg	Iron 1.0mg

Exchanges: ½ Starch, ½ Fat

Chinese Chicken Salad

2 (4-ounce) skinned, boned chicken breast
    halves
1 (10-ounce) package frozen broccoli
    flowerets, thawed
½ cup sliced water chestnuts, drained
½ cup mandarin oranges in light syrup,
    drained
⅓ cup unsweetened orange juice
3 tablespoons cider vinegar
1 tablespoon low-sodium soy sauce
2 teaspoons sugar
1½ teaspoons dark sesame oil
1 teaspoon grated orange rind
¼ teaspoon salt
¼ teaspoon ground ginger
⅛ teaspoon dried crushed red pepper
4 cups shredded napa cabbage
2 tablespoons chow mein noodles
1 tablespoon sesame seeds, toasted

Place chicken in a nonstick skillet; cover with water. Bring to a boil; cover, reduce heat, and simmer 15 minutes or until chicken is done. Cut into strips.

Combine chicken, broccoli, water chestnuts, and mandarin oranges.

Combine orange juice and next 8 ingredients in a bowl. Pour juice mixture over chicken mixture, and toss gently. Arrange 1 cup cabbage on each of 4 serving plates. Top with chicken mixture; sprinkle with noodles and sesame seeds. Yield: 4 (1-cup) servings.

Per Serving:

Calories 199	Carbohydrate 22.5g	Fiber 2.8g
Fat 5.1g	Cholesterol 36mg	Calcium 89mg
Protein 17.5g	Sodium 335mg	Iron 1.8mg

Exchanges: 2 Very Lean Meat, 1½ Starch, ½ Fat

Lemon Tea Cakes

1¼ cups sifted cake flour
⅛ teaspoon baking powder
2 teaspoons grated lemon rind
¼ cup margarine, softened
⅓ cup sifted powdered sugar
1 egg white
2 tablespoons low-fat buttermilk
    Vegetable cooking spray
¼ cup sifted powdered sugar
1 tablespoon lemon juice

Combine cake flour, baking powder, and lemon rind in a small bowl, stirring well; set aside.

Beat margarine at medium speed of an electric mixer; gradually add ⅓ cup powdered sugar, beating mixture until light and fluffy. Add egg white; beat well. Add flour mixture to margarine mixture alternately with buttermilk, mixing well. Freeze 10 minutes.

Turn dough out onto a lightly floured surface. Roll dough to ¼-inch thickness; cut into rounds with a 1½-inch round cutter.

Place rounds on cookie sheets coated with cooking spray. Bake at 375° for 6 to 8 minutes or until edges are lightly browned. Remove to wire racks, and let cool completely.

Combine ¼ cup powdered sugar and lemon juice in a small bowl, stirring until smooth. Drizzle glaze over cookies. Yield: 40 cookies.

Per Cookie:

Calories 30	Carbohydrate 4.5g	Fiber 0.0mg
Fat 1.2g	Cholesterol 0mg	Calcium 3mg
Protein 0.4g	Sodium 15mg	Iron 0.3mg

Exchange: ½ Starch

Sunset Supper

Marinated Vegetable Salad (page 227)

Spicy Grilled Tuna (opposite page)

Sunset Supper

Fruit Juice Cooler
Spicy Grilled Tuna
Marinated Vegetable Salad

Serves 6
Total calories per serving: 396
24% calories from fat
Supper on the table in: 45 minutes

Fruit Juice Cooler

2 cups cranberry juice cocktail, chilled
2 cups unsweetened pineapple juice, chilled
2 cups lime-flavored mineral water, chilled

Combine cranberry juice and pineapple juice in a large pitcher; cover and chill. Gently stir mineral water into juice mixture just before serving. Serve over ice. Yield: 6 (1-cup) servings.

Per Serving:

Calories 97	Carbohydrate 24.3g	Fiber 0.1g
Fat 0.1g	Cholesterol 0mg	Calcium 17mg
Protein 0.3g	Sodium 20mg	Iron 0.3mg

Exchange: 1½ Fruit

Spicy Grilled Tuna

1 tablespoon onion powder
1 tablespoon dried basil
2 teaspoons dried thyme
½ teaspoon ground white pepper
½ teaspoon black pepper
¼ teaspoon ground red pepper
6 (4-ounce) tuna steaks (½ inch thick)
Vegetable cooking spray
Fresh thyme sprigs (optional)

Combine first 6 ingredients in a small bowl; stir well. Rub tuna steaks with pepper mixture.

Coat grill rack with cooking spray; place on grill over medium-hot coals (350° to 400°). Place tuna on rack, and grill, covered, 4 to 5 minutes on each side or until tuna flakes easily when tested with a fork. Transfer to individual serving plates. Garnish with thyme sprigs, if desired.
Yield: 6 servings.

Per Serving:

Calories 171	Carbohydrate 1.8g	Fiber 0.3g
Fat 5.7g	Cholesterol 43mg	Calcium 26mg
Protein 26.7g	Sodium 45mg	Iron 2.1mg

Exchange: 3 Lean Meat

Marinated Vegetable Salad

1 (14-ounce) can artichoke hearts, drained
   and halved
1 (8-ounce) package sliced fresh mushrooms
1 medium zucchini, cut into very thin strips
¼ cup sliced green onions
½ cup fat-free Italian dressing
¼ cup balsamic vinegar
4 cups torn green leaf lettuce
1 cup cherry tomatoes, halved
4 ounces part-skim mozzarella cheese, cut into
   ½-inch cubes
¼ cup sliced ripe olives
2 tablespoons freshly grated Parmesan cheese

Combine first 4 ingredients in a heavy-duty,
zip-top plastic bag. Pour dressing and balsamic
vinegar over vegetable mixture; turn bag to coat.
Cover and marinate in refrigerator up to 4 hours,
turning bag occasionally.

Remove vegetables from marinade, discarding
marinade. Combine vegetable mixture, lettuce,
tomato halves, mozzarella cheese, and olives in a
large bowl; toss gently to coat. Sprinkle with
Parmesan cheese. Yield: 6 (2-cup) servings.

Per Serving:

Calories 128	Carbohydrate 15.3g	Fiber 1.6g
Fat 4.6g	Cholesterol 12mg	Calcium 201mg
Protein 9.2g	Sodium 449mg	Iron 2.2mg

Exchanges: ½ Starch, 2 Vegetable, 1 Fat

It's in the Bag

One of our Test Kitchens' favorite ways to
marinate food is in a zip-top plastic bag. It's handy,
there's no mess to clean up, and the bag takes up
little space in your refrigerator. You just turn the
bag over occasionally to make sure the food is
coated to absorb the flavor.

Meal Plan for Sunset Supper

- Prepare the vegetables and marinade for Marinated Vegetable Salad and
  marinate in the refrigerator up to 4 hours.

- Combine and chill fruit juices.

- Prepare Spicy Grilled Tuna for grilling.

- While the tuna cooks, finish the salad.

- Right before mealtime, mix the Fruit Juice Cooler.

Meatless Night

Macaroni Casserole
Spicy Cornbread Muffins (1 each)

Serves 4
Total calories per serving: 500
17% calories from fat
Supper on the table in: 1 hour

Spicy Cornbread Muffins
(opposite page)

Macaroni Casserole (opposite page)

Macaroni Casserole

1 (8-ounce) package elbow macaroni,
    uncooked
2 tablespoons minced fresh parsley
1 tablespoon minced fresh chives
2 teaspoons dried oregano
½ teaspoon salt
½ teaspoon pepper
2 cups 1% low-fat cottage cheese
¼ cup skim milk
    Vegetable cooking spray
½ cup (2 ounces) shredded reduced-fat
    Cheddar cheese
1 (8-ounce) can no-salt-added tomato sauce
¼ cup fine, dry breadcrumbs
2 tablespoons freshly grated Parmesan cheese
    Cherry tomato slices (optional)
    Fresh oregano sprigs (optional)

Cook macaroni according to package directions, omitting salt and fat. Drain and place in a large bowl. Combine parsley, chives, dried oregano, salt and pepper; sprinkle over macaroni, tossing to combine.

Place cottage cheese and milk in container of an electric blender or food processor; cover and process until smooth. Add to macaroni mixture, tossing to combine.

Spoon half of macaroni mixture into a 1½-quart baking dish coated with cooking spray. Sprinkle with half of Cheddar cheese, and top with half of tomato sauce. Repeat layers. Sprinkle with breadcrumbs and Parmesan cheese. Bake at 375° for 30 minutes or until golden and bubbly. Garnish with cherry tomato slices and oregano sprigs, if desired. Yield: 4 (1¾-cup) servings.

Per Serving:

Calories 398	Carbohydrate 59.5g	Fiber 2.8g
Fat 5.7g	Cholesterol 15mg	Calcium 268mg
Protein 27.1g	Sodium 990mg	Iron 3.4mg

Exchanges: 2 Lean Meat, 3½ Starch

Spicy Cornbread Muffins

1½ cups yellow cornmeal
1 teaspoon baking soda
½ teaspoon salt
1 teaspoon sugar
2 egg whites
¼ cup picante sauce
3 tablespoons vegetable oil
1 (8-ounce) carton plain nonfat yogurt
    Vegetable cooking spray

Combine first 4 ingredients in a large bowl; make a well in center of mixture. Combine egg whites and next 3 ingredients; add to dry ingredients, stirring just until moistened. Spoon batter into muffin pans coated with cooking spray, filling two-thirds full. Bake at 425° for 18 to 20 minutes. Remove from pans immediately. Yield: 1 dozen.

Per Muffin:

Calories 102	Carbohydrate 13.9g	Fiber 1.7g
Fat 4.0g	Cholesterol 0mg	Calcium 40mg
Protein 2.9g	Sodium 287mg	Iron 0.6mg

Exchanges: 1 Starch, ½ Fat

Meal Plan for Meatless Night

- First, prepare Macaroni Casserole.
- While it bakes, assemble Spicy Cornbread Muffins.
- Bake casserole, then turn oven temperature to 425°, and bake the muffins.

Seafood Supper in a Snap

White wine (6 ounces)
Broiled Shrimp Kabobs
Orange Rice
Steamed asparagus (¾ cup)
Dinner Rolls (1 each)

Serves 8
Total calories per serving: 516
9% calories from fat
Supper on the table in: 1 hour, 15 minutes

Broiled Shrimp Kabobs (opposite page)

Broiled Shrimp Kabobs

2 pounds unpeeled large fresh shrimp
1 cup chopped onion
4 cloves garlic, minced
⅓ cup fat-free Italian dressing
¼ cup lemon juice
¼ cup low-sodium soy sauce
2 teaspoons ground ginger
3 lemons
   Vegetable cooking spray

Peel shrimp, leaving tails intact. Place shrimp in a heavy-duty, zip-top plastic bag. Combine onion and next 5 ingredients in a small bowl; stir well, and pour over shrimp. Seal bag securely, and shake well. Marinate shrimp in refrigerator at least 40 minutes, turning bag occasionally.

Remove shrimp from marinade, reserving marinade. Pour marinade into a small saucepan; bring to a boil. Remove from heat, and set aside.

Cut each lemon into 8 wedges. Thread shrimp and lemon wedges alternately onto 8 (12-inch) skewers. Place kabobs on rack of a broiler pan coated with cooking spray. Broil 5½ inches from heat (with electric oven door partially opened) 4 minutes on each side or until shrimp turn pink, turning and basting often with marinade. Yield: 8 servings.

Per Serving:

Calories 129	Carbohydrate 5.5g	Fiber 0.4g
Fat 1.9g	Cholesterol 154mg	Calcium 61mg
Protein 20.9g	Sodium 453mg	Iron 2.6mg

Exchanges: 3 Very Lean Meat, 1 Vegetable

Orange Rice

1½ cups water
1½ cups unsweetened orange juice
2 teaspoons reduced-calorie margarine
1½ teaspoons chicken-flavored bouillon granules
1½ cups long-grain rice, uncooked

Combine first 4 ingredients in a saucepan; bring to a boil. Add rice. Cover, reduce heat, and simmer 30 minutes or until liquid is absorbed and rice is tender. Yield: 8 (¾-cup) servings.

Per Serving:

Calories 154	Carbohydrate 32.9g	Fiber 0.4g
Fat 1.1g	Cholesterol 0mg	Calcium 14mg
Protein 2.9g	Sodium 165mg	Iron 1.5mg

Exchange: 1½ Starch

Meal Plan for Seafood Supper in a Snap

- Marinate the shrimp for Broiled Shrimp Kabobs.

- For 8 servings of steamed asparagus, purchase 2 pounds fresh asparagus spears. Snap off tough ends, and remove scales from spears. Arrange asparagus in a steamer basket over boiling water. Cover and steam 8 to 10 minutes or until asparagus is crisp-tender. If desired, sprinkle with fresh lemon juice. Set aside; keep warm.

- Cook the rice; about 10 minutes before the Orange Rice is done, broil the kabobs.

- Serve rolls with dinner, allowing 1 per person. Pour each guest a glass of wine—enjoy!

Metric Equivalents

The recipes that appear in this cookbook use the standard United States method for measuring liquid and dry or solid ingredients (teaspoons, tablespoons, and cups). The information in the following charts is provided to help cooks outside the U.S. successfully use these recipes. All equivalents are approximate.

Equivalents for Different Types of Ingredients

A standard cup measure of a dry or solid ingredient will vary in weight depending on the type of ingredient.

A standard cup of liquid is the same volume for any type of liquid. Use the following chart when converting standard cup measures to grams (weight) or milliliters (volume).

Standard Cup	Fine Powder (ex. flour)	Grain (ex. rice)	Granular (ex. sugar)	Liquid Solids (ex. butter)	Liquid (ex. milk)
1	140 g	150 g	190 g	200 g	240 ml
¾	105 g	113 g	143 g	150 g	180 ml
⅔	93 g	100 g	125 g	133 g	160 ml
½	70 g	75 g	95 g	100 g	120 ml
⅓	47 g	50 g	63 g	67 g	80 ml
¼	35 g	38 g	48 g	50 g	60 ml
⅛	18 g	19 g	24 g	25 g	30 ml

Dry Ingredients by Weight

(To convert ounces to grams, multiply the number of ounces by 30.)

1 oz	=	¹⁄₁₆ lb	=	30 g
4 oz	=	¼ lb	=	120 g
8 oz	=	½ lb	=	240 g
12 oz	=	¾ lb	=	360 g
16 oz	=	1 lb	=	480 g

Length

(To convert inches to centimeters, multiply the number of inches by 2.5.)

1 in					=	2.5 cm		
6 in	=	½ ft			=	15 cm		
12 in	=	1 ft			=	30 cm		
36 in	=	3 ft	=	1 yd	=	90 cm		
40 in					=	100 cm	=	1 m

Liquid Ingredients by Volume

¼ tsp					=	1 ml		
½ tsp					=	2 ml		
1 tsp					=	5 ml		
3 tsp	=	1 tbls			=	½ fl oz	=	15 ml
		2 tbls	=	⅛ cup	=	1 fl oz	=	30 ml
		4 tbls	=	¼ cup	=	2 fl oz	=	60 ml
		5⅓ tbls	=	⅓ cup	=	3 fl oz	=	80 ml
		8 tbls	=	½ cup	=	4 fl oz	=	120 ml
		10⅔ tbls	=	⅔ cup	=	5 fl oz	=	160 ml
		12 tbls	=	¾ cup	=	6 fl oz	=	180 ml
		16 tbls	=	1 cup	=	8 fl oz	=	240 ml
		1 pt	=	2 cups	=	16 fl oz	=	480 ml
		1 qt	=	4 cups	=	32 fl oz	=	960 ml
						33 fl oz	=	1000 ml = 1 l

Cooking/Oven Temperatures

	Fahrenheit	Celcius	Gas Mark
Freeze Water	32° F	0° C	
Room Temperature	68° F	20° C	
Boil Water	212° F	100° C	
Bake	325° F	160° C	3
	350° F	180° C	4
	375° F	190° C	5
	400° F	200° C	6
	425° F	220° C	7
	450° F	230° C	8
Broil			Grill

Index

Recipes in red are superquick.

Tips and Techniques

Apples, baking, 44
Bagel chips, making, 10
Bananas, freezing, 23
Biscuits, secret to perfect, 31
Blackening technique, broiler method, 95
Breadcrumbs, making soft, 184
Bread shell, type of, 157
Bread toppers, types of, 36
Bruschetta, making, 13
Bulgur, definition of, 132
Buttermilk, for flavoring, 140
Cabbage, cooking red, 176
Capers, definition of, 91
Cheese
    freezing, 111
    Gruyère, 148
    Swiss, 148
Cheesecake, helpful hints about, 60
Cheese, cottage, uses for, 140
Cilantro, uses for, 26
Cleanup tips, 86, 90, 135
Coriander, uses for, 26
Cornbread, helpful hints about
    baking, 28
Couscous, definition of, 165
Crabmeat, in appetizers, 98
Creamer, nondairy, 53
Croutons, as a soup topper, 144
Dental floss, for easy slicing, 38
Dutch baby, definition of, 34
Egg roll wrappers, uses for, 17
Egg whites, whipping, 61
Extracts, as substitutes for
    liqueurs, 34, 45
Fish
    cooking tip, 97
    grouper, 93
    orange roughy, 93
Freezing
    bananas, 23
    cheese, 111
    meatballs, 15
    meat, for easy slicing, 72
    salads, 123
    soup, 147
Garlic
    grilled, 210
    inserted in a roast for flavoring, 74
    minced from a jar for fresh, 167
Ginger, crystallized, 42
Goat cheese, 118
Herbs, 8
Jambalaya, definition of, 83
Jicama, definition of, 122

Kitchen shears, for chopping
    herbs, 178
Lasagna noodles, no-cook, 120
Low fat
    condiments, 17
    fruit topping, 141
    milk in soup, 156
    salad dressing, 141
Marinate
    food in a plastic bag, 136
    for flavoring and tenderizing, 70
Meatballs, making ahead and
    freezing, 15
Meat, freezing and slicing, 72
Microwave
    chicken, cooking, 153
    muffins, reheating, 30
    tortillas, warming, 110
Milk powder, instant nonfat dry,
    as a thickener, 182
Mustard
    Chinese, 17
    Dijon, as a thickener, 74
Oil, olive
    types of, 179
Onions, Vidalia, 182
Orange
    rind, for flavoring, 46
    rind, grating, 136
Oysters, shucking, 18
Pasta, substitutions for, 167
Pears
    as sandwich topper, 160
    coring, 171
Pepper
    black, 173
    white, 150
Pine nuts, definition of, 105
Pita chips, making, 10
Polenta, definition of, 165
Popovers, equipment for making and uses
    for, 32
Pork, tips on buying a roast, 81
Posole, variation of, 133
Potatoes, hash brown, 183
Prunes, flavor variation of, 170
Radicchio, definition of, 127
Rice
    cooking tip, 107
    crust, 102
    brown, instant, 107
    topping for, 73
Salad dressing, as a low-fat topping for
    fruit, 141

Salads
    congealed, unmolding, 131
    freezing, 123
    greens, types of, 138
    main dish, 213
Salsa, 109
Sauce, sweet-and-sour, 17
Scallops, buying and storing, 99
Seasoning blend, 100
Soup
    freezing, 147
    low-fat milk in, 156
    reheating, 147
    serving suggestion, 144
Sour cream, for flavoring, 109
Soy sauce, 17
Spinach, buying fresh, 187
Substitutions
    for amaretto, 34
    for canned corn, 129
    for Cointreau, 46
    for fresh corn, 165
    for fresh garlic, 167
    for ginger liqueur, 123
    for Gruyère cheese, 148
    for half-and-half in soup, 156
    for hoisin sauce, 79
    for kalamata olives, 115
    for pasta, 167
    for praline liqueur, 45
    for prunes, 170
    for tomato paste, 115
    for Vidalia onions, 182
    for whipping cream in soup, 156
    for yogurt flavors, 50
Succotash, ingredients for, 155
Toasting
    coconut, 52
    pecans, 162
    squash seeds, 146
Tomatoes
    uses for plum, 116
    health benefits of, 188
Tortellini, definition of, 134
Tortilla chips, making, 10
Tortillas, serving suggestion, 157
Turkey, uses for leftovers, 160
Vegetables, steaming, 204
Vinegars
    making your own, 218
    red wine, 8
Waffles, tips on freezing Belgian, 33
Wine, red, 155
Wonton wrappers, where to find, 17

Acknowledgments

Oxmoor House wishes to thank the following merchants:

Antiques & Gardens, Birmingham, AL
Barbara Eigen Arts, Jersey City, NJ
Biot, New York, NY
Bridges Antiques, Birmingham, AL
Carolyn Rice Art Pottery, Marietta, GA
Cassis and Co., New York, NY
Christine's, Birmingham, AL
Cyclamen Studio, Inc., Berkeley, CA
Daisy Arts, Venice, CA
Interlude, Birmingham, AL
The Loom Company, Aletha Soule, New York, NY
Potluck, Accord, NY
Savoir Vivre International, San Francisco, CA
Union Glass, San Francisco, CA

Contributing photographers:
Ralph Anderson: pages 21, 51, 180
Edward Badham: pages 66, 192
Jim Bathie: pages 13, 22, 41, 139
Randy Mayor: pages 16, 103
Howard L. Puckett: page 31

Contributing photo stylists:
Cindy Manning Barr: page 31
Kay E. Clarke: pages 13, 16, 22, 41, 139
Iris Crawley O'Brien: pages 159, 175, 190, 218

Source of Nutrient Analysis Data:
Computrition, Inc., Chatsworth, CA and
information provided by food manufacturers